H. H. FARMER

RECONCILIATION AND RELIGION
Some Aspects of the Uniqueness of Christianity as a Reconciling Faith

Front cover:

Herbert Henry Farmer
Courtesy of Westminster College, Cambridge

H. H. FARMER

RECONCILIATION *and* RELIGION

SOME ASPECTS OF THE UNIQUENESS OF CHRISTIANITY AS A RECONCILING FAITH

GIFFORD LECTURES   UNIVERSITY OF GLASGOW   1951

Edited and introduced by C. H. Partridge

The Edwin Mellen Press

Library of Congress Cataloging-in-Publication Data

Farmer, Herbert Henry, 1892-
  Reconciliation and religion : some aspects of uniqueness of
Christianity as a reconciling faith / H.H. Farmer ; edited and
introduced by C.H. Partridge.
      p. cm.-- (Texts and studies in religion ; v. 78)
  "Gifford lectures, University of Glasgow, 1951."
  Includes bibliographical references.
  ISBN 0-7734-8353-5
  1. Christianity--Essence, genius, nature. 2. Reconciliation-
-Religious aspects--Christianity. 3. Personalism. I. Partridge,
Christopher H. (Christopher Hugh), 1961- . II. Title.
III. Series. IV. Series: Gifford lectures ; 1951.
BT60.F37   1998
230--dc21   98-20123
                                                                              CIP

This is volume 78 in the continuing series
Texts and Studies in Religion
Volume 78 ISBN 0-7734-8353-5
TSR Series ISBN 0-88946-976-8

A CIP catalog record for this book is available from the British Library.

The Edwin Mellen Press   The Edwin Mellen Press
         Box 450   Box 67
   Lewiston, New York   Queenston, Ontario
   USA 14092-0450   CANADA L0S 1L0

The Edwin Mellen Press, Ltd.
Lampeter, Ceredigion, Wales
UNITED KINGDOM SA48 8LT

Printed in the United States of America

For

George & Dorothy Partridge

my wonderful parents

CONTENTS

FOREWORD

The first series of H. H. Farmer's Gifford Lectures, delivered in 1950, soon after his appointment as Norris-Hulse Professor of Divinity at the University of Cambridge, England, was eventually published in 1954 under the title *Revelation and Religion* (J. Nisbet and Co., London). Farmer gave them the sub-title *Studies in the Theological Interpretation of Religious Types*. It is clear from the text of the lectures that he was intent on giving a *theological* interpretation of the empirical fact of religion in human experience. Moreover, his was an attempt to give a *Christians* interpretation of religion.

Farmer knew that he was entering demanding territory and that there had not been many who had gone before him. He readily confessed his own sense of being a student of such matters. None the less, the book was received warmly by reviewers who often remarked on the urgency of the topic, the clarity of the presentation, and the serious and demanding nature of the argument.

The second series of Gifford Lectures, however, remained unpublished until now. Dr. Christopher Partridge gives some of the known reasons for this in the Preface to this present volume. Undoubtedly Farmer's modesty and his appreciation of the demanding nature of the subject he had taken had something to do with it.

In this volume we now have the second series of lectures, first delivered in 1951. These lectures compliment and advance the argument of *Revelation and Religion* and represent a sustained attempt by a notable British theologian to think through the issues involved in affirming the critical uniqueness of Christ and the normative nature of the religion which bears His name, if not always His spirit. It is easy to recognise the dated style of these lectures. However, they are important for the following reasons.

First, they are what they attempt to be, namely, a serious theological interpretation of the fact of religion. Any contemporary reader will be aware of the continuing power and influence of religion in the world community. Plurality of religious expression can be found in all the major cities of the world. And, sadly, religion in its corrupt forms remains one of the most deeply divisive and disrupting of factors in the search for world peace and justice. The topic, therefore, remains urgent.

Second, this further series of Gifford Lectures with its subtitle *Some Aspects of the Uniqueness of Christianity as a Reconciling Faith* help Christians reflect theologically on the nature of their own convictions. Since Farmer gave the lectures there has been a steady flow of varied literature on the pressing question of Christ's uniqueness and the claims Christians make for the work God did in Him. Again the topic is urgent and we can be grateful for Farmer's thoughtful systematic approach to the subject. If he wanted to give a theological interpretation of the fact of religion he desired even more that it be a Christian account.

I am delighted that *Reconciliation and Religion* is published. As far as I can judge, Dr. Partridge has faithfully represented Farmer's full and partially corrected text. He is to be congratulated on his careful work which enables us all to read Farmer's lectures today.

Brian Haymes
Bristol Baptist College

PREFACE

Several years ago, like many postgraduates cautiously but excitedly embarking upon the doctoral voyage, I was clear about the general area I wanted to explore, but uncertain as to the theologians I wanted as travelling companions. The general area I was intending to explore was the theology of religions and the particular theologians I was considering were primarily German, namely Friedrich Schleiermacher, Paul Tillich, Karl Barth and Emil Brunner, the reading of whose works eventually led me to concentrate on the thought of Brunner. Although greatly stimulated by his arguments, I wasn't satisfied with his rejection of Schleiermacher's work. At this point, although I had come across Farmer's *The World and God* on the shelves of the Divinity library at Aberdeen University, I was by no means familiar with his work. However, whilst browsing in a second-hand book shop, I came across his first series of Gifford lectures, *Revelation and Religion*. Intrigued by the title, I took it off the shelf, flicked through it and was interested to find a critique of Brunner which raised similar concerns to my own. Needless to say, I bought the book. On reading further, I discovered that Farmer was clearly working with some form of personalist encounter theology similar to Brunner's— which I had become convinced had much to offer—and that he was offering a constructive and interesting alternative which was far more positive about Schleiermachian insights. The more I read the more I enjoyed his arguments and style of writing. It wasn't long before I was searching for more of this down-to-earth, passionately Christian, personalist theology. I had found my travelling partner.

Since my research at that time was principally concerned with the construction of a Christian theology of religions, Farmer's Gifford lectures, which constitute his fullest treatment of the subject, were of primary importance. As you might imagine, I was therefore rather dismayed to discover that the second series of these lectures had never been published. Furthermore, my initial enquiries into the whereabouts of the original manuscript were not encouraging. I was, for example, told by one correspondent that Farmer had been so unhappy with them that he had burned them. This, of course, turned out not to be the case as I discovered when the late Rev. Lesslie Newbigin put me in touch with Farmer's daughter and son-in-law, Mrs Mary and Rev. John Williamson, who were from the outset interested in my research and always enormously helpful. To my great relief, they informed me that the lectures were still extant and that they had been sent to Dr Brian Haymes, Principal of Northern College, Manchester (now Principal of Bristol Baptist College). A keen student of Farmer, Dr Haymes not only encouraged contemporary Farmer studies, but also wanted to see the lectures published. However, having little time to spend on the work himself, he very kindly handed them over to me.

Although by this time I was nearing the end of my doctorate, on reading through them I recognised the importance and contemporary relevance of what I was reading for theologians who were seeking to construct a Christian theology of religions which, whilst being fair to the facts of religious history, nevertheless sought to hold on to the traditional doctrine of Christ's uniqueness and finality. Although there will be those who are not persuaded by Farmer's thesis, there can be few who will not admire his careful arguments, his creativity and the overall cogency and consistency of the work. Certainly, I am confident that there will be many who will be greatly stimulated by what he has to say.

Excited by the work and encouraged by Dr Haymes, I wrote back to Rev. and Mrs Williamson in order to enquire as to their feelings concerning the editing and publication of the lectures. After meeting with other members of the family, they concluded that I should prepare them for publication and seek a publisher. Hence, after a further discussion with Dr Haymes, I proceeded to work on the text.

One of the concerns of Farmer's family was that, in their words, "our father's own humility towards his work should be respected." This has always been my concern. Although, because of the copious hand written comments on the text itself and various separate scraps of paper, it has sometimes been difficult to discern precisely what amendments he would have wanted to make to the original lectures, every effort has been made to reproduce faithfully what Farmer wanted to convey. To this end the work includes several features: (a) The book opens with an introductory essay discussing the principal areas of Farmer's thought, the aim being to contribute to an informed reading of the text. (b) Throughout I have included footnotes which refer the reader to relevant passages in Farmer's published works as well as, less frequently, other significant texts. (c) In some cases, where an important passage has had a line drawn through it and no alternative rendering has been given by Farmer, it has been placed in the footnotes. (d) Although Farmer more often than not failed to provide references, every effort has been made to track down the origin of quotations. (Sometimes the books referenced in the footnotes are later editions of those which would have been used by Farmer.) (e) The book concludes with the most comprehensive bibliography to date of Farmer's writings.

One of the disadvantages of reproducing, as far as possible, the lectures as Farmer wrote them, is that some of the language, although quite intelligible, seems dated. This is particularly the case concerning his use of non-inclusive language. I mention this because, had Farmer written this book today, he would have almost certainly used inclusive language. He had a sensitivity to such issues and a positive attitude regarding the role of women in the Church and the university.

As to the work itself, although there were originally ten lectures, several of these have been brought together: (a) the first two ("Introductory" and "Religion and Theology") were brought together by Farmer to form the first chapter; (b) lectures 5 and 6 ("Morality and Religion") were brought together;

as were (c) chapters 7 and 8 ("The Significance and the Non-significance of the Self").

Although the work never found its way to the publishers, it is clear that Farmer initially intended the lectures to be published. I say this for two reasons: (1) half of his written lectures were later prepared as chapters; and (2) in the first series of published lectures he explicitly states that "the second series of these lectures [are] to be published later."[1] Moreover, parts of them were produced as articles and pamphlets. For example, "Monotheism and the Doctrine of the Trinity", *The Christian Person and Morality* and parts of *The Word of Reconciliation* can all be traced back to work done for these lectures. However, he seems, by the late 1950s, to have abandoned the idea of publishing them as a single work. As to why he came to this conclusion, I suggest the following interrelated reasons. Primarily, it seems to me, he felt that they would no longer command much interest. He simply felt that they, along with his theology generally, were rather "old hat". Although his later writings indicate that he had himself not departed from his thesis in *Reconciliation and Religion*, in the years that had passed since their delivery things had moved on. For example, it took him until 1954 to publish the first series, by which time Tillich had hinted at a similar thesis in the first volume of his *Systematic Theology*.[2] Indeed, Farmer's Preface to *Revelation and Religion* shows traces of this emerging lack of confidence in the importance of his work. After humbly questioning his "fitness for the task", he writes the following, which, significantly, comes immediately after a paragraph commenting on the importance of his work as the filling of a gap in contemporary systematic theology:

> Since writing this last paragraph I have read Professor Tillich's first volume of his *Systematic Theology*, and I am interested to observe that, in some paragraphs of the long introductory section, he confirms what I have just said. He speaks of the need in systematic theology

---

[1] H. H. Farmer, *Revelation and Religion*, p.70 n.

for what he calls a "theological history of religion", by which he means what I mean by a "theological interpretation of religion". He says that such a theological history of religion has not so far "been theoretically conceived and practically established". "A theological history of religion", he adds, "should interpret theologically the material produced by investigation and analysis of the pre-religious and religious life of mankind. It should elaborate the motives and types of religious expression, showing how they follow from the nature of the religious concern and therefore necessarily appear in all religions, including Christianity in so far as it is a religion. A theological history of religion also should point out demonic distortions and new tendencies in the religions of the world, pointing to their Christian solution..." (p.44). These words seem to me to indicate very well some of the things I have attempted to do in the following pages.[3]

Furthermore, not only did Tillich become increasingly interested in this subject, publishing his *Christianity and the Encounter of the World Religions*[4] in 1963, but ever greater numbers of theologians (some with far greater knowledge of the history of religions) were producing important studies in the area.

One can understand, therefore, why a humble thinker like Farmer became increasingly reluctant to publish. Indeed, it has to be said that, had he still felt his work to be necessary, it would have required extensive revision in order to accommodate contemporary thought on the subject. Furthermore, being familiar with Farmer's writings and having spoken to people who knew him, I am convinced that he would not have been satisfied with the idea of publishing for the sake of publishing. He wrote because he wanted to make a difference

---

[2]London: Nisbet, 1953.

[3]H. H. Farmer, *Revelation and Religion*, p.ix.
[4]New York & London: Columbia University Press, 1963.

to contemporary Christian faith and to challenge contemporary critiques of the Christian worldview. Unless he really believed his work to be relevant and necessary he would have been very unhappy about publishing it.

Bearing the above in mind, it comes as no surprise to learn from his daughter, Mrs Mary Williamson, that, as time went on, he became very unsatisfied with the material, and eventually gave up the idea of revising it for publication. This needs to be borne in mind when reading through the lectures. This is material with which Farmer was unhappy.

So why publish it? Firstly, like the students of any thinker or movement, the increasing numbers of scholars interested in the study of Farmer are keen to have access to all his writings, particularly his most important—and these lectures are, by far, his most important unpublished writings.

Secondly, as interest in interfaith dialogue progresses and as theologies of religions are debated, those Christians who are unhappy with the various 'pluralist' hypotheses, and who want to retain some understanding of Christian uniqueness, are looking to the past for wisdom. As is so often the case in the history of ideas, a light from the past can be used to guide us into the future. This, I am convinced, is the case with Farmer's thought. Although there are undoubtedly discussions and ideas in his books which are outdated and, to some extent, unhelpful, there is a great deal that is powerful, fresh and thought provoking. These lectures will not only provide food for thought for the student of Farmer, they will, I believe, provide stimulation for tired theologians of religions seeking new ideas and fresh insights which might be used in the construction of a specifically *Christian* thesis.

Thirdly, several years ago, Eric Sharpe asked, "Why, in the matter of recent Christian thought, should it be assumed that almost the only modern theologians worthy of the name are all Germans?" He went on to bemoan the fact that this has led English-speaking students to "ignore and undervalue home-grown products." "Let the theologian study Barth, Brunner, Bultmann and Bonhoeffer, Moltmann, Tillich and Käsemann by all means. But have Maurice, Forsyth, John and Donald Baillie, Temple, Ramsey, Oman, Quick and Farmer nothing to teach him? And how often do any of these figure in conventional theological syllabuses?"[5] It is hoped that, along with the recent and very welcome interest in, for example, Forsyth, the Baillies and Oman,[6] the present volume will contribute to the steadily growing revival of interest in. British theology generally and Farmer in particular. In short, the present volume should be of interest to the following: (a) those interested in Farmer's thought; (b) those interested in personalist theology, of whom Farmer was, following Oman, one of the foremost British exponents; (c) those generally interested in British theology; (d) those who aim, like Farmer, to set forth the content of the Christian revelation and faith in such a way that their uniqueness and finality within the history of religions will be, to some extent, validated; (e) those generally interested in the theology of religions.

Finally, the lectures are worth publishing because they are, quite simply, excellent. Each time I have set aside my day to day academic chores to sit down and work on them, I have been rewarded. This, as I'm sure many careful readers will agree, is a stimulating and exciting work. Although it is undoubtedly a little dated, I have found them to be more worthwhile and personally helpful than many of the more contemporary theological texts that I feel the need to struggle through. This is good, solid, carefully crafted theology.

---

[5]E. J. Sharpe, *Understanding Religion* (London: Duckworth, 1983), p.15.
[6]E.g.: T. Hart (ed.), *Justice the True and Only Mercy: Essays on the Life and Theology of Peter Taylor Forsyth* (Edinburgh: T. & T. Clark, 1995); several of Forsyth's works have recently been published by New Creation Publications Inc. (Blackwood, Australia); D. Fergusson (ed.), *Christ, Church and Society: Essays on John Baillie and Donald Baillie* (Edinburgh: T. & T. Clark, 1993); S. Bevans, *John Oman and His Doctrine of God* (Cambridge: Cambridge University Press, 1992).

ACKNOWLEDGEMENTS

I am keenly aware that this work is not simply the result of my labour, but rather came into being because of the numerous kindnesses of many people. In this respect, I would first and foremost like to express my gratitude to the family of H. H. Farmer and particularly to Mrs Mary Williamson and Rev. John Williamson for going out of their way to make these lectures available to me, for entrusting me with the editorial work and for their continual encouragement since our initial contact in 1993.

I am enormously grateful to Dr Brian Haymes who has always been supportive and helpful and who kindly agreed to write the Foreword. Likewise, I am grateful and to Professor Trevor Hart who gave me much invaluable advice in the initial stages of the project, to my friend and colleague Dr. Eric Christianson who kindly read the text and sifted out several errors and to Ms Helen Hughes who so diligently and knowledgeably proofread the work.

Finally, my thanks are due to Professor Herbert Richardson, the Director of the Edwin Mellen Press, who not only enabled the work to reach its published form, but whose enthusiasm for the project and for the work of Farmer generally I found most inspiring.

Christopher Partridge
Chester
July, 1998

INTRODUCTION

THE CHRISTIAN PERSONALISM OF
H. H. FARMER
Christopher H. Partridge

Biographical Notes

Herbert Henry Farmer (1892-1981), son of Mary Ann and William Charles Farmer (a cabinet-maker), was born in Highbury, London, 27th November, 1892. He had three older brothers and no sisters. After attending Owen's School in Islington, in 1911 he went to study at Peterhouse, Cambridge. There he read for, and (in 1914) took first class honours in, the mental and moral sciences tripos. He was consequently elected Burney student in the philosophy of religion. Being a conscientious objector, instead of entering the military, he worked as a farm labourer at Histon, near Cambridge. In 1916 he entered Westminster College, Cambridge to prepare for ministry in the Presbyterian Church of England and graduated with distinction in 1917. In 1919 he was ordained and became the minister of a church in Stafford. Whilst in Stafford, it is also worth noting, he did a bit of part-time lecturing in psychology at the Selly Oak Colleges, Birmingham. In 1922 he moved to St Augustine's Presbyterian Church in New Barnet, London (where he remained until 1931). A year later, in 1923, he married Gladys Sylvie Offord.

His period at New Barnet was a significant time for Farmer the preacher and scholar. During his years here he was to see an enormous growth in his reputation and popularity.[1] In 1927 he published his first book, a well-received collection of sermons entitled *Things Not Seen*. This was followed in 1929 by the publication of his equally well-received volume, *Experience of God*. This led to an invitation, a year later, to give the Carew Lectures[2] at Hartford Theological Seminary in Connecticut, the substance of which (along with the Russell lectures delivered at Auburn Theological Seminary, New York, in 1934) provided the basis for his important and influential work, *The World and God: A Study of Prayer, Providence and Miracle in Christian Experience* (1935). Shortly after the delivery of his 1930 Carew lectures, he was appointed as Riley Professor of Christian Doctrine and Ethics at Hartford Theological Seminary. An excited letter from a well-wisher to the seminary's president, R. W. Barstow, gives us some indication of Farmer's popularity at this time: "I most heartily congratulate President Barstow and The Hartford Theological Seminary on the announcement that Rev. Herbert H. Farmer has accepted the appointment to the Riley Chair of Christian Doctrine. Mr Farmer has already come to be regarded as one of the front rank men of his day in the field of systematic theology. His brilliant record at Cambridge University, his power as a preacher and lecturer among college men, his experience as a pastor, his record as an author, his proved acceptability as a teacher and preacher before American audiences indicate that his coming to America is an event of first-class importance to the theological world of this country".[3]

---

[1] For a good outline of the philosophical and theological context of Farmer's thought see D. C. Lapp, "The Context and Contribution of the Theology of H. H. Farmer" (unpublished doctoral thesis: University of Ottawa, 1975), ch.1.

[2] *Lecture 1*: "The Doctrine of the Ideal Man"; *lecture 2*: "The Conception of the Norm and Nature of Religion"; *lecture 3*: "The Norm and the Growth of Religious Experience and Knowledge"; *lecture 4*: "The Norm and the Problem of Apocalyptic"; *lecture 5*: "The Norm and the Doctrine of God".

[3] Hartford Seminary Library: Item No. 11948.

Although he made many friends at Hartford and clearly greatly enjoyed his time in America,[4] one gets the impression that he was pleased, in 1935, to return to what he affectionately termed his "homeland"[5] in order to succeed his mentor and friend, John Oman, as Professor of Systematic Theology and Apologetics at Westminster College, Cambridge. Indeed, the family returned to England several times during his four year period at Hartford, and, in 1933, Gladys Farmer stayed in England to have their third child.[6]

Again, his growing importance as a theologian during these early years is indicated by the fact that he received an honorary Doctorate of Divinity from Glasgow University (1936) and was appointed Stanton Lecturer in Philosophy of Religion at Cambridge University (1937-1940). Along with these marks of recognition, in July, 1937, he was invited to speak, along with Emil Brunner, Reinhold Niebuhr, Paul Tillich and William Temple, at the conference on Church, Community and State which sought to "understand the true nature of the vital conflict between the Christian faith and the secular and pagan tendencies of our time, and to see more clearly the responsibilities of the Church in relation to that struggle."[7] Not one for speculative theology, discussions such as these appealed greatly to Farmer as being of central importance to the theological task. However, perhaps more significantly,

---

[4]That this is so, is warmly expressed in a short poem he wrote for the Faculty-student Banquet in 1935—shortly before returning to England: "America, After Four Years. Things I have Loved" (Hartford Seminary Library: Item No. 11956). The poem concludes,
  "...I have loved Hartford with its parks and noble trees,
  And most of all its friendly people, and in this, at least, my wife agrees.
  You have made it quite apparent e'en to our dense, benighted pates,
  That the nicest people in all the earth inhabit the United States."
[5]Letter to R. W. Barstow, 5th August, 1933 (Hartford Seminary Library: Item No. 11956).
[6]Letter to R. W. Barstow, 26th July, 1933 (Hartford Seminary Library: Item No. 11926).
[7]J. H. Oldham, in N. Ehrenström et al., *Christian Faith and the Common Life*, Church, Community and State Series, vol.4 (London: George Allen & Unwin, 1938), p.vii. Farmer's paper, published in this volume is entitled, "The Revelation in Christ and the Christian's Vocation", (pp.143-172).

particularly regarding his argument in the present volume, he was invited to take part in the International Missionary Council Meeting at Tambaram, Madras in December, 1938. In response to Hendrik Kraemer's important volume written for discussion at the Conference, *The Christian Message in the Non-Christian World*, and as a result of those and subsequent discussions, Farmer produced a paper for the first volume of the Tambaram series, *The Authority of the Faith.*[8] Although Farmer fundamentally agreed with the central thesis of Kraemer's book and was clearly happy to affirm the exclusivist emphases of the Tambaram findings,[9] he nevertheless did question some of the more Barthian beliefs. For example, in accordance with his understanding of the nature of revelation (which is discussed below), he questioned the tendency to play down any understanding of divine revelation and human response in other faith communities. Indeed, many years later, Kraemer recorded his agreement with Farmer's criticism that he had neglected the awareness of God which is to be found in non-Christian faiths.[10]

In 1938 he published a second very successful volume of sermons, *The Healing Cross.* This was followed in 1941 by *The Servant of the Word*, his influential Warrack lectures on preaching—delivered at St Mary's College, University of St Andrews and New College, University of Edinburgh. Regarding these latter two works, the late Professor Donald MacKinnon made the following insightful comment: "...to read these two books together provides the critical student of religious language with an indispensable introduction to evaluation of the preacher's address as a fundamental

---

[8] H. H. Farmer, "The Authority of the Faith", in W. Paton (ed.), *The Authority of the Faith*, Tambaram Series, vol.1 (London: Oxford University Press, 1939), pp.163-180.

[9] See "The Faith By Which the Church Lives" and "The Witness of the Church in Relation to the Non-Christian Religions, the New Paganisms, and the Cultural Heritage of the Nations", in W. Paton (ed.), *The Authority of the Faith*, Tambaram Series, vol.1, pp.183-216.

[10] H. Kraemer, *Religion and the Christian Faith* (London: Lutterworth, 1956), p.316

dimension of that language."[11] A year later in 1942 he produced his personal favourite, *Towards Belief in God*, an updated and thoroughly revised version of his earlier study, *Experience of God*. 1946 saw the publication of his Lyman Beecher lectures, delivered at Yale University. These lectures, published under the title *God and Men*, function as an accessible introduction to his personalist theology. Three years later, in 1949, not only was he appointed as a visiting lecturer in theology to the University of Toronto, but, more significantly, he succeeded C. H. Dodd as the Norris-Hulse Professor of Divinity at Cambridge University, where, shortly afterwards, he was made a Fellow of Peterhouse (1950). In 1951 perhaps the most important of his many articles was published as the lead essay in the twelve volume *Interpreter's Bible*, "The Bible: Its Significance and Authority". It was at this high point in his academic career when he was invited by the University of Glasgow to give the prestigious Gifford Lectures (1950-1951). The first series of these lectures was published in 1954 as *Revelation and Religion: Studies in the Theological Interpretation of Religious Types*. The second series, *Reconciliation and Religion: Some Aspects of the Uniqueness of Christianity as a Reconciling Faith*, is here published for the first time.

Although Farmer officially retired in 1960 in order to spend more time with his family, he did continue to lecture and write until 1966. In 1961 he delivered the Ayer lectures at Colgate-Rochester Divinity School in New York and the Earl lectures at the Pacific School of Religion, as well as lecturing at Knox College, Dunedin and Ormond College, Melbourne. In 1966 the lectures were brought together in his final volume, *The Word of Reconciliation*. Whilst, perhaps because of the changing theological climate,

---

[11]D. M. MacKinnon, "Farmer, Herbert Henry (1892-1981)", in *The Dictionary of National Biography 1981-1985* (London: Oxford University Press, 1990), p.136.

this volume was not as well received nor as widely read as his earlier works, it was (to quote Professor MacKinnon again) "a profound essay in the theology of the Atonement...suffused with Farmer's own reverent, yet always restlessly interrogative spirit."[12]

Farmer's writings were popular and influenced a generation of theologians because, not only do they demonstrate a broad learning and grasp of theology and philosophy, and a lucidity and clarity of thought which make them accessible to a wide readership, they also reveal an unusual spiritual depth. Passages from his books were often cited in devotional works such as Leslie Weatherhead's *A Private House of Prayer* and Rita Snowden's *People are People*.[13] For example, in his *Thinking Aloud in War-Time*, Weatherhead writes, "When the flowers of the city pulpit are sent to the sick, we attach a card to them on which are printed, at my request, some significant words of H. H. Farmer."[14]

Finally, it is probably true to say that he was not only amongst the most important British theologians this century, but also the best known British preacher of the academic community of his generation. "Of all the university sermons preached in Edinburgh University in the last twenty years", says James S. Stewart (himself, of course, an outstanding and influential preacher), "perhaps the most memorable was one by Dr Herbert Farmer of Cambridge on sin and forgiveness...Now, Dr Farmer, of course, has written abstractly as a theologian on the nature of sin. He could have done something of that kind in the Cathedral and been quite effective...[However] there can be no doubt that the great congregation that thronged the Cathedral that night, left with a far

---

[12]Ibid., pp.136-7.
[13]L. D. Weatherhead, *A Private House of Prayer* (London: Hodder & Stoughton, 1958), p.268; R. F. Snowden, *People are People* (London: Epworth, 1971), pp.20, 131.
[14]L. D. Weatherhead, *Thinking Aloud in War-Time* (London: Hodder & Stoughton, 1939), pp.152-3.

acuter sense of the wrath and love of God than the most able abstract generalisation on human sinfulness could possibly have given."[15] Again, the late Donald MacKinnon records that Farmer was "one of the finest preachers I have ever heard."[16] John Hick also recalls that Farmer was one of the two best preachers he has heard, the other being Reinhold Niebuhr.[17]

Although MacKinnon, Farmer's friend and successor at Cambridge, related to me that he had visited Farmer during his retirement and had been surprised at the extent of his knowledge about contemporary developments in theology, and although he continued to preach for some years after his retirement, Farmer's final years sadly saw a decline in his mental and physical abilities. He died at his home on 13 January 1981 aged eighty-eight.

Radical Personalism

Farmer's critique of Kraemer was informed by a conviction which runs like a thread through all his work, including the present volume, namely that God is actively and constantly revealing himself to the souls of men and women, and moreover, that this is the underlying reason for the rise of human religion. More accurately, "living religion" is the result of, on the one hand, the initiative of divine *revelation* and, on the other hand, humanity's self-conscious *apprehension* of, and response to, that divine approach. That is to say, revelation is, to a large extent, defined in terms of religious experience: "all religious experience, if it is living and formative, has the quality of revelation in it, has within it the sense that the divine Thou makes himself

---

[15]"The Imagination in Preaching"—a tape recording of lecture delivered at Union Theological Seminary, Richmond, Virginia. The tape is now held in the Union Theological Seminary Archives.
[16]"Aspects of Kant's Influence on British Theology", in G. MacDonald Ross & T. McWalter (eds.), *Kant and His Influence* (Bristol: Thoemmes Antiquarian Books, 1990), p.353.
[17]Stated in a private letter to G. D'Costa. See G. D'Costa, *John Hick's Theology of Religions: A Critical Evaluation* (London: University Press of America, 1987), p.10.

known to man in his own personal situation."[18] Although this clearly shows Farmer's thought to be continuous with that of, for example, Friedrich Schleiermacher, Wilhelm Herrmann, and John Oman, as evident in his response to Tambaram, it should not be considered to be antithetical to that represented by Karl Barth, Emil Brunner and Hendrik Kraemer. As will become clear, because God is personal there must be an objective self-disclosure before anything at all can be known about him. Revelation is, in other words, a distinctively interpersonal event in which God takes the initiative: *"The essence of religion in all its forms is a response to the ultimate as personal."*[19] The sphere of religion is "the sphere of the personal, and to penetrate deeply into one is always to penetrate deeply into the other."[20] Revelation presupposes a "world of persons"—something which, according to Farmer, is particularly the case in Christian experience.

As personal beings we are constituted by the nature of the relationships we form with other persons, particularly the relationship we form with God— God, the neighbour, and the self constitute "an ultimate and continuous order of personal relationships."[21] It is important to grasp what is being said here. Farmer is not simply saying that we are in relation with other persons and with God; he is saying that persons are always in relation with God *in and through* their relationships with one another; and persons in relation with God are likewise persons in relation with one another *in and through* their relationship with God. "The self does not stand in two relations, one to God and one to his neighbour, but in *one relation* with as it were two poles; he is related to his

---

[18]H. H. Farmer, *The World and God*, p.83.
[19]Ibid., p.28.
[20]Ibid., p.32.
[21]Ibid., p.13.

neighbour in God and to God in his neighbour; it is a single and quite indiscerptible continuum of order."

Indeed, we are "persons" only because we exist in this bipolar relationship: "man is only distinctively man at all because...he stands, right down to the innermost core and essence of his being, in the profoundest possible relationship to God all the time in an order of persons...For when God creates man he creates that relationship by the same act."[22] Farmer thus emphatically repudiates the idea that a person's relationship to God begins or ceases at the point where that person begins or ceases to profess faith in Christ, or even to believe in God.

By implication then, we encounter God in fundamentally the same way that we encounter other persons, God's approach to humanity being in accordance with the very fabric of "the world of persons" in which we exist. Hence Farmer often begins his discussions of God as personal with a discussion of our own personal existence. An underlying reason for this is that because in dealing with personhood we are dealing with the ultimate nature of reality which cannot be described in terms other than its own, personhood can only really be understood firsthand; we need to reflect on our own experience. "We must assume that any man knows through his own self-awareness what it means to be a person, because he is one."[23]

> When I talk to my neighbour over the garden hedge it is quite impossible for me, even for a moment or two, to react to him as I do to the dog, even though I may call him one to my wife afterwards. Nor am I in the least danger of confusing him suddenly with the radio which is talking, possibly far more intelligently, through a window.

---

[22]H. H. Farmer, *God and Men*, p.68.
[23]Ibid., p.33.

And the reason for this is not merely that external appearances and other coincident conditions make such a confusion impossible. There is also something peculiarly and intrinsically coercive and self-evident in the immediate relationship into which both have come through that conversation...As I talk to him, hear his views, say things which he repudiates, listen to things which I repudiate, sense feeling passing from one to the other—I just know, directly and indubitably, that I am in that quite distinctive relationship with that quite distinctive sort of being which I call personal...Theoretically I should be bound to admit, if I paused for a moment and thought about it, that such an inference might be all wrong; my neighbour, after all, might, theoretically, be an elaborate mechanism or a hallucination. But when I am in practical rapport with him, I just know that such an idea is silly, if not meaningless. I am emphatically not here working with inferences, which might conceivably be mistaken. I *know* immediately that I am in a personal world, a personal dimension with him.[24]

Although, because we are physical beings, our awareness of one another is clearly mediate, this does not alter the fact that it also seems to be, at the same time, immediate.

But what, in this "psychical immediacy", is the key element by which we know that we have encountered a person? What comes across as central in our relations with a person that is lacking in our relations with a dog or a goldfish? Following a stream of thought which goes back to Kant, Farmer's answer is, quite simply, "will". "'Will' means 'person'; in and through the resistance of values the dimension of the personal is immediately known."[25] That is to say,

---

[24]H. H. Farmer, "Experience of God as Personal", pp.241-2.
[25]H. H. Farmer, *The World and God*, p.24.

within all personal relationships there is an awareness of a will "standing over against our own in a certain polarity or tension", presenting itself to us as "an inaccessible source of activity, continuously creating, as it were, an invisible frontier between [another's] being and ours, a frontier where there is always at least potential resistance, and over which there is no passing save in so far as he invites us so to do."[26] This, of course, must not be taken to mean that we only encounter persons in hostile situations of resistance or pressure, for the type of resistance that he has in mind is the basis of *all* personal relationships. He simply means that in encountering a person we encounter a will which limits our own. Thus, if we are not to treat another's will as something to be manipulated (thereby depersonalising the encounter), it must be respected and dialogued with. "The resistance of a will can never be overcome save by what we call agreement or reconciliation."[27] To clarify the point he offers the following illustration:

In the laboratory dealing with my earthworms, my microscope, my reagents of various sorts, I am, so far as my own will is concerned, in a very real sense a dictator...my will is the only will at work in the situation...I manipulate things as I wish...I do not ask the earthworm's permission to put him under the microscope; there is no permission to ask. But when I step into my own home amongst persons I am in a different world. Why? Because my will now undergoes a new and altogether different check or limitation, the limitation of other intelligent, self-directing, self-conscious, *personal*, wills besides my own. The will of another person confronts me with an independent and inaccessible source of activity which I know I am not able, and ought

---

[26]Ibid., p.19.
[27]Ibid., p.21.

> not to try, to manipulate and control into an instrument of my own will;
> and the other person himself knows that I cannot and ought not to do
> so.[28]

The point is that, in a fully personal relationship, the inaccessibility of another's will, its independence and self-determination in the face of external pressure is essential. This is most clearly evident in a situation of *trust*, trust being a relationship in which the awareness of another as personal is at its most developed stage. The more we are certain of the unalterable consistency of a person's will the more that person is deemed trustworthy; alternatively, the more we consider a person's will to be manipulable by other persons or external events the less we feel we can trust them. "This might be said to be what personality supremely is, namely that type of conscious being who is capable of entering into a relationship of trust."[29]

In the world of persons therefore there is both community and individuality. Persons are independent sources of activity, neither accessible to, nor controllable by one another, and yet, at the same time, unable to isolate themselves from each other. We are "free of one another, and yet bound to one another." Each will limits and conditions the other, whilst, at the same time, being free of the other. A dog may be stubborn, a tree may not move to let you pass, but neither, though frustrating, offer a personal value-resistance to your will. Likewise, vegetation and animals are unable to "co-operate" with you on a personal level. Hence, it is specifically the awareness of "the other as potentially co-operative in his resistance, or as potentially resistant in his co-operation, [which] lies at the heart of our awareness of personality in one

---

[28]H. H. Farmer, *God and Men*, p.43.
[29]H. H. Farmer, *The World and God*, p.21.

another."[30]   Indeed, freedom is recognised as the chief characteristic of the human person. For Farmer it is almost tautologous to say that a person's will is "free", for a will that is limited and conditioned in such a way that it is not free would not, by definition, be self-directing, and, therefore, neither would it be personal. A person whose will is suppressed and manipulated is treated more as an "it" than a "thou"; the relationship becomes merely functional and instrumental, and a functional and instrumental relationship is not a personal relationship in the sense in which Farmer understands the term. Here then is the very essence of the personal world: that wills are both free and yet condition and limit one another.

However, that said, how are we to account for the harmony and unity so central to society, not to say to family life? How do we account, in other words, for the meeting of minds between persons? For, if one will were to exert itself in such a way that it forced or dominated another it would simply depersonalise the situation and thereby frustrate any personal ends. For example, a "100 per cent dictator" would not be a person, "he would simply be a peculiar source of overriding energy, strictly comparable to a gale or a man-eating tiger."[31] So, in a nutshell, how does one will condition another so that the latter will remains free? "It can do so", argues Farmer, "only by confronting [the will] as an inescapable *claim*."[32] "Harmony between human persons only becomes possible when each, as he confronts the other, recognises himself to be under a certain constraint—the constraint of what we call claim: the other has claims upon me, I have claims upon the other."[33] Put simply, claim allows a relationship between two personal wills to be of such a

---

[30]Ibid., pp.22-3.
[31]H. H. Farmer, *God and Men*, p.49.
[32]H. H. Farmer, *The Servant of the Word*, p.42 (my emphasis).
[33]H. H. Farmer, *God and Men*, pp.48-9.

kind that each is conditioned by the other whilst remaining free of the other. Claim is not compulsion! I can freely reject it. That said, I *cannot* avoid being conditioned by it. It forces me to exercise my freedom in deciding to accept it or reject it, at which point it enters into my history: it conditions me. Claim is, therefore, an essential component of the world of persons, it belongs to the very structure of the personal dimension. It is an ultimate of the personal world, an indefinable, "its impact [having] to be felt to be known, and it is not analysable into other notions."[34] As soon as I become aware of a person, I become aware of a claim upon me. Indeed, failure to recognise this claim is not merely to treat the other as less than personal, but also to treat myself as such, for "if it is the mark of a person to confront me with claim, it is equally the mark of my being a person that I should recognise myself to be under the claim."[35]

Turning now to the specific apprehension of God as personal, Farmer insists that underlying everything exists not "an impersonal Moral Order" or "a Creative Life Force", but "an infinite mind, not without kinship to our own."[36] Thus, "the supernatural is not the idea of the contranatural, but rather the idea of the ultimate as personal; it indicates a reality which is not part of the natural order, nor yet separate from it, nor active only in suspension of it, but *above* it, in the sense of ruling it to the ends of a personal kingdom in which man is called to have a part."[37] This being so, it follows that what is central to one sphere should likewise be central to the other; the experience of other persons and the experience of God being intimately bound up with one another. In accordance with this he posits a view of ultimate reality

---

[34]Ibid., p.43.
[35]Ibid., p.49.
[36]H. H. Farmer, "Science and God", pp.175.
[37]H. H. Farmer, *The World and God*, p.111.

sometimes termed "ethical theism", "which takes as its central ideas the idea of personality and the idea of goodness. God is an infinite, personal reality Who has created, and is unweariedly interested in, the highest good of finite persons".[38] That is to say, for Farmer the term "God" signifies two broad understandings of ultimate reality, both of which necessitate divine personality: (a) rational intelligence and purposeful will; and (b) absolute goodness and the consequent intention to bring about what is "wholly good". That this is so, he argues, is confirmed by the fact that the two primary elements in the human awareness of God are "absolute demand" and "final succour".

Absolute Demand and Final Succour

I'm sure that, like myself, those familiar with Farmer's work will immediately think of these two terms when they hear his name mentioned. Although initially used by Oman, Farmer distinctively developed them and made them his own. Indeed, the centrality of this understanding of the human apprehension of God to Farmer's thought is clearly and interestingly apparent in his Gifford Lectures. Hence, in what was his fifteenth Gifford lecture (wholly devoted to divine demand and succour), he makes the following comment: "I am conscious that by this time I must have spoken of these two things almost to the point of exhaustion; but it is the facts which are to blame. We have maintained again and again, both in the previous volume and in this, that these two elements are right at the centre of the living awareness of God, and the fact that we are always encountering them, no matter from what angle we approach and explore religious experience and thought, is but a verification

---

[38]H. H. Farmer, *Towards Belief in God*, p.17.

of that assertion." [39] The sense of God "as absolutely demanding will [and] as the promise and source of all good can be discerned, in however rudimentary or corrupt form, in most, if not all, spontaneous and living religion." [40] We consider each in turn.

1. Absolute demand. Because the awareness of God happens in the sphere of our wills, just as we cannot reason from the physicality of humans to their personality, so we cannot argue the case for a personal God from the fact that the world looks as though it might have a personal purpose behind it. Rather, the experience of God as personal is *"self-authenticating and able to shine in its own light* independently of the abstract reflections of philosophy, for if it were not, it could hardly be a living experience of God as personal." [41] Hence, he states—in a passage which reminds one very much of Barth—"If we...ask how we would expect such a reality to disclose itself to us, the answer can only be that we can have no such expectancy about the matter at all; for in the nature of the case there are no parallels, no analogies on which expectancy may be based...we shall *just know* that we are dealing with God..." [42] That is to say, we become aware of God as personal by becoming aware of, and responding to, "certain value-resistances, thrust down into the midst of our own values and preferences, of such a nature that we cannot but know them to come from the Eternal." [43] Through the impact of these absolute values "there is perceived what may be called..."ontal depth" or "the dimension of the eternal"...like a promontory jutting out into the sea from some vast, misty, dimly sensed *hinterland* of mountains..." [44] Such value-resistances are

---

[39]Below, p.85. See also his comments in *Revelation and Religion*, pp.63ff, 138ff, 149ff, 152ff.
[40]H. H. Farmer, *Towards Belief in God*, p.60.
[41]H. H. Farmer, *The World and God*, p.158 (my emphasis).
[42]H. H. Farmer, *Towards Belief in God*, p.40 (my emphasis).
[43]H. H. Farmer, "Experience of God as Personal", p.243.
[44]H. H. Farmer, *The World and God*, p.26.

apprehended as absolute, sacred and unconditional, calling for obedience literally at any cost. Indeed, even the most basic instinct of all, that of survival, the preservation of one's life, is relegated to second place. As an example Farmer cites the report of Captain Oates, who, in order to save the lives of his companions, rather than allow them to carry his frost-bitten body over the Antarctic wastes, left his tent whilst they slept and struggled out into a blizzard never to be seen again. "This was", he says, "calm, unadulterated self-immolation, with no hot emotion, no public applause, no ecstatic vision to urge him on: there was just something within the Captain's soul which pointed the way to death, and there was the quiet bowing of his spirit to it."[45] Such acts, he points out, fill our beings with a sense of *reverence*, "a sense of something infinitely worthwhile and *sacred*."[46] Here is a self-sacrificial act of obedience to that which we instinctively recognise to be good and right; hence, our paradoxical feeling that in such destruction of life, life is fulfilled. The word "sacred" is, therefore, particularly appropriate, since the content of his action is fundamentally the same as the content of any specifically "religious" action. For, in the history of religions the central category of "the sacred" has always signified "the impact of a higher world upon men's spirits" and the intrinsic absolute demand of surrender and obedience. "No unbiased student of the religious history of mankind could fail to sense the presence of something extraordinarily gripping in the idea of God in the lives of men and women. The word "God" comes...saturated with the blood and tears of martyrs."[47] His point is that

---

[45]H. H. Farmer, *Experience of God*, p.32.
[46]Ibid., p.33.
[47]H. H. Farmer, *Towards Belief in God*, p.39.

God enters human experience in a living and coercively real way. God comes in the call of things so sacred and absolute that they must not be put into the balance with anything else whatever. This is what lies behind the obstinacy and the capacity for martyrdom of religious people. This is what lies behind the fact that sacrifice runs like a red streak through all religion from its most primitive form upwards. The mother casting her babes to Moloch and Damien giving up all to tend the lepers stand in a direct line of succession with one another; they are both bowing their heads, the one primitively, fearfully, superstitiously, the other with the full light of knowledge which has come through Christ, to a haunting, divine presence in their hearts, which reveals itself only through its insistence on an absolute surrender of this life to itself.[48]

Moreover, we are aware that we have indeed apprehended *another will*, and not merely our own desires or anthropomorphic projections (as Feuerbach claimed), because of its *unconditionality*. That is to say, whereas that which I impose upon myself by my own will can, in the final analysis, be set aside, particularly in the face of personal extinction, an *unconditional* demand cannot. Therefore, by definition, such a demand is not my own. Hence, "Whoso says God, says, for the religious mind, the ultimate WILL haunting the soul with the pressure of an unconditional value, with the demand for an unconditional obedience; and whoso says the pressure of an unconditional value, the demand for an unconditional obedience, says, for the religious mind, the ultimate WILL of God."[49] That is not to say that one feels the impact of unconditional value and then *goes on* to deduce from that the awareness of an

---

[48]H. H. Farmer, *Experience of God*, p.39.
[49]H. H. Farmer, *The World and God*, p.24.

ultimate holy purpose as the best explanation for it. No, for Farmer, this would be philosophy, not living religion. Rather, the awareness of God is given *immediately* in and through the impact of unconditional value itself. There is a coerciveness, a certain compelling unanalysable immediacy, in the apprehension of God, a sense of something standing over against us, independent of us, "'hitting' us and demanding adjustment from us."[50]

Finally, the absolute demand constitutes a "claim" upon our wills. It does not override our personal freedom. Quite simply, God's claim on me meets me the moment I encounter him, and sin (according to Farmer) is fundamentally the fact that we have rejected, and do reject, this claim of God upon us. Furthermore, to say that God claims us means that, in John Baillie's words, "however much we try to keep to ourselves, yet he will not leave us to ourselves. It means that he invades even our 'ultimate heart's occult abode'. It means that his is a love that has claimed us from the beginning, and that to the end refuses to let us go."[51]

2. Final succour. At the heart of the apprehension of God there is, inseparable from the awareness of "absolute demand", an awareness of *ultimate* or *final succour*. God is not merely encountered as an absolute will claiming us for himself, but also as "the promise and source of all good". "I do not believe that God ever comes livingly to a man or a woman without making a claim, a demand. Nor does he ever come without proffering strength and succour."[52] Again, "To know God livingly and fully as personal he must be apprehended at one and the same time as 'consuming fire' and as 'refuge and strength.'"[53] These twin perceptions are given in and through one another:

---

[50]H. H. Farmer, *Towards Belief in God*, p.22.
[51]J. Baillie, *Our Knowledge of God* (London: Oxford University Press, 1939), p.13.
[52]H. H. Farmer, *The Servant of the Word*, p.67.
[53]H. H. Farmer, *The World and God*, p.26.

the absolute demand which impacts the human soul provides succour, in that it opens up the way to a person's highest good. Indeed, it is crucial to Farmer's thesis, and particularly to his notion of reconciliation, that God's purpose, which discloses itself to humanity in absolute demand, also discloses itself as seeking humanity's "highest and richest personal life": "It is of the highest significance to say that a demand which asks, if necessity should arise, the surrender of this life and all its delights, is, in and through that very demand, pointing the way to man's highest blessedness."[54] God's will, though it circumscribes human desires, is thus apprehended as fully trustworthy. Operating in the same world of values—indeed, as the ground of that world— God seeks the fulfilment of the human personality. His will, in its very resistance, is, therefore, "in a unique and ultimate way, co-operative."[55] It both resists our human wills and yet enables us to achieve self-realisation as persons. Hence the truth of Jesus' words, "...whoever loses his life for my sake will find it" (Matt. 10:39): "the only way to have the deeper nature released is to have some greater demand addressed to it."[56] Thus, as was pointed out in the illustration of Captain Oates' self-sacrifice, paradoxically we feel that in such destruction of life, life is fulfilled: in bowing to the absolute demand one ascends to the heights of personhood.

The fact that living religion does provide succour in helping us to achieve self-realisation is, of course, no accident; it is fundamental to who we are as human persons living in the world. As such, it is therefore pragmatically verifiable.

---

[54]H. H. Farmer, *Towards Belief in God*, pp.51-2.
[55]H. H. Farmer, *The World and God*, p.25.
[56]H. H. Farmer, *The Healing Cross*, p.141.

The Pragmatic Element of Religious Conviction

Corresponding to the apprehension of God as "demand" and "succour" Farmer identifies two elements of conviction: the coercive and the pragmatic. These, along with a third "reflective" element,[57] are another important aspect of his theology.[58] Early on in his theological career he made it clear that one of his principal theological aims was to explain the grounds for theistic belief; a task which he understood to be both descriptive and apologetic, in that he sought to describe, critically interpret and defend the reasonableness of "the elements of conviction". These elements, he believes, are basic in the formation of theistic belief. It is important to understand at this point that, as with the twofold apprehension of God, there is an intermingling of the elements of belief. For the purposes of analysis one is forced to divide what is in reality, according to Farmer, a very complex and continuous process: "In actual experience our convictions are, as it were, deposited out of a stream of experience in which at any given moment the inescapable compulsions of truth and fact and the experimental ventures and verifications of pragmatic faith are in continual, eddying interplay with one another."[59] The awareness of God, in other words, represents a perceptual synthesis of all three elements, which, though logically distinguishable, should not be interpreted as separate cognitive faculties. Though, of course, these criteria cannot be applied with any mathematical

---

[57]The third element is the result of "a peculiar combination of the other two" (*Experience of God*, p.24). We are not fully satisfied, he argues, unless our beliefs have been "reflectively submitted to the criticism of reason, and unless they harmonise with other knowledge and, in general, help them to give [us] a satisfying philosophy of life taken as a whole" (ibid., p.23).
[58] The importance of the elements of conviction to Farmer's thought are discussed in detail in Brandt Boeke's excellent dissertation, "The Knowledge of God in the Theology of H. H. Farmer" (unpublished doctoral thesis: Princeton Theological Seminary, 1987), chs. 4-7.
[59]H. H. Farmer, *Towards Belief in God*, p.27.

precision—and thus cannot produce mathematical certainty—they do provide, for the believer, "an indispensable guide":

> If a belief (1) shines in its own light with a certain inherent compellingness, (2) "works" in the sense of both satisfying our nature and of helping in the practical task of managing our world, (3) reveals on examination both internal consistencies and external harmony with other experience and knowledge, then we have in regard to it as full an assurance of truth as it is possible for a human mind to have and it ought ever to ask.[60]

Having already noted something of the compellingness of religious conviction—to which I will be returning below when I consider its self-authenticating nature—my present concern is with its practical aspect: the succour of theism.

Farmer begins his discussion of theistic verification "with a rather obvious fact, namely that all experience comes to us through intercourse between our minds and the world, or environment, in which we live...There must be objects experienced and a consciousness which experiences those objects."[61] This characteristic Farmerian emphasis on both the subjective and objective dimensions of knowing reveals an affinity to Kantian and neo-Kantian emphases upon the inseparability of the subjective processes of apprehension and the reality of an objective referent. Apprehension of our environment, whether natural or supernatural, necessarily involves an interplay between the world and ourselves, an interplay which is, moreover, fundamental to our evolution as persons.

---

[60]Ibid., p.28.
[61]Ibid., p.20.

This latter point needs some elucidation. His thesis is that the individual evolves by the continual process of harmonisation: we seek to harmonise ourselves with our environment by avoiding destructive forces and utilising beneficent ones. That is to say, not only does the environment demand that we adjust ourselves to it, but there is an inborn impulse to meet the challenge— urged on by self-preservation and the desire to develop. Hence (and here we see a distinct epistemological realism in his thought—and thus a parting of company with Kant), because life is all the time an adjustment to the world, the distinction between truth and falsity is paramount; we need to know the truth about our environment in order to adjust ourselves correctly to it. "The two things are inseparable. The distinction between fact and fiction, truth and falsity...only has meaning in relation to a vital impulse within the living creature to live accordingly to that distinction...In its effort to adjust itself to the facts, the living being maintains and develops itself, unfolds its latent powers."[62] Moreover, this adjustment is governed by what he refers to as our "immanent teleology": the blueprint, so to speak, of an organism present in the earliest moments of its life. We have, in other words, an "interest" in becoming what we were created to be—"interest" being broadly "a response to [an] environment taking an organically relevant direction through feeling."[63] We feel a sense of well-being, a certain healthiness, when we are in a harmonious relationship with our environment; when we are living in accordance with our immanent teleology. Thus, "the functional and teleological unity of the organism enters as a determinant into the consciousness."[64]

---

[62]Ibid., p.22.
[63]H. H. Farmer, *The World and God*, p.40.
[64]Ibid., p.40.

Germane to this, and important for understanding Farmer's thesis, is his treatment of analytic and synthetic apprehension. *Analytic apprehension—* logical or empirical analysis proceeding solely by deductive or inductive inference—refers to the way in which the mind attempts to deconstruct, or break down, what it apprehends. Such apprehension allows one to see the constituent parts of a whole and the various ways they interconnect. "The process is essentially one of abstraction; that is to say, it is a process of isolating in thought aspects of the situation which in fact are not met in that isolated form at all."[65] In contrast, *synthetic apprehension* fuses impressions together into "significant totalities". However, whereas the analytic response can be volitional—a physicist purposes to break down the universe into its constituent parts—the synthetic approach cannot. Of course, to a certain extent, the impulse to analyse is inborn; but, to synthesise impressions, he argues, by a deliberate act of the will into total significant situations is impossible—"the mind must fuse [impressions] in a sort of intuitional flash which is as a rule quite beyond volitional control."[66] The reason for this is that the synthetic response to the world is part of what is "essentially a feeling response", the term "feeling" referring to an awareness (not necessarily a fully self-conscious or explicit awareness) of "the *significance* of a situation *for the individual's own life.*"[67]

The point is that our intuitive, synthetic apprehension of the world serves the evolutionary impulse to know the facts of our environment and, thereby, to discover how we fit into it—*its significance for ourselves.* Indeed, he insists that the valuation of one's experience and environment is the primary mode of knowledge; all knowledge reflects our personal values, our inner and

---

[65]Ibid., p.32.
[66]Ibid., p.34.
[67]Ibid., p.35 (my emphasis).

instinctive drive for self-realisation. In Oman's words, "We cannot know without interest."[68] "We know all environment, not as impact or physical influx, but as meaning: and this meaning depends on [among other things]...the unique character of the feeling it creates...[and] the unique value it has for us..."[69] This is attained by synthetic apprehension; we synthetically perceive the significance of situations in relation to our own interest. In this context Farmer emphasises the importance of "wishful thinking": *what we want to be the case* determines the significance of our environment for us. Although it is advisable to guard against wishful thinking, since it can lead to problematic, egocentric, fantastical conclusions, "our wishes and desires, if they be of *the right sort*, may be an indispensable factor in knowing *realities of a certain order.* Why not?...[There] is certainly truth of feeling as well as truth of exact logical statement and proof."[70] He thus rejects the idea, as does William James,[71] that because one *wishes* a belief to be true, for that reason, one should conclude its falsity. Wishful thinking can be a cognitive manifestation of our teleological interest.

The argument is that the charge against religion of "wishful thinking" is not wholly unfounded. For, as an aspect of our primal interest, intrinsic to our immanent teleology as "persons", it operates as a key factor in our apprehension of God. Hence, in his discussion of the "Inner Roots of Personal Religion",[72] Farmer contends that the awareness of God corresponds to "the fundamental interest of the personality". Religion, in other words, is "rooted in the deepest interest of the human organism, the interest which it has in

---

[68]J. Oman, *The Natural and the Supernatural* (Cambridge: Cambridge University Press, 1931), pp.5-6.
[69]Ibid., p.58.
[70]H. H. Farmer, *God and Men*, p.30 (my emphasis).
[71]Cf. W. James, "The Will to Believe", in W. James, *The Will to Believe and Other Essays in Popular Philosophy* (New York: Dover, 1956).
[72]H. H. Farmer, *The World and God*, ch.2.

fulfilling itself, in becoming that which by the primordial constitution of its being it is intended to be."[73] We are religious by design. However, it is important to understand that this is not merely a natural function akin to the leaves of a plant turning toward the sun. In the human consciousness, the urge towards maturity becomes, in the pursuit of an ideal life, a fully self-conscious purposive interest: we *actively seek* meaning; we rise above the impersonal forces of nature in our desire for harmony and self-realisation. This, he argues, is the deepest, most pervasive and formative aspect of humanity, manifest in our unconscious processes and, on the highest level, in ideals, aspirations, feelings of guilt and remorse and, supremely, in the moral and religious life.

> It is some confirmation of the rightness of thus relating the awareness of God on its subjective side to the immanent teleology which constitutes man specifically man, that religion is in some ways the most distinctive of human functions; there is nothing even dimly suggestive of it in animal life...It is further confirmation that religion, perhaps more than any other interest, inevitably grows feeble and corrupt if it be isolated from the other interests of life, instead of informing and giving meaning and direction to them all. And it is still further confirmation that it has been possible for different thinkers, each with a show of truth, to discover the essence of religion in one or other of the three fundamental aspects of consciousness. Some, like Hegel, have sought to centre religious need and truth in reason; others, like Kant, in the will; others, like Schleiermacher, in feeling. Each is right, and yet is in a measure wrong. For religion is in some way a

---

[73]Ibid., p.39.

response of the whole personality, thinking, willing, feeling. It is the personality grasping, intuiting something through its own profound interest in its own fullest realisation.[74]

Hence, returning to the element of "succour", put simply, the theist should discover the truth of Psalm 27.13 ("I am confident of this: I will see the goodness of the Lord in the land of the living"), "that to serve God *is* to walk the way of increasing blessedness and victory even in this present life, that, to put it very vulgarly, religion does in fact deliver the goods".[75] His argument is that, "of the various interpretations of life which are open to us to adopt and live by, that which in practice proves to be more satisfying to our whole nature is the more likely to be true. *Per contra*, that which in practice leaves us frustrated, unhappy, in unresolved conflict with ourselves and with our world, is less likely to be true."[76] This clearly functions as a basic presupposition in the minds of most people: if a philosophy of life is fundamentally at odds with the facts—as most people understand them—it is unlikely to gain widespread acceptance. And it does not do so for the reasons outlined above: what is considered "false" is not considered "good"—truth, we feel, is good to know; "a man gains in well-being by knowing the truth; and that which in the long run is not good to know, brings with it no enhancement or enrichment...is not likely to be true." As we have seen, this deep-seated pragmatic conviction is allied to synthetic apprehension; it motivates the human quest for knowledge and leads us to construct vast unifying theories and interpretative systems. Continually feeling ill at ease with our environment, "misfits" in the world, we seek to adjust ourselves to it; we seek to know the truth, to be rightly related to

---

[74]Ibid., pp.41-2.
[75]H. H. Farmer, *Towards Belief in God*, p.52.
[76]Ibid., p.24.

reality. However—and this is important—unlike the rest of life, problems arise when we humans realise that the task of adjustment and harmonisation lies *permanently beyond us*. Though Farmer discusses several areas in which this is evident (memory, imagination, consciousness of being a "self" and the tensions inherent within human society), the basic issue is most concisely stated in a memorable early sermon entitled "The Dilemma of Godlessness". Comparing humanity to a spider fruitlessly trying to spin a web on the edge of a rock where the currents of air immediately blow the fine strands away, he asks, "What are these creatures—what am I—rushing up to town in automobiles and swaying railway trains, selling this, buying that, tapping out letters and invoices on writing machines, phoning hither and thither, eating, drinking, love-making, money-making?"[77] His point is that when one concentrates merely on one's physical existence there seems to be a hollow meaninglessness at the heart of it all. To contemplate seriously one's life with no external reference leads to a sense of its meaninglessness and a philosophy which, in many cases, becomes very debilitating, not to say destructive: "man's dignity begins to vanish away. He becomes simply a rather pathetic animal, carried along by instincts and desires whose objects have no more permanence and significance than the honey after which the ants run in accordance with *their* instincts and desires. With this tragic difference, however, *he knows* that that is how things are."[78] Unlike other creatures, *Homo sapiens* need to know that their lives have meaning. And this need cannot be satisfied by their natural environment. As long as a plant has sun, water and fertile soil its needs are met. Not so for the human. Our world is, so to speak, too small for us. This is why, he argues, theism provides succour. In

---

[77]H. H. Farmer, *The Healing Cross.*, p.2.
[78]Ibid., p.5.

the words of Oman, we are shown "a world really big enough to breathe in."[79] When we apprehend God we discover that there "*is* an environment larger than this world in relation to which alone can man's true life be realised."[80] A significant element, therefore, in final succour is the assurance that there is this "invisible, intangible world, a supra-mundane, supernatural reality to which man must be rightly related if he is to fulfil his own distinctive nature and destiny."[81] More specifically, there is provided in the apprehension of God "an explicit and living conviction, so mediated that directly the mind contemplates it and relates it to the facts it becomes possessed again by the sense of its truth, that behind all the challenges of life there is a divine purpose which is Love..."[82] Hence, the theist no longer experiences the universe as hostile to his or her needs; no longer is it considered ultimately to be a frustration to our immanent teleology; our deepest interests and "wishes" as persons can be realised. Encompassing the universe there is a purpose of love; underlying it, one who seeks our highest good; encountering us, a God who is our "final succour". Thus it is that "in religion the spirit of man discerns itself to be at home in the universe."[83] Hence, theism, in making sense of the world, meets a basic human need, and is, thereby, pragmatically verified.

The Self-authenticating, Coercive Element of Religious Conviction

However, theism does not merely provide succour, in that, in our apprehension of God, we are also aware of "sacred value". This is why, in addition to the descriptions of religion mentioned above, there are also those which emphasise obedience, abasement, dependence and submission to moral duty.

---

[79]Cited in H. H. Farmer, *Towards Belief in God*, p.59.
[80]Ibid., p.75 (my emphasis).
[81]Ibid., p.74.
[82]H. H. Farmer, *Experience of God*, p.62.
[83]H. H. Farmer, *The World and God*, p.42.

Moreover, in thus confronting us God is, again, responding to an intrinsic "personal" need. Because our destiny as responsible persons requires that we should, to some extent, be in charge of it, we need to: (a) be aware, however dimly, of the immanent norm of our nature and to co-operate with it; and (b) rise above animal instinct and take responsible control of our destiny. Both these requirements are fulfilled by the impact of unconditional values. "[In] the awareness of unconditional values the norm of [the] whole organism, its deep urge towards its own self-realisation, breaks into the self-consciousness of man."[84] That is to say, in our apprehension of the divine we become aware of what we *ought* to be—of what we were created to be. Our obedience to this "ought", therefore, frees the urge towards self-realisation and we move on to "a new level of insight and power". On the other hand, if our lives are marked by disobedience, moral failure and sin there is "a progressive degradation and disintegration of the whole personality on all its levels, running out into debased and unnatural physical appetites as luridly pictured in the first chapter of the Epistle to the Romans."[85] As to the impact of sacred values releasing us from a merely instinctive existence, to quote Oman again, the moment humanity said, "'this is sacred, this is not the realm of ordinary values'...he had said to his world as well as to himself, 'Thou shalt not'. Forthwith he began to be master of himself, and, thereby, master in his world. Then, in some true sense of the word he began to be free. Thus by the judgement of the sacred, man was set free from the leading strings of nature..."[86]

Therefore, living religion, the divine-human encounter, is rooted in our humanity and fundamental to our self-realisation as persons. This is why, he argues, in various ways and to varying extents, a large proportion of

---

[84]Ibid., p.45.
[85]Ibid., p.46.
[86]J. Oman, *The Natural and the Supernatural*, p.85.

definitions of religion seem to support the notion that in religion the human soul "achieves, or maintains, or affirms, its essential selfhood in and through an awareness of its essential unity with the ultimate ground and meaning of the world."[87] Moreover, because his thesis understands our environment to be one congenial to *personal* self-realisation, responsive to our "interest" as personal beings, it demonstrates the appropriateness of understanding this ultimate ground as *personal*. Put simply, only a personal being could provide a universe with a character congenial to the highest values and strivings of personal beings.

Now, of course, this argument is based on certain presuppositions and is not intended as a rational proof of God's existence. For Farmer, final proof can only be given in a self-authenticating, coercive divine-human encounter.

We need now to consider more closely this understanding of a "self-authenticating" and "immediate" theological epistemology. Perhaps the best way to do this will be to provide (a) a brief outline of some of the criticisms that have been levelled against Farmer's thesis and (b) a summary evaluation of their adequacy.

In his 1936 review of *The World and God* F. R. Tennant is particularly critical of Farmer's claim that God is immediately known in and through the experience of demand and succour. He accuses him of "not being sufficiently alive to the difference between certainty in the sense of personal convincedness and certainty in the sense of an objective and logical characteristic of some propositions—which sense alone is involved when knowledge is being discussed."[88] In the following decades it was argued that logical positivism and subsequent linguistic analysis undermined any

---

[87]H. H. Farmer, *The World and God*, p.43.
[88]F. R. Tennant, Review of *The World and God* , in *Mind* 45 (1936), p.243.

epistemology based on the immediacy of experience: "The notion of existential encounter is not enough to support a theological position epistemologically...The divine-human encounter is nothing like as straightforward as Farmer and others suggest."[89] "'I have had an experience of God' is not valid as a claim to objective knowledge of God...[for] there are no tests available to give grounds for the statement."[90] This is a point that has been forcefully argued by Antony Flew, C. B. Martin, and Ronald Hepburn. All three would agree with Stephen Neill that "philosophical thinking of [Farmer's] type now seems to belong to a rather remote world. The thinking of the older generation of philosophers was formed before linguistic analysis or logical positivism had been heard of...[Linguistic philosophy] presented a pistol at the heads of all theologians: when theologians speak are they speaking of anything at all, and is it possible to attach any meaning at all to their utterances?"[91] Metaphysical statements, it is argued, are "meaningless" because their truth or falsity cannot be empirically established. Statements are only meaningful to the extent that they can be "scientifically" verified; to the extent that they adhere to the basic rules of logic.

In *God and Philosophy*, which is a fairly ruthless and blunt assault on theism, Flew provides a chapter on religious experience in which Farmer, John Baillie, and H. D. Lewis are singled out for attack. Flew's basic objection seems to be as follows. In the words of Hobbes, "if any man pretend to me that God hath spoken to him...immediately, and I make doubt of it, I cannot easily perceive what argument he can produce to oblige me to believe it...To say he hath spoken to him in a dream, is no more than to say he dreamed that

---

[89]B. Haymes, "The Theology of H. H. Farmer" (unpublished Master's thesis: Exeter University, 1972-3), pp.113-4.
[90]B. Haymes, "The Supernatural is Personal", in *The Baptist Quarterly* 26 (1975), p.10.
[91]S. Neill, "Theology 1939-1964", in *The Expository Times* 64 (1976), p.23.

God spoke to him..."[92] Hence, Farmer's assertion that experience of God is "self-authenticating" is of little value, in that it involves *only* experience without any *falsifiable* reference to anything beyond—and in claiming immunity from philosophical criticism, is both illogical and unobtainable. Thus, in a similar way to Tennant, Flew wants to draw a distinction between "biographical" and "epistemological" questions. That I believe I have encountered God is *biographically* true. That belief, however, says nothing as to whether I *actually* have. Certainty, says Tennant, "is a matter of personal biography, while philosophies are concerned with public truth."[93] Moreover, all talk "about either inter-personal relations or belief in a person presupposes the truth of the presupposition that the other person does objectively exist."[94] But this is precisely what is in question. Thus Farmer's claim to have had an encounter with God amounts to little more than "gratuitous and parochial dogmatism."[95] In the final analysis, if God is disembodied, his existence cannot be established, therefore propositions about him cannot be verified or falsified.

However, as Ronald Hepburn points out,

The main features of this approach can only be welcomed by the philosopher of religion. If the methods of verification that philosophers bring to religious statements are suitable for confirming the existence of *objects*, and if God is "irreducibly *Subject*", irreducibly *personal*, the application of these methods will quite misleadingly (perhaps falsely) proclaim that God does not exist. This warning is salutary...to the linguistic philosopher whose "hangover"

---

[92] A. G. N. Flew, *God and Philosophy* (London: Hutchinson, 1966), p.126.
[93] F. R. Tennant, Review of *The World and God*, p.242.
[94] A. G. N. Flew, *God and Philosophy*, p.135.
[95] Ibid., p.137.

from positivism tempts him to think of verification as *par excellence*
the confirmation of scientific hypotheses.[96]

Nevertheless, Hepburn does want to question the validity of an entirely self-
authenticating knowledge of God. Are there no checking procedures? Can we
not have *both* encounter *and* reasoned theistic argumentation? And do not the
obvious differences between God and humans invalidate the personalist
analogy between meeting people and meeting God?

Noting (approvingly) that Farmer emphasises the fact that "although
personal knowledge of people is in some sense direct or immediate, it is by no
means independent of 'bodily manifestations'", Hepburn feels that "it is
doubtful whether [he] holds on to his own insight consistently."[97] His unease
is due to Farmer's central concepts of "trust" and "will". As we have seen, a
person is "that type of conscious being who is capable of entering into...a
mutual relationship of trust", personal relationship being an "ultimate polarity
of wills". Taking "will" as the common factor, he provides an account of the
personal knowledge of God by asserting that an awareness of absolute,
unconditional values is none other than an awareness of the will of God. "And
'will' means 'person'." Farmer thus speaks of an immediate, self-
authenticating, personal encounter: God is "known only through direct
perception". Hepburn, however, complains that by using the word "will"
Farmer has made "the transition from human to divine encounters...look
deceptively smooth."[98] To say that "will" means "person" is, he believes,
misleading, in that a "sense of will", apart from bodily evidence, does not
guarantee the existence of a person. For example, he makes the point that a

[96]R. Hepburn, *Christianity and Paradox: Critical Studies in Twentieth-Century Theology*
(London: Watts, 1958), pp.29-30.
[97]R. Hepburn, *Christianity and Paradox*, p.40.
[98]R. Hepburn, *Christianity and Paradox*, p.40.

soldier can be given the courage to fight on because he believes that back at home his mother is willing him to do so, when in fact, unknown to him, his mother recently died. His awareness of will is not therefore dependent on the existence of a person. There are likewise many situations in which people are deceived by, or deluded about, a sense of will.

That said, can we be mistaken about absolute values? Hepburn agrees that this is fairly solid ground, but argues that there is an inconsistency in Farmer's thought which allows him to identify these values with the will of God. Farmer's assertion that unconditional value judgements can be satisfactorily accounted for only by understanding them as the will of God, assumes the premise that God's will is itself unconditionally good. If this was not the case, then "the fact that he backed up some moral judgement of ours would do nothing to settle the question of its absoluteness or even its rightness."[99] The implication of Hepburn's point is probably best understood if we reduce it to the following syllogism: (a) The value of unconditionality is applied to that which God wills; (b) God's will is itself unconditionally good; therefore, (c) God's will is unconditionally good because what he wills he wills! This is, to say the least, problematic. Hepburn thus argues that the judgement that God's will is *unconditionally* good must be a *human* value-judgement. "But if we can make this one judgement, it can no longer be said that the sense of unconditional obligation is understandable only as encounter with God's will."[100] Indeed, as he points out, Farmer himself concedes that "it is not possible to exclude logically all other possible causes of the unconditionality of the moral imperative."[101] Farmer thus tacitly admits that the sense of absolute value does not *necessarily* imply an encounter with God.

---

[99]Ibid., p.42-3.
[100]Ibid., p.43.
[101]Ibid., p.43.

Although the above critics make some important points, they do not, I believe, do justice to Farmer's cumulative thesis. Several points need to be considered: (1) Farmer is surely right to emphasise the *primacy* and *immediacy* of the coercive element in belief: "We believe in God, in part at any rate, because we cannot help it, because something "hits" us immediately out of our world, something, which in its essential impact upon our spirit, comes as the call of God to us."[102] As with our conviction about any truth, we become aware of an objective fact demanding adjustment from us. This is why it is always very difficult for atheistic régimes to stamp out religious belief, for "in religion there enters the human mind a compulsion more powerful than even powerful impulses like fear, hunger and sex."[103] Indeed, as H. D. Lewis argues, many of the sophisticated arguments and conclusions of "reflective religion...turn upon an alleged immediacy of encounter with the divine, much of the philosophy of religion having been prompted and given its direction by inspired and gifted mystics who...make a special claim to immediate experience of God..."[104] The point is that in religious experience persons become convinced of an objective fact confronting them. As Simone Weil put it, "We experience the compulsion of God's pressure."[105] That it is God's pressure is, of course, open to question since it cannot be empirically and publicly verified.

(2) Although the believer does not stand before a bodily manifestation as such, arguably becoming aware of God is similar to the way persons become aware of other persons—and, as with cognition of God, the believer's encounter with another human person yields immediate knowledge, which is

---

[102]H. H. Farmer, *Experience of God*, p.40.
[103]H. H. Farmer, *Towards Belief in God*, p.51.
[104]H. D. Lewis, *Our Experience of God* (London: Collins, Fontana, 1970), p.347.
[105]S. Weil, *Waiting on God*, tr. by E. Craufurd (London: Collins, Fontana, 1959), p.14.

not only non-inferential, but also incommunicable, just as all the basic elements of human experience are incommunicable. "Who could describe light and colour to one who has known nothing but darkness?"[106] The point is that these mundane epistemological facts concur with theological epistemology. In a similar way to knowing other persons, it is not "possible to describe the compelling touch of God otherwise than as the compelling touch of God. To anyone who has had no such awareness of God...it will be quite impossible to indicate what is meant."[107] In the final analysis, as Hendrikus Berkhof has pointed out, "the functional adequacy of language can be judged only by the person who through the medium of this language understands what this language tries to say."[108]

(3) However, there is far more to Farmer's argument than the mere assertion that the self-authenticating and incommunicable nature of religious experience is unavoidable. He holds that there *is* a society of tests and checking procedures which enable us to distinguish awareness of God from fantasy. As we have seen, he acknowledges that, because of the dangers of "wishful thinking", claimed encounters may have more to do with psychology than theology: "a belief is not necessarily true because it lays hold of the mind with a certain intrinsic compelling power."[109] He would thus agree with Flew that the claim "I have had an experience of God" does not in itself verify that experience. As with other experiences, and particularly personal relationships, there is an element of trust, confirmed over time by pragmatic and reflective verification.

---

[106]C. B. Martin, *Religious Belief* (Ithaca: Cornell University Press, 1959), p.69.
[107]H. H. Farmer, *Towards Belief in God*, p.40.
[108]H. Berkhof, *Christian Faith: An Introduction to the Study of the Faith* (Grand Rapids: Eerdmans, 1979), p.67.
[109]H. H. Farmer, *God and Men*, p.21. Experience clearly shows that "it is possible for false beliefs...to take possession of men's minds" (p.18).

My point is that Flew, Hepburn and Martin all fail to mention the crucially important three elements of conviction, let alone their interrelatedness.[110] Farmer never asserts that the element of direct awareness is the *only* element in the establishment of religious conviction which need be considered. "It is our thesis", he states, "that it is *only one* element, though a quite indispensable one."[111] Indeed, Tennant's critique seems to be based on a misunderstanding of precisely this point. Farmer does not believe, as Tennant insists he does, that "religious experience involves direct apprehension of a real realm...and is *sufficient of itself*, or without presuppositions derived elsewhere, to vouch for the reality of that realm."[112] Although Farmer would not, of course, be happy with Tennant's "rational theology", he nevertheless does have a place for rational reflection. He is keen to balance the subjectivity of the coercive element in religious belief with the objectivity of rational verification provided by the pragmatic and reflective elements. Thus, to Hepburn's question, "Can we accept that sharp division—either arguments for God *or* personal encounter; nothing in between?"[113] Farmer would answer in the negative. He does not try to defend (as perhaps Brunner did) the validity of an *entirely* self-authenticating knowledge of God and an experience which claims immunity from all philosophical criticism. As F. G. Healey has pointed out, "the words of Farmer to which Hepburn refers more than once—"the Christian experience of God as personal, which in the nature of the case must be self-authenticating and able to shine in its own light independently of the abstract reflections of philosophy..."—those very words are embedded within the context of a discussion about miracles and the laws of nature, and how scientific and

---

[110] On this see B. Boeke, "The Knowledge of God in the Theology of H. H. Farmer", chs. 4-7.
[111] H. H. Farmer, *Towards Belief in God*, pp.40-1 (my emphasis).
[112] F. R. Tennant, Review of *The World and God*, p.242 (my emphasis).
[113] R. W. Hepburn, *Christianity and Paradox*, p.30.

religious views might be set in some sort of organic relation to one another."[114] Hence, he rejects the notion that religious belief is "unconditional" in the sense that it allows no further verification beyond immediate encounter. Although he recognises the dangers of rationalism, his understanding of "self-authenticating" does not mean that intuitive apprehension is veridical in the sense that it lies beyond the need or possibility of scrutiny or confirmation.

(4) It would seem that because of the common stock of "personalist" epistemological terms (such as "I-thou", "intuition" and "immediate apprehension"), critics have assumed that such as Martin Buber, John Baillie, Brunner and Farmer are investing them with the same meaning. This, however, is a mistake. Certainly in Farmer's case, but most probably in John Baillie's also, Buber's influence was limited and has been greatly overstated.[115] There is certainly not the consensus that Flew and Hepburn seem to think there is. One cannot simply assume that Farmer is saying the same thing as Brunner and Buber.

(5) As to Flew's contention that "all assertion must involve a theoretical possibility of error proportionate to its content", Illtyd Trethowan has argued that a theoretical possibility of error does not logically refute the fact that we actually know things: "Knowledge of the truth", he says, "is always self-authenticating in the sense that it is always a matter in the end of my *seeing* something."[116] Therefore, in defence of Farmer and H. D. Lewis he argues that, "What they are claiming...is an awareness of God. The fact that this

---

[114]F. G. Healey, "Introduction" to *Prospect for Theology: Essays in Honour of H. H. Farmer* (Welwyn: Nisbet, 1966), p.28.
[115] See my discussion of this point in *H. H. Farmer's Theological Interpretation of Religion* (Lampeter: Edwin Mellen Press, 1998), pp.37-45.
[116]I. Trethowan, *The Absolute and the Atonement* (London: George Allen & Unwin, 1971), p.23.

claim cannot be falsified is nothing against it. Nor can Flew's falsification principle show that the claim is without content."[117]

(6) Finally, Farmer makes it clear that, as far as he is concerned, theistic proofs are "as religiously improper as they are philosophically inadequate"— God's existence is indemonstrable. Quite simply, he never attempts to provide a rational demonstration of the relationship between the claims "I have had an experience of God" and "God exists".

To sum up: Farmer's use of the term "self-authenticating" is far more qualified than his critics suggest. Hence, although his thesis "sounds at first like retiring into the inaccessible shelter of one's own subjective feelings",[118] we have seen that several points need to be borne in mind: (a) The coercive element's presence, in however compelling a form, "establishes no right to dispense with the tests of practical experience and of the acutest reflection we can command."[119] (b) There is, in the final analysis, nothing particularly reprehensible about the claim to a direct encounter and an ultimately incommunicable experience. "It is a perfectly proper thing for a religious man to say: 'I have a direct experience of a certain kind of reality, and behold, I find it so unique that I cannot describe it in terms of anything lying outside that direct experience itself.'"[120] (c) It is all too easy to be led astray by slippery words like "private" and "subjective". An experience, he points out, might be private and subjective in the sense that it is incommunicable, but not in the sense that it mediates a reality closed off to the experience of all, and thus incapable of being formulated in a system of generally accepted propositions. Indeed, modern research has established both "how widespread

---

[117]Ibid., p.23.
[118]H. H. Farmer, *Towards Belief in God*, p.40.
[119]Ibid., p.41.
[120]Ibid., p.41.

religious experience is in human life from the lowest stages to the highest",
and "how impressively unanimous such religious awareness is that at its heart
there is something incommunicably peculiar to itself, both in respect of the
reality disclosed through it and in respect of the response which it evokes in
the soul."[121] One is, therefore, not left alone pondering one's own subjective
experiences, but rather one exists as part of (to use Polanyi's phrase) a
community of verifiers. Hence, to quote Healey:

> If the religious way of knowing is unique, it is so, not on account of
> uniqueness in psychological ways of apprehending, but on account of
> the uniqueness of what is apprehended. If it is incommunicable, that is
> because the apprehending must in the case of each person be his own.
> It is not incommunicable, however, in the sense that one person cannot
> express to another enough to enable him, if he will, to recognise from
> his own experience what is being talked about. A good deal of
> Farmer's work... is directed to just that aim.[122]

Having said that, in the final analysis it should be reiterated that religion
cannot provide empirical verification of its claim that in encountering absolute
values one encounters the divine will. This is a statement of "faith". We rest
on an "invincible surmise", reflectively verified. To the unbeliever Christian
theism can be shown to be internally coherent and at least as persuasive as any
other worldview; to the believer divine personality and goodness can be
systematically shown to be the most faithful interpretation of his or her
religious experience. In Farmer's writings we see an attempt to present (in
Hick's words) "Christian theism as a coherent possibility, which gains the

---

[121]Ibid., p.42.
[122]F. G. Healey, "Introduction" to *Prospect for Theology*, p.29.

believer's allegiance through the compelling quality of his own religious experience, and which finds confirmation both in the pragmatic outworking of his faith and in rational reflection upon human experience as a whole. This is not a way of thinking which eschews logic and relies solely upon a unique, incommunicable, self-certifying experience of encounter with God."[123]

The Uniqueness and Finality of the Christian Revelation and Faith: the Gifford Lectures

Farmer's Gifford Lectures constitute his most important work on religion and religions.[124] Indeed, according to Hendrik Kraemer, they were "a very important event in English theological writing on [the] subject."[125] Having said that, Farmer had been interested in Christian theology's relation to "living religion" *per se* and other religions for many years (probably the result, as in most things theological, of Oman's influence). This interest is evident in *The World and God* (1935) in which he developed an understanding of revelation which was able to include both God's activity in other faiths and the uniqueness and finality of his revelation in Christ. It is also evident in *Experience of God* (1929), and even in his first volume of sermons, *Things Not Seen* (1927). Having said that, it was clearly his participation in the International Missionary Council Meeting at Tambaram, Madras, which focused his scattered thoughts on the subject, particularly as regards the uniqueness and finality of the Christian revelation and faith. "We came increasingly to see", he says, "that the great non-Christian religions...are in a very real sense all wrong: that is wrong as "alls", as totalities—and must be all

---

[123] J. Hick, "A Philosopher Criticises Theology", in *The London Quarterly* 187 (1962), p.105.
[124] For a fuller discussion of his Gifford Lectures see C. H. Partridge, *H. H. Farmer's Theological Interpretation of Religion: Towards a Personalist Theology of Religions* (Lampeter: Edwin Mellen Press, 1998), chs. 2, 5, 6.
[125] H. Kraemer, *Religion and the Christian Faith* (London: Lutterworth, 1956), p.219.

wrong, despite incidental and isolated rightnesses, for the reason that they leave, not having Christ, the absolutely basic problem of man's situation unsolved. Built upon another foundation, organised around another centre, they are radically and totally different; and if Christianity be right, they must be in a radical and total way wrong."[126] This passage, taken from a sermon delivered shortly after his return from Tambaram, although showing the influence of Kraemer's Barthian "biblical realism", does emphasise a conviction which is evident throughout his writings (particularly immediately post-Tambaram)—namely, that "God's historic act of Incarnation in Jesus Christ 'for us men and our salvation'" is "radically discontinuous" with the history of religions. It is arguable that had it not been for Tambaram he would not have written the Gifford Lectures he did write a decade later. They would possibly have lacked their emphasis on discontinuity and been far more Schleiermachian.

Having said that, he did not depart from the Schleiermacher-Otto-Oman line of thought. The Gifford Lectures are, in part, an attempt to understand Christian *discontinuity* within an essentialist *continuity* thesis worked out in terms of a personalist encounter theology. Hence, as a consistent development of his earlier work, what he has left us with is a theology of religions which seeks to combine an understanding of persons in other faith communities as those "in conversation" with God (this fundamental encounter being understood as the underlying "essence" of religion—"living religion"), with an understanding of the normativity and finality of the Christian revelation and faith.

We turn now to his understanding of the "essence" of religion, "religion" *per se*. "I shall assume that there is underlying all genuinely religious

---

[126]H. H. Farmer, "The One Foundation", p.206.

phenomena a common defining essence of some sort, by which they are constituted genuinely religious phenomena and distinguished from other phenomena which merely look like religion or are usually closely associated with religion."[127] It is this *common defining essence* which he has in mind when he speaks of "religion", or rather, what he prefers to call, *"living religion"*. That is,

> religion so to speak at its point of vital origin, religion as it continually and spontaneously springs up in the soul of man and in the midst of human life and history in creative and originating energy...the source of its vitality, when it has vitality, and of its power to persist as a distinctive and irreplaceable factor in human affairs...We may say that our interest is in Religion with a capital R, the vital essence of religion as distinct from what is merely the routine of religion or merely consequential upon it or parasitic to it.[128]

In short, he makes a distinction which has often been made between the essence and manifestation of religion.

Farmer's understanding of religion is governed by "God's self-disclosure in the Incarnation and in particular by his disclosure therein of his personal nature and his personal purpose towards man."[129] Thus, "whenever religion arises with some degree of spontaneous, creative, living power, it does so because at that point ultimate reality is disclosing itself *as personal* to man."[130] Of course, as he anticipates, one could argue that this assumption is rather

---

[127]H. H. Farmer, *Revelation and Religion*, p.24.
[128]Ibid., pp.24-5.
[129]Ibid., p.27.
[130]Ibid., p.28 (my emphasis).

arbitrary, particularly in view of the fact that some religions have an impersonalistic conception of ultimate reality? However, he wants to say that, although it is admittedly an "assumption", it can be viewed as "a basic element in a hypothesis". Thus, "what begins as an apparently arbitrary assumption will, we hope, be revealed in due course as an element in an interpretative theory which is at least sufficiently justified to be worthy of consideration."[131] Another criticism which could be levelled against Farmer's work is that it compromises, if not denies, Christian uniqueness. That is to say, it might be argued "that to find the clue to the essence of all living religion in the Christian faith lands us in the serious error of putting Christianity into the general class of religions along with other religions."[132] However, that Farmer does not compromise Christian uniqueness and yet maintains an essentialist position is an important aspect of his Gifford Lectures, and something he sought to do in *The World and God*.

It is Barth (and following him, Kraemer) who most famously rejects the notion that Christianity, rooted in God's revelation in Christ, is *a religion* along with other religions. Religion is "unbelief" (*unglaube*). "It is the attempted replacement of the divine work by a human manufacture. The divine reality offered and manifested to us in revelation is replaced by a concept of God arbitrarily and wilfully evolved by man."[133] Thus, "No undertaking subjects men to so severe a judgement as the undertaking of religion."[134] However, it is Barth's fellow countryman Emil Brunner to whom Farmer particularly responds. For reasons very similar to Barth's, Brunner

---

[131]Ibid., p.29.
[132]Ibid., p.30.
[133]K. Barth, *Church Dogmatics* I/2, tr. by G. T. Thompson & H. Knight (Edinburgh: T. & T. Clark, 1956), p.302.
[134]K. Barth, *The Epistle to the Romans*, tr. by E. C. Hoskins (Oxford: Oxford University Press, 1933), p.136.

declares that "The Christian faith...is not '*one* of the religions of the world.'"[135]
"[Christian] revelation is different from all that has been claimed to be
revelation in the world of religions...[Indeed] those religions of which we
might think they are the closest to the biblical gospel are its most violent
opponents."[136]

As we have seen, Farmer was clearly not unsympathetic to such
sentiments. He too wanted to "preserve unimpaired the claim which
Christianity implicitly makes." The revelation of God in Christ is, he insisted,
the "absolute, unconditional final approach of the Eternal to the human
soul."[137] Therefore, the religions of the world are, in the final analysis (to
quote again from his 1939 BMS sermon), "in a very real sense all
wrong...Built upon another foundation, organised round another centre, they
are radically and totally different; and if Christianity be right they must be in a
radical and total way wrong."[138] Yet we have seen that he also insisted, in his
Gifford Lectures, that this need not entail a denial that Christianity is one of
the world's religions. "Brunner appears to overlook the possibility that
Christianity might *both* be in a class by itself *and* in the general class of
religions at the same time."[139] And he does so, according to Farmer, because
he has failed to make a crucial distinction between a "general defining
concept" and a "normative defining concept"—a simple distinction which
Farmer developed on the basis of principles drawn from R. G. Collingwood's
An Essay on Philosophical Method. This distinction is central to both series of
Gifford Lectures and thus needs to be understood in order to grasp his overall

---

[135]E. Brunner, *Revelation and Reason: The Christian Doctrine of Faith and Knowledge*, tr. by
O. Wyon (London: SCM, 1947), p.258.
[136]E. Brunner, *The Scandal of Christianity* (London: SCM, 1951), p.50.
[137]H. H. Farmer, "Christianity and the World To-Day", in *Missionary Review of the World* 58
(1935), p.115.
[138]H. H. Farmer, "The One Foundation", p.206.
[139]H. H. Farmer, *Revelation and Religion*, p.31.

argument. I begin with a simple introduction to Collingwood's thesis before going on to explain Farmer's use of it.

Collingwood points out that although the problem of philosophical method has always been important, "there are reasons for thinking it a problem of peculiar importance to-day [1933]."[140] One reason is that, although there is an increasing variety of ideas on offer and a widespread interest in the problem of method, "it has not yet been directly faced as a distinct problem, as Descartes faced it in the *Discours* or Kant in the *Critique*. Consequently philosophers of all schools are still in varying degrees...under the domination of methodological ideas inherited from the nineteenth century, when philosophy was in various ways assimilated to the pattern of empirical science."[141] That is to say, philosophers were working with methodological presuppositions more appropriate to the exact and empirical sciences. Philosophy, however, is a specific enquiry with its own distinct method. He thus considers such logical processes as classification, definition and deduction in order to demonstrate that they assume a form peculiar to philosophy. For example, though philosophy, like science, is concerned with something "universal" (over against historical thought which is concerned with something "individual"[142]) the philosophical notion of "the universal", or "the concept", is distinctive.

Collingwood demonstrates this thesis in a discussion of logic and ethics. For example, "traditional logic regards the concept as uniting a number of different things into a class",[143] on the grounds that each of the members share a common characteristic, and are, therefore, instances of the concept. Furthermore, the concept unites two distinct kinds of plurality, namely,

---

[140]R. G. Collingwood, *An Essay on Philosophical Method* (Oxford: Oxford University Press, 1933), pp.4-5.
[141]Ibid., p.7.
[142]"Truth as such, not this or that truth; art as such, not this or that work of art" (Ibid., p.26).
[143]Ibid., p.27.

"individual instances" (e.g. colours) and "individual differentiations" (e.g. blue). However, whereas in science, as a rule, one can easily classify one's data in this way (e.g. lines are either curved or straight; organisms are animals or vegetables), this is not true in philosophy. "The specific classes of a philosophical genus do not exclude one another, they overlap one another. This overlap is not exceptional, it is normal."[144] To take an example from ethics, motives have traditionally been divided up according to desire, self-interest and duty. But it is impossible to demonstrate that a given action consists of only one of these motives. Actions are, to some extent, always the result of mixed motives. "[In] our ordinary thought about moral questions...we habitually think in terms of concepts whose specific classes, instead of excluding one another, overlap."[145] Indeed, even logic and ethics themselves overlap, since "thinking is a labour to which ethical predicates may attach."[146] This being the case, the classification theory in philosophy needs to be modified. For, if it is not, argues Collingwood, we will be led into one, or perhaps both, of two fallacies. Farmer neatly summarises them: "Either we shall disqualify the ambiguous instances (i.e. those that fall into more than one class), rule them out of consideration, and confine ourselves to what appear to be pure uncontaminated examples of their class; or, avoiding this, we shall suppose that where the two classes overlap the defining concepts of both of them must be identical even if they are differently expressed."[147]

Collingwood's discussion turns next to the notion of "a scale of forms", which operates neither deductively nor inductively—it neither begins from, nor terminates in generalisations. He begins by asking what kind of

---

[144]Ibid., p.31.
[145]Ibid., pp.42-3.
[146]Ibid., p.43.
[147]H. H. Farmer, *Revelation and Religion*, p.32.

differences must exist between the species of a philosophical concept in order to allow them to overlap. Are they, for example, differences of degree? Obviously not, as this would hardly lead to an overlap—the point at which any one specific species began would be the point at which another ended. What about differences of kind? These are equally unable to provide an explanation, since they too do not allow for overlap. He thus makes the point that when we come to consider the overlap of species or classes, the distinction between differences in degree and kind cannot be applied in the mutually exclusive way in which it usually is. On the contrary, *differences of degree and kind are combined* so that the members of a species may differ from one another in *both* degree *and* kind at the same time. That is to say, on a scale of degrees whenever a variable reaches a "critical point" a new specific form suddenly comes into being. Though there are non-philosophical examples of a scale of forms, such as, for example, ice, water, and steam which differ both in degree, as hotter and colder, and in kind, as specifically different states of the same substance, the variable, unlike a philosophical scale of forms, is not identical with the essence. Whilst the generic essence of ice, water, and steam is H_2O, the variable is heat, which in one of the forms is absent. In the philosophical scale "the variable is identical with the generic essence."[148] For example, Plato's procedure in the *Republic* is typical of philosophical definitions, in that he begins from the minimal idea of the State as a primitive economic structure, and progresses towards the ideal, which is at the same time the *real* State. Therefore—and this is important for understanding Farmer's thesis—"the result of this identification is that every form, so far as it is low in the scale, is to that extent an imperfect or inadequate specification of the generic essence,

---

[148]R. G. Collingwood, *An Essay on Philosophical Method*, p.60.

which is realised with progressive adequacy as the scale is ascended."[149] As John Passmore puts it, "A philosophical definition...is the discovery of the ideal form, by reference to which its imperfect embodiments can be placed."[150] In Farmer's words, "things may sometimes be properly considered to constitute a single class, not because they are related to one another as fully co-ordinate species of a general type or essence, expressible in a general concept or *Allgemeinbegriff*, but because they are in varying ways and degrees individual expressions of, or approximations to, an ideal type or essence, expressible in a normative concept or *Normbegriff*."[151]

It should now be coming clear as to how Collingwood's thesis enabled Farmer to affirm both the continuity and the discontinuity of the Christian revelation and faith with other religious traditions. Basically his argument is that Brunner, in denying that Christianity is a religion, had failed to avoid the above mentioned fallacies. Concentrating on Christianity's distinctive characteristics, and following traditional logic, Brunner reached the inevitable conclusion (in accordance with the first fallacy) that Christianity is not a religion, or, if it is, others are not. Again, following traditional logic, he argues that if we begin with the thought that all religions must somehow belong together, there is (in accordance with the second fallacy) no essential distinction between them. Hence, to assert a common religious essence is to undermine the uniqueness of the Christian faith. Therefore, Christianity is either not a religion, or if it is, we must say that it is the *true* religion and that all the others are false. But, asks Farmer, what is meant by the term "false" in this context? "If it means *wholly* false in the sense that there is, in other faiths, no apprehension of, or relation to, divine reality, then it certainly becomes a

---

[149]Ibid., p.61.
[150]J. Passmore, *A Hundred Years of Philosophy* (Harmondsworth: Penguin, 1968), p.304.
[151]H. H. Farmer, *Revelation and Religion*, p.34.

question whether they can be religions at all."[152] Brunner, unlike Barth, would agree with this—which, it has to be said, makes his thesis rather problematic. We must, he states, quoting I. A. Dorner, "'either deny heathenism the right to bear the name of religion at all or we must admit that in it we see God's acts and his revelation, even though this is said in a broad sense.' There are phenomena in the religions of non-Christian peoples which 'we must refer back to stirrings of the divine Spirit in their hearts.'"[153] Again, according to Brunner, behind all religion "there lies, on the side of God, truth, communication, the testimony of the Creator-God to himself."[154] So, Brunner seems to reject the idea that other faiths are *wholly false*, thereby forfeiting their right to be called "religions". The point is that this leads to some confusion in Brunner's thought, for surely, having affirmed this, he cannot then deny that Christianity is, in some sense, "a religion" along with other religions. Yet this is precisely what he seems to do. In other words, without any explanation, he rather confusingly wants to affirm a radical discontinuity whilst, at the same time, maintaining that there is a continuity—understood in terms of a divine-human encounter or "the stirrings of the divine Spirit in [human] hearts", the Spirit of the same God who is revealed supremely in Jesus Christ.

Farmer's argument is simply that "these confusions can be avoided if we take note of what Collingwood calls the 'overlap of classes', and in particular the possibility of a 'scale of forms' which...the overlap of classes involves...Applying this to the relation of Christianity to other religions, it becomes possible to maintain that Christianity has something in common with

---

[152]Ibid., p.33.
[153]E. Brunner, *Revelation and Reason*, p.263 (I. A. Dorner, *Christliche Glaubenslehre*, p.679); H. H. Farmer, *Revelation and Religion*, p.33.
[154]Ibid., p.262.

other religions in respect of which it differs from them in degree, and yet also has within it that which makes it incommensurable with them, makes it different from them in kind."[155] Taking the scale of forms, at the apex of which is the ideal, he argues that if that ideal were ever fully realised, whilst not falling out of the class of which it was the realisation, it would nevertheless be different in kind from its less perfect manifestations. That is to say, it would, on the one hand, be in the same class "as the most remote, fragmentary, or distorted expressions of the ideal", and, on the other hand, since "the ideal realisation occurred only once, and...in the nature of the case...could occur only once", in "a very radical way" it constitutes a unique 'class by itself'."[156] Thus his point is, quite simply, "The living essence of religion is revealed once and for all, in its sole perfect manifestation, in the Christian revelation and in the relation with God which that revelation makes possible for men, and it is exemplified in other religions in varying degrees of incompleteness, fragmentariness, distortion and perversion. In other words, *there is given to us through the Christian revelation the normative concept of religion.*"[157] Christianity differs in both degree and kind from other religions, and can, therefore, as the "ideal", be described as the unique and final *religion.* Hence, although his Gifford Lectures show that he still wanted to affirm the central thrust of his earlier post-Tambaram Baptist Missionary Society sermon, his use of Collingwood enabled him to modify a rather Brunnerian stance in order to accommodate his essentialist convictions. Hence, for example, although Christianity and other faiths have much in common, such as the apprehension of divine demand and succour, the present volume argues that only in the Christian revelation and faith are these elements convincingly

---

[155]H. H. Farmer, *Revelation and Religion*, pp.33-4.
[156]Ibid., p.34.
[157]Ibid., pp.34-5.

reconciled in a way that does not diminish either. In this and other respects
the Christian faith is shown to be normative. As such the Christian thinker is
in a unique position to provide a theological interpretation of religious history.
Situated at the apex of the scale of religious forms or types, as the ideal type of
religion, the Christian faith provides an elevated position for the reflective
theologian to survey the whole of religious history. The Christian alone can
truly discern where living religion surfaces in the broad sea of faiths.

Now, this raises the further and more basic question concerning why there
is religious plurality in the first place. In other words, if there is one
underlying, self-disclosing ultimate reality, as Farmer claims there is, then
why is there such a variety of responses to it? Although Farmer doesn't
explicitly address the question as such, it is clear that had he done so his
answer would have been set in a fundamentally hamartiological context.

As we have seen, humans are primarily and distinctively persons living in
a single bipolar relationship with other persons and with God. Hence, we can
never, so to speak, become "godless". "For when God creates man, he creates
a relationship by that same act—without the relationship there would be no
man."[158] And what constitutes this relationship is, quite simply, the divine
"claim". We can accept this claim or reject it, live in rebellion or in
obedience, but the claim is always there, and thus so is the relationship.
Furthermore, as we have seen, he introduces the notion of "claim" because he
believes it to convey an understanding of the approach of God which does not
violate human freedom—the freedom of the will being fundamental to
responsible personhood. Our relationship with God must therefore be the
result of a free response to his claim upon us. Hence his stress upon the
necessity of an "epistemic distance" between God and humanity; a distance

---

[158]H. H. Farmer, *God and Men*, p.68.

which allows us to make meaningful and responsible decisions uncoerced by the awesome presence of God. "God's will must bring man's will into harmony with itself, not by any exercise of *force majeure*, but always by eliciting from man his own...spontaneous surrender to it in obedience and trust."[159] That is to say, the "epistemic distance" is the necessary context in which the approach of God to the souls of men and women can take place. John Hick, a student and friend of Farmer whose early thought was clearly indebted to that of his teacher, and who has very effectively developed this particular aspect of Farmer's thought in his pluralist philosophy of religion, neatly summarises the point: "in order to freely *come* to God man must not be created in the immediate presence of his maker but at a distance from him—not a spatial but an epistemic distance, constituted by the circumstance that man has been brought into being in a world and as part of a world in which God is not compulsorily evident, and in which awareness of the divine Thou includes a free interpretative act, traditionally called faith."[160] Again: "Only when we *voluntarily* recognise God, desiring to enter into relationship with him, can our knowledge of him be compatible with our freedom, and so with our existence as personal beings. If God were to reveal himself to us in the coercive way in which the physical world is disclosed to us, he would thereby annihilate us as free and responsible persons...If man is to be personal, God must be *deus absconditus*."[161]

These notions of an epistemic distance and human freedom are basic to what has been called "the sacramental principle." For Farmer, God must deal with humanity and communicate himself to us by means of signs and symbols in order to protect human personality and allow us to enter into a truly

---

[159] H. H. Farmer, *The World and God*, p.70.
[160] J. Hick, *God and the Universe of Faiths* (London: Collins, Fount, 1977), p.54.
[161] J. Hick, *Faith and Knowledge* (London: Collins, Fount, 1978), pp.134-5.

personal relationship with him. We have been created with a genuine, though relative, autonomy in relation to God. That is to say, we have been created with cognitive freedom; we are born into a creaturely sphere which God has set at an epistemic distance from himself.

Turning now to the specific question of sin, to exercise our freedom negatively, to reject the claim, is not to nullify the divine-human relationship, but to live, in Brunner's words, as "man in revolt". "Man is the being who is responsible...Responsibility is the presupposition of the fact that man is able to be a sinner."[162] "We are so made", says Hendrikus Berkhof, "that we need to find the anchoring of our life in the holy love of God by seeking our security in him and by being obedient to him. Sin is the refusal to find our anchoring there."[163] Sin, in Farmer's words, is the "great refusal which man persists in making at the centre of his being, that centremost point where the claim of God...meets him and constitutes him a distinctively human person."[164] It therefore constitutes "a specifically *religious* category." That is to say, when we speak of "sin" we are speaking not of a crime, or a vice in which the reference to God is not present, we are rather "seeking to indicate something in which the profoundest and most far-reaching responses of [the] soul to the Eternal as personal are involved."[165] To quote Brunner again: "Sin ought not to be confused with vice...Sin belongs to a quite different category from that of vice and virtue. Vice and virtue belong to the empirical sphere, to that of the "qualities". But sin, like faith, lies beyond the empirical sphere, in the sphere of man's relation to God. Indeed they are his relation to God; the one is

---

[162]E. Brunner, *Man in Revolt: A Christian Anthropology*, tr. by O. Wyon (London: Lutterworth, 1939), p.73.
[163]H. Berkhof, *The Christian Faith*, p.189.
[164]H. H. Farmer, *God and Men*, pp.70-1.
[165]H. H. Farmer, *The World and God*, p.185.

negative the other is positive."[166]   Thus, where sin is mentioned in Scripture, "the human being is seen as the "person before God"; there he stands within the dimension of responsibility, of responsible personal existence."[167]   Sin must therefore be treated with the utmost seriousness, for it is understood to be a refusal to respond to the divine demand. It is a disobedience, which involves alienation in "the most fundamental of all personal relationships." "[The] ground-tone which abides throughout, is the sense of being in conflict...with the Eternal Personal."[168]   In the final analysis, therefore, sin is a profound egocentricity over against God.

Moreover, because sin is a perversion of "the most fundamental of all personal relationships" it is bound to permeate our existence as a whole. That is to say, individual sin cannot be contained within individuals. Hence:

> No individual can be judged wholly responsible for the state of
> darkness in which he dwells. If it is always in a measure the result of
> his own insincerity, it is also in a measure the result of other people's.
> For the insincerities of individuals organise themselves into social
> systems, with their enormous power to shape every new personality
> which is born into them. Every individual, himself swiftly victimised
> as soon as he is born, is soon in turn victimising others, and so the
> process goes on, until a cosmos, or as Ritschl called it, a kingdom of
> evil, with a frightful power of self-perpetuation and renewal, is brought
> into being. The inner life of the individual thus becomes, not a clear-
> cut issue between the higher and the lower, between conscience and

---

[166]E. Brunner, *The Christian Doctrine of Creation and Redemption: Dogmatics* vol.2, tr. by O. Wyon (London: Lutterworth, 1952), p.106.
[167]Ibid., p.104.
[168]H. H. Farmer, *The World and God*, pp.188-9.

instinct, but a confused cock-pit of forces, some of them unconscious and even uncontrollable, in which it is impossible to say where personal choice and responsibility begin and end.[169]

In other words, we are not wholly responsible for our sin, but neither are we without responsibility. He would thus agree with Brunner that whilst to be a sinner means to be engaged in rebellion against God—sin not being a quality or substance but always an act—sinfulness is a fate as well as a choice. We are "slaves to sin". Thus, unlike many of his contemporaries, Farmer insisted on the "deep and abiding truth of the so-called doctrines of 'original sin' and 'total depravity.'"[170] The truth of original sin being that we are born into a close-knit, human, personal order, which is in fact no longer an order, but rather a *dis*-order, and a disorder which "instantly becomes part and parcel of our personal existence, even before we become conscious of ourselves as persons and can be deemed in any way responsible for it...Sin thus meets and conditions us at the very point of our origin: it is *original* sin."[171] "Total depravity" on the other hand, does not mean that everything in human existence is "foul, beastly and depraved", for this is quite clearly not the case. It rather indicates that "everything in human life is affected by the fundamental wrong relationship to God which lies at the very root of man's being."[172] The totality of a human's being is affected in the sense that anything we do *can* become utterly corrupt, and even when it does not and indeed reflects divine truth, it does so inadequately and falteringly. We always, as Paul says, "fall short of the glory of God".[173] Hence, although obviously

---

[169]Ibid., pp.195-6.
[170]H. H. Farmer, *God and Men*, p.80.
[171]Ibid., pp.80-1.
[172]Ibid., p.81.
[173]Romans 3.23.

differing from Augustine in some respects, Farmer agrees with his twofold aim both to represent sin as a dominant drive, and humanity as bound together in a solidarity of guilt (though not a biological solidarity). "We are not", as Brunner puts it, "dealing with *chromosomes* and *genes*."[174]   Sin is simply "appallingly contagious", "like leprosy in the sphere of the spirit."[175]

As to the consequences of sin, the most fundamental and obvious is an epistemic "blindness": the inability to discern the truth concerning God, oneself and the true meaning of one's life. We become increasingly unable to know the nature of God's will for us, and claim upon us, and even, indeed, to know that there is a personal God at all. Seeing reality from a wrong centre (from the self rather than from God and his claim upon us), the myopic sinner distorts the available data and thereby misinterprets the true nature of ultimate reality and the epistemological predicament of humanity. In short, as we reflect on the nature of existence and ultimate reality, there takes place, in varying degrees, an unconscious, but, nevertheless, very profound, egocentric twisting and distorting of the data.

The history of religions therefore—including Christianity when it is not true to the revelation of God in Christ—is the history of sinfully distorted human responses to the claim of God. Take for example the *Bhakti* tradition within Indian thought. This, he argues, is

the welling up of something in the nature of living religion, and may be taken...to reveal the continuous pressure of the divine personal self-disclosure amidst all the darkness and perversion of human life and thought. But though there is thus a breaking away from the dominant

---

[174]E. Brunner, *The Christian Doctrine of Creation and Redemption*, p.104.
[175]H. H. Farmer, *Things Not Seen*, pp.138, 157.

[*Vedantic*] tradition into a world of personal relationships and categories, the break-away...is not complete. On the contrary, the impersonal system of thought, with its accompanying mental attitudes...still drifts back...like a mist between the soul and God, muffling and distorting, if not at times, preventing, the full personal encounter.[176]

And such distortion cannot be checked by the devotees because it is in the main not recognised for what it is. This is not to say that other religions have no conception of sin, for many quite clearly do. The point is that as a result of their hamartiological blindness, they have, at best, an inadequate understanding.

Furthermore, the only remedy for this condition is one appropriate to its nature, namely, one which deals with the profound tear in "the fabric of the I-thou world".[177] Such is found only in Christ. Whereas "other religions than Christianity teach that God forgives sin...none makes this truth so basic and central in its message."[178] Indeed, for Farmer, "everything distinctive of the Christian life is indissolubly bound up at some point with the experience of God's forgiveness mediated through his revelation of himself in Christ."[179] The point is that the obedient Christian is increasingly brought "*out* of falsehood and illusion *into* an ever clearer insight into the true divine order..."[180] Unless one undergoes a "fundamental re-orientation of the whole life in relation to God", any view of reality will be, at best, viewed through the

---

[176]H. H. Farmer, *Revelation and Religion*, p.158.
[177]H. H. Farmer, *The Servant of the Word*, p.43.
[178]H. H. Farmer, *The Healing Cross*, p.113.
[179]Ibid., p.113.
[180]Ibid., p.116.

cracked and distorting spectacles of sin. Thus, in his 1939 address to the Baptist Missionary Society, he stated that other faiths

> must not be judged by incidental fine qualities and insights which may be discerned in them...but as highly complex, powerful, all-embracing systems or organisms of belief, culture, morality, social structure, philosophy, which hold and shape the whole life of those who have a part in them. Considered as such totalities or systems or organisms...they are in a very real sense all wrong: that is to say wrong as "alls", as totalities—and must be all wrong, despite incidental rightnesses, for the reason that they leave and must leave, not having Christ, the absolutely basic problem of man's situation unsolved.[181]

This accounts in part for the plurality of religions. Because "sin organises itself into social systems, which, [are] entrenched in the habits and traditions of a whole class of people",[182] one's religious response will not only be distorted, but it will be moulded by those habits and traditions. Environment, family, friends, interests, culture all play a dominant role in a person's interpretation of ultimate reality. In other words, because a person interprets reality from an egocentric perspective, everything that has gone into moulding that person will necessarily influence, if not dictate, their understanding of reality. And although the interpretation may not be wholly false, it will, to a significant degree, have the stamp of the interpreter upon it. Hence, it follows, that since there are many interpreters, influenced by many cultural and environmental factors, there will be many interpretations of the one divine

---

[181]H. H. Farmer, "The One Foundation", p.206.
[182]H. H. Farmer, *Things Not Seen*, p.157.

reality, and many answers to the problems posed by the various tensions discussed in the present volume of Gifford Lectures. Indeed, Farmer would agree with Hick that "the different encounters with the divine which lie at the basis of the great religious traditions... [are] encounters from different historical and cultural standpoints with the same infinite divine reality and as such they lead to differently focused awarenesses of that reality."[183] "These encounters have taken place within different human cultures by people of different ways of thought and feeling, with different histories and different frameworks of philosophical thought, and have developed into different systems of theology embodied in different religious structures and organisations. These resulting large-scale religio-cultural phenomena are what we call the religions of the world."[184] That said, from a Farmerian perspective, Hick's comments suffer from a conspicuous lack of hamartiological content. And a thesis which fails to take sin seriously is bound to misinterpret the data and thereby be fundamentally flawed. A sound hamartiology, for example, leads us to the conclusion that there will, in varying degrees, be inadequate and, indeed, false interpretations of ultimate reality—not merely different ones.

Finally, it has to be said that it is not merely hamartiological blindness that accounts for religious plurality, but also the very nature of God.

If God be a reality then He is, by definition, an infinitely rich and all-inclusive reality, in some sense penetrating and pervading all else. Small wonder then, that the reports men give of him and of his dealings with them, whilst having much in common, should be so

---

[183]J. Hick, *God and the Universe of Faiths*, p.141.
[184]Ibid., p.143.

various. A variety of apprehension does not point to the unreality of an
object so much as to its richness and complexity. It is, for example, of
a rich and complex personality like, say, Gladstone, that men give
varying reports.[185]

Hence, for Farmer (again, in a similar way to Hick), there can be many *true*
understandings of God within other faith communities, but, he argues (unlike
Hick), to the extent that they contradict the revelation given in Christ, they
must be considered flawed. Conversely, to the extent that they concur with
that revelation they can be said to be true.

This brings us to another issue discussed particularly in the first series of
Gifford Lectures, namely the distinction between divine self-revelation and the
human discovery of God—a distinction which Barth, Brunner and Kraemer
make much of. Farmer, although accepting the distinction, qualifies it. It
concerns, he argues, not a person's activity or passivity as such, but rather the
object of religious apprehension and the relationship it initiates. That is to say,
the distinction is between "a reality and a relationship which are not personal
and a reality and a relationship which are." *Revelation* is central to an I-thou
relationship, whereas *discovery* is central to an I-it relationship. This is the
principal reason why philosophy must be rejected as a method of establishing
the personal nature of the ultimate. Such knowledge is only given in a direct
personal encounter which, in the case of a disembodied, absolute Subject,
must be initiated by that Subject. It can never be the result of merely human
reflection. This, of course, follows on from what was said earlier about the
apprehension of God in our discussion of Farmer's "radical personalism".

---

[185]H. H. Farmer, *Towards Belief in God*, p.134.

Farmer felt that a loss of the sense of the personal in modern thought had led to an increasing obsession with "monism" which had, in turn, led to a situation in which revelation and discovery have been virtually collapsed into one another. Even when the word "revelation" is used in respect of the knowledge of God, "the thought of God's personal activity is often not present, or, if present, is so in such an attenuated form that the word discovery would be just as appropriate."[186] In other words, by "monism" Farmer referred to thought which failed to distinguish between, or at least obscured the duality between, God and the rest of creation. This, in turn, resulted in a loss of the sense of the supernatural aspect of reality, leaving only an empty naturalism— God is not that which stands over against human persons, a being who is personal and thus must disclose himself to human persons.

> In the century since Hegel such ideas, without the precision given them by the philosophers, have become very widespread, partly through the influence of Hegelian schools of thought, but more because of the fact that they have become fused with the doctrines of evolution and the supposed immutable laws of nature, as these have been popularised by science; so that increasingly the conception of the universe as a monistic system has become almost unconsciously part of the mental furniture of the modern man. In so far as such ideas receive articulate expression, it is usually in the form of some vague "life force" philosophy.[187]

---

[186]H. H. Farmer, *The World and God*, p.82.
[187]Ibid., p.3.

He thus attacked the immanentist process thought of, for example, Henry Nelson Wieman as the "translation of Christian belief into the idiom of Bergson and Whitehead." Although Wieman sought to be a Christian philosopher, Farmer complains that nowhere in his work is there any mention of what was quite central to Jesus' personal life, namely, "his profound and unique filial consciousness of God as transcendent personal will of righteousness and love."[188] This neglect of the personal all but emptied his thought of religious, not to say Christian, content. Basically, as Farmer understands him, under the pressure of "the rational-empirical methods and the findings of science" Wieman produced "a newer naturalism", "a philosophy in search of a religion."[189] No longer does knowledge of God depend on his personal activity, for the ultimate is neither transcendent nor personal. He simply rehearses the arguments of scientists and philosophers who speak of an "underlying order being revealed in the events of nature and history" and yet leave out the idea of personal purposive activity. As far as Farmer is concerned, anything short of "a pungent and living sense of divine purpose or will actively dealing with [persons] so insistently and directly that they can no more disregard it than they can someone hammering at the door", is not revelation.[190] And "living religion" is always the human response to the self-revelation of God: it is the divine-human encounter, never simply the human quest for the divine.

Inextricably linked with these issues, are those surrounding "natural theology", a subject which Farmer takes up at the beginning of his first series

---

[188]Ibid., p.116.
[189]Ibid., p.117. The final comment is simply a reversal of Whitehead's statement that "Christianity is a religion in search of a philosophy."
[190]H. H. Farmer, *The World and God*, p.84.

of Gifford Lectures.[191] Farmer understands the term "natural theology" to refer to a reasoned argument aimed at convincing the rational mind of the existence and nature of "the one supreme, personal, self-subsistent Mind, to whose good, wise, creative, ruling purpose the world (including man) owes its existence, nature, coherence, and destiny."[192] One of Farmer's key points is that there is in the human mind "a profound inward connection" between "natural theology" and "natural religion". Therefore, his argument is that if natural theology has any ability to convince, it does so because "something of natural religion or natural religio-theism is concomitantly active in [the] mind."[193] A good illustration of the point is provided by some comments he makes concerning Kant's moral argument for the existence of God. In order to grasp the force of this illustration we need briefly to remind ourselves of Kant's main points. On the basis of his assertion that it is illegitimate to use theoretical reason beyond the range of one's experience, Kant argued that we cannot ascertain the existence of God by simply using the traditional ontological, cosmological or teleological arguments. However, this does not mean that it cannot be established, only that it has to be established on a different ground. He found this different ground in the sphere of ethics, arguing that God, moral freedom and immortality are necessary presuppositions in the operations of moral reason. For example, on the basis of his assertion that we have an obligation to perfect virtue, he argued that there must necessarily be an afterlife, since it would be ridiculous to expect a person to progress to moral excellence in the short time he or she has on earth.

---

[191] The Gifford Lectures, endowed at the Scottish Universities of Aberdeen, Edinburgh, Glasgow and St Andrews by the will of Lord Adam Gifford (1820-87), seek to promote "the study of natural theology in the widest sense of the term." Having said that, as evidenced by the fact that Barth and Brunner were Gifford lecturers, the founder's terms have been interpreted very generously indeed.

[192] H. H. Farmer, *Revelation and Religion*, p.2.

[193] Ibid., p.9.

Again, the principal of justice requires that a perfectly good person should be rewarded with perfect happiness. Since this is manifestly not the case in this life, the presupposition of morality must be that there is a God who is willing and able to provide such happiness in the afterlife. Thereby Kant, starting from an absolute, autonomous moral imperative, sought to demonstrate the necessity for belief in God. Religious beliefs are made necessary by the contradiction which would otherwise exist between the moral imperative and the natural order. Having said that, he insisted that "it is not meant by this that it is necessary to suppose the existence of God."[194] In other words, there is *no logical necessity* to believe in God's existence from the fact of the moral imperative. Such a conclusion must always be an "act of faith". On the other hand, he wants to say that it is unreasonable *to accept* the moral imperative and yet, at the same time, *not to accept* that there is a guarantee more ultimate than the phenomenal world. Farmer suggests that the source of this dubiety in Kant can be found in the fact that he was "already conscious in his own soul of the profound inward connection of morality with religion; he was already aware of God in and through his awareness of the absolute demand of morality; the two—the categorical imperative and God—were, so to say, given together."[195] (Indeed, it is worth noting that Farmer's understanding of the "absolute demand" is not a little indebted to the Kantian concept of the categorical imperative.) The point is that Kant apprehended morality's "metaphysical depth" and on that basis produced his "moral argument". In other words, inductive reasoning towards theism always involves, as a key element in it, certain prior religious insights and convictions. Hence, Farmer's oft quoted statement that "natural theology can only make progress towards its

---

[194]Kant, "The Existence of God as a Postulate of Practical Reason", in J. Hick (ed.), *The Existence of God* (London: Macmillan, 1964), p.139.
[195]H. H. Farmer, *Revelation and Religion*, pp.147-7.

desired haven when it allows its sails to be filled in part by the wind of natural religion."[196] This, of course, is far from saying that reason is wholly redundant or unimportant—we have already mentioned his emphasis on the reflective element of conviction in religious belief. Indeed, as part of our God-given status as persons, one can say that "it is by reason and reason alone that man is able to become aware of God's approach to the soul..."[197] Or, in Austin Farrer's words, "we cannot acknowledge or master what [God] reveals without the use of our reason. Therefore all his self-manifestation is also our discovery of him, and all revealed theology is rational theology."[198] So, although "not by any means indispensable to the religious life, nor by itself...able to produce and sustain the religious life", reason does have a place within theology.[199] It not only allows us to make sense of revelation, it also provides "confirmatory considerations which present themselves when we bring the thought of God with us to the interpretation of the world and man's place in it. It is a question of coherence of the belief with the facts, particularly with the fact of the existence of man..."[200] Indeed, this use of reason to establish grounds for theistic faith is evident throughout Farmer's work. "We are entitled", he says, "to expect that belief in God...should provide us with a reasonable and credible philosophy, with a principle of interpretation of the world in its broad aspects and constitutive principles which shall be as convincing as any other philosophy or interpretation, and more so than most."[201]

---

[196]Ibid., p.13.
[197]H. H. Farmer, *The World and God*, p.87.
[198]A. Farrer, *The Glass of Vision* (London: Dacre Press, 1948), p.2.
[199]H. H. Farmer, *Towards Belief in God*, p.114.
[200]Ibid., p.182.
[201]H. H. Farmer, *Towards Belief in God*, pp.112-3.

Moreover, from an evangelistic perspective, "we cannot exclude the possibility that the argument itself may at any moment penetrate to deeper levels of the mind than the discursive intellect to which it primarily appeals, and so will play a part in calling into activity the religious response to the world on which it depends in part for its force."[202] This is always a possibility because, since the human is a single entity, "thought is related to the deepest ground of our being as persons."[203] That said, as we have pointed out, our religious response is *sui generis* in that it cannot be generated in the first instance by rational arguments. So although all argument is, to some extent, abstract, generalised and reflective, it does not follow that it is of little value, since "like a dully glowing and smouldering piece of wood it may, plunged into the oxygen of an individual history, become brightly incandescent and even burst into flame."[204]

However, in the final analysis, he would have agreed with Italo Mancini's comment that "if philosophy's highest achievement is to speak about God, religion's minimum is to be able to speak *with* God and this can only happen on God's initiative."[205]

We turn now to a brief examination of the method Farmer utilises in his Gifford Lectures to study the religious essence and to construct a scale of religious types. At the beginning of the first series, originally announced under the title *The Theological Interpretation of Religion*, he states that it is his intention to develop and stimulate "the interpretation of religion from the standpoint of the Incarnation."[206] He was concerned that there had been "little

---

[202]H. H. Farmer, *Revelation and Religion*, p.15.
[203]Ibid., p.15.
[204]H. H. Farmer, *Towards Belief in God*, p.63.
[205]I. Mancini, "Philosophy of Religion", in M. Eliade & D. Tracy (eds.), *What is Religion?: An Enquiry for Christian Theology*, Concilium 136 (Edinburgh: T. & T. Clark/New York: Seabury Press, 1980), pp.64-5.
[206]H. H. Farmer, *Revelation and Religion*, p.viii.

attempt to provide, not a merely descriptive and classificatory phenomenology of religion, but a philosophy of it carefully wrought out in the light of its many and varied concrete manifestations."[207] On the one hand, Christian theologians didn't seem to consider a theological interpretation of religion an integral part of their work. And on the other hand, much previous historical and phenomenological work had been done, consciously or unconsciously, on the basis of presuppositions which were "usually remote from the central affirmations of the Christian faith".[208] Although there were exceptions, such as Oman, on the whole, Farmer believed that his audience at Glasgow, in February 1950, witnessed "a preliminary 'blazing of the trail'"[209]—though Eric Pyle has commented that "Farmer has done more than blaze a trail", and his work is "much less...preliminary than his humility led him to suggest."[210]

Farmer begins with an outline of the phenomenological method of "seeking to uncover the essence of religion by examining as many as possible of the established and generally recognised forms which the religious life of mankind has historically assumed, and analytically abstracting from them what they all have in common. You strike out all the differences and what is left gives you the general concept of religion, or *Allgemeinbegriff*...[which] is then identified with the essence of religion."[211] But, he argues, "inward *Tiefe* cannot possibly be discerned merely by bringing a detached analytical mind to their outward manifestations and summing up likenesses in a general concept."[212] His argument is that a phenomenology which seeks to investigate the essence of religion, has, by that very fact, ceased to be an objective

---

[207]Ibid..
[208]Ibid..
[209]Ibid., p.viii-ix.
[210]E. H. Pyle, "Diagnoses of Religion", in F. G. Healey (ed.), *Prospect for Theology*, p.204.
[211]H. H. Farmer, *Revelation and Religion*, p.43.
[212]Ibid., p.44.

examination and become a philosophy. For, "the notion of a purely detached, objective study, whatever meaning and application it may have in other spheres, is certainly not applicable here. It is an *ignis fatuus.*"[213]   Although such a method has the appearance of objectivity, the data supposedly being catalogued in a neutral and descriptive way, when a scholar draws upon that data in order to try and uncover the general underlying idea of religion he or she has passed out of the sphere of description and into the sphere of interpretation.   Thus the claim that such a phenomenology is a descriptive science is invalid, since any conclusion that the phenomenologist subsequently reaches is subjectively conditioned.   After all, is not the description of religious phenomena *per se* interpretative?   "For how is it possible to know what facts to include in your review unless you already have in advance some idea of what religion essentially is?"[214]   That is to say, how does one distinguish between elements which are common to all religions because they are truly religious, and elements which are just linked to the phenomenon of religion, but are not fundamentally religious?   For example, he makes the point that "at one time nearly everybody took animism to be a form of religion; but today that is denied by many.   Is primitive Buddhism a religion or merely a humanistic philosophy?   Are we to include animism and original Buddhism in our review of religious facts or not?   The answer given is bound to depend, consciously or unconsciously, on a preconceived idea of what religion essentially is."[215]   Or, as Oman puts it, "we very much need a view of religion to know what are the relevant facts and how far they have significance.   If we do not know already what religion is, we can no more hope

---

[213]Ibid., p.43.
[214]Ibid.
[215]Ibid., p.43 n.

to reconstruct a living religion out of a mere welter of facts than if we had never seen a tree to construct it out of sawdust."[216]

Hence, bearing the above in mind, "We have no option but to follow the method which has been called "productive empathy": the method, that is to say, of penetrating to the living essence of religion, as it lies behind and within its manifestations, by feeling our way into it on the basis of our own inner religious faith and experience."[217] Although the method is that of the German thinker Georg Wobbermin,[218] Farmer refers to him only rarely, and then only to his study in the psychology of religion, *Das Wesen der Religionen* (*The Nature of Religion*). However, it is probably true to say that he was influenced by him more than his characteristic paucity of references suggest. Indeed, the fact that he refers solely to the first edition of 1921 suggests that his acquaintance with Wobbermin goes back to the early years of his theological career. We begin, therefore, with a brief introduction to the relevant aspects of Wobbermin's thesis.

Although rarely referred to, when he is, it is as "the inventor of the religious-psychological circle"—the context for productive empathy. To understand his concept of a religious-psychological circle we first need to know that he begins by making a sharp distinction between a psychology of religion which presupposes the existence of religion in the observer, and one which is concerned with religious phenomena and makes no such presupposition. Only the former, he argues, can arrive at a true understanding of religion, since the latter deals merely with the externals. His argument is that since religion is fundamentally one of the facts of inner experience, in

---

[216]J. Oman, *The Natural and the Supernatural,* p.57.
[217]H. H. Farmer, *Revelation and Religion,* p.45.
[218]Georg Wobbermin (1869-1943), Professor of Systematic Theology at Göttingen, was one of the first to introduce the psychology of religion into German theology.

order to understand it a psychological analysis is necessary. However, such an analysis cannot be prosecuted from some neutral vantage point, for no such point exists. Therefore, one must investigate on the basis of a previously formed understanding of the nature and truth of religion *per se*. The point is that, in the final analysis, Christian theology is necessary for a "Christian science of religion", since "the investigator of religion can only be sure of understanding, in the fullest sense of the word, the innermost depths of that religion which produced his own religious experience...And it follows from this that a conclusion can be reached only after the faith content of Christianity has been unfolded."[219]

The religio-psychological circle is the method used to investigate these innermost depths. By examining one's own religious experience one develops a sensitivity for the specifically "religious", as distinct from the merely external and institutional. The investigator then turns his or her "sharpened eye" to other religions, more equipped to be able to make the same distinction, and thereby come closer to determining the nature (*Wesen*) of religion, "the purest form of the specifically religious element in the total historical complex of the religious life."[220] Having done this, the scholar returns again to his or her firsthand experience, his or her eye having been further sharpened, and so on. As long as this circular activity is carried out, the investigator's sensitivity to the essence of religion is increased.

But where does "productive empathy" come in? Quite simply, it is "the unique instrument" of the religio-psychological circle. It is the *feeling-into-process* which constitutes the very basis of the circle. "Only with the aid of productive empathy can the religio-psychological circle draw nearer and

---

[219]Ibid., p.44.
[220]Ibid., p.8.

nearer to its goal..."[221] It is *productive* empathy because it "reveals itself as a *creative* continuation or rebirth of experience".[222] What he seems to be saying is that it is an empathy which *produces* ever greater levels of sensitivity to, and therefore empathy with, another's religious experience; it is an empathy which provides access into purer, deeper levels of the specifically "religious" elements of experience. Hence, Wobbermin defines his approach as "the method of the religio-psychological circle moved by productive empathy."[223]

Furthermore, as is clear from even a superficial reading of *The Nature of Religion*, Wobbermin, like Farmer, though to a far greater extent, is significantly indebted to Schleiermacher. Indeed, his motto for the religio-psychological method is: "*Back to Schleiermacher and from Schleiermacher forward!*"[224] Basically, he believed that, although Schleiermacher's theory is unavoidably limited (because of the lack of psychological research at the turn of the nineteenth century), his fundamental convictions are correct: "all conceptual forms of expression of religion, its dogmas and its creeds, are of a secondary order and...can only be rightly understood from the basis of inner-religious experience."[225] The religio-psychological circle, he argues, helps to demonstrate the validity of Schleiermacher's thesis, in that it successfully works on the basis of a distinction between the external trappings of religion and its inner essence. Hence, the nature of religion "*must be that fundamental underlying motive of religious life common to all forms of religious expression.*"[226] Indeed, the term "religious-psychological circle" is only "a technical description of the process which [Schleiermacher] used in his

---

[221]Ibid., p.8.
[222]Ibid., p.8 (my emphasis).
[223]Ibid., p.19.
[224]Ibid., p.xi. "[A] return to Schleiermacher simply must be demanded" (pp.14-5).
[225]Ibid., p.14.
[226]Ibid., p.42.

treatment of the problem of the nature of religion...already observable in the *Reden über die Religion.*"[227] "Religion is grounded in the subjective consciousness, i.e. in the affective and volitional life of man, and in such a way that it is entirely conditioned by the ego-function, and that its conviction and its conceptual content, including all the formation of ideas developed therein, must be understood in reference to the underlying religious experience."[228]

It is not hard to see why Farmer found this approach so attractive: it operates with presuppositions very similar to his own. Any discipline "whose subject is the human spirit and its concerns", must come to terms with the fact that an examination of empirical and essentially passive data, as in a laboratory, is impossible. "The very nature of the reality with which we are dealing gives us no option but to work on the basis of our own religious sense."[229] Although, as Wolfhart Pannenberg has pointed out, this opens the gate to subjectivism,[230] Farmer argues that it "does not permit us to remain enclosed within our own subjectivity."[231] The student of religion must take due account of the facts of religious history. That is to say, although there is an obvious danger of becoming Procrustean, this can be mitigated to some extent by recognising one's own standpoint and by allowing the facts to speak for themselves. He thus rejects the traditional phenomenological use of empathy (*Einfühlung*) on the basis of *epoché* and adopts instead a method of empathy which functions on the basis of the student's presuppositions. We must "take what we derive from our own religious sense into the field of

---

[227]Ibid., p43.
[228]Ibid., p.53.
[229]H. H. Farmer, *Revelation and Religion*, p.46.
[230]W. Pannenberg, *Systematic Theology*, vol.1, tr. by G. W. Bromiley (Edinburgh: T. & T. Clark, 1991), p.134 n.
[231]H. H. Farmer, *Revelation and Religion*, p.46.

religion generally and...bring it into reciprocal interplay with what is there presented to us."[232] Indeed, he believes that this will serve, not only as a guide which will enable us to work through the great multitude of religious facts, but also as an edifying and constructive help to our own faith, "ridding it both of misconception and of superficiality."[233] In short, what he is commending is more accurately described as "the method of the religio-psychological circle moved by productive empathy".

As to the normative essence of religion (the distillate which emerges as a result of reflection upon one's Christian religious experience), Farmer suggests that there are seven essential elements, all of which he discusses at length in the present volume. The first six concern the apprehension of God as: (1) ontologically other; (2) axiologically other; (3) personal; (4) "asking all" from the worshipper ("absolute demand"); (5) "giving all" to the worshipper ("final succour"); and (6) intimately present and active within the worshipper's own being. Finally, (7) there is an aspect of the Christian's apprehension of God which pervades the whole encounter, namely, a distinctive "element of feeling", a "distinctive feeling-tone which *reverberates through the whole being* when God is livingly encountered".[234] These seven elements, always present in Christian worship, constitute the normative defining concept of religion. That is not to say that the worshipper will always be aware of all seven elements to the same degree. Obviously some elements may become more dominant than others in the worshipper's mind. However, "in anything that can be properly called a distinctively Christian encounter with, and apprehension of, God, the other elements are always there as

---

[232]Ibid., p.46.
[233]Ibid.
[234]See ibid. chs. 3 and 4.

overtones, qualifying the whole awareness."[235]   In the present volume of
lectures he examines the tensions that these elements produce, such as, for
example, the tension between the apprehension of God as intimately present
and active within the worshipper's own being.[236]   Again there is a tension
between God as asking all from the worshipper and God as giving all to the
worshipper.[237]   Needless to say, his argument is that these tensions are
reconciled/unified in the Christian revelation and faith.

However, his point in the first series of lectures is that it is these seven
elements that constitute the *Normbegriff* (normative defining concept) of
religion. It is on the basis of these that he seeks to interpret the wider field of
religious phenomena. In other words, having analysed the essential elements
of the Christian experience of God, we are, according to Farmer, in a position
to do two things:

> first, we are able to discriminate and set on one side as not essentially
> religious those beliefs and attitudes which, because they have been,
> and can still be, closely associated with religion, are much too easily
> assumed to be religious beliefs and attitudes and classified with them.
> Second, we are able, in the sphere of the genuinely religious, to
> formulate a classification of types, or scale of forms, under the
> normative concept of religion which is given to us through the
> Christian revelation and experience.[238]

---

[235]Ibid., p.81.
[236] See below, ch.2.
[237] See below, ch.3.
[238]H. H. Farmer, *Revelation and Religion*, pp.86-7.

His analysis of the seven elements of living religion enables him to "elucidate and interpret the immense and highly complex field of religious, or ostensibly religious, facts": it provides him with "a basis for a broad classification of religious types", which constitute "a scale of forms ranged under the normative concept of religion...found in the Christian revelation and experience."[239] Indeed, half of the first series of Gifford Lectures (five of ten lectures) are devoted to an exposition and illustration of this scale of forms. However, it is perhaps worth noting that, for the purpose of classification, he omits all but incidental reference to the seventh element, since a distinctive feeling-tone characterises *all* living religion. The other six elements, on the other hand, will, in living religion, be present in varying degrees and in a variety of forms.

As we have seen, for Farmer non-Christian faiths are "distorted manifestations of the full and unitary relation to God as personal which is alone realised, or at least realisable, in the Christian revelation and experience".[240] This distortion consists in the fact that they lack a balanced unity of the elements—something which he makes much of in the present volume.[241]

One or other of the elements as it were breaks loose and obtains a position of obsessive dominance; the result of this is that not only are the remaining elements in varying degrees distorted and weakened— indeed at times almost completely suppressed—but also the dominant element itself, lacking the check and completion of the others, becomes increasingly subject to perversion and error. The process may be

---

[239]Ibid., p.113.
[240]Ibid., p.114.
[241] See ch.1 below.

compared to what sometimes takes place in the body when one group
of cells, growing unduly, establishes itself tyrannically over the other
cells, whilst at the same time needing them in order to live at all; by so
doing it may in the end cause the breakdown of the whole organism.[242]

Clearly such an understanding of revelation and religion provides us with an
effective basis for a classification of religious types, in that we are able to
produce a scale of religious forms according to the elements which assume
dominance, and the degree to which they do so. That said, Farmer's aim is
simply to identify dominant trends, not neatly to construct boxes into which
religious phenomena can easily be placed. As he points out, living religion
will always have "fringes, penumbras, nuances of thought and feeling,
fluctuations of emphasis, to which any system of classification must fail to do
justice. Always we have to remember the subtle variableness and fluidity of
religion as livingly experienced, as *erlebt*, especially on its hidden inward
side."[243] Indeed, it is possible that two or more elements may achieve
dominance simultaneously, in which case "overlaps and cross-divisions of
various kinds arise."

Finally, it needs to be understood that he is operating with two
fundamental categories: "substantival" religion and "adjectival" religion.
Substantival religion is "religion as constituted by the awareness of the
specifically religious objective reality"[244]—the living essence of religion.
Hence, he works on the basis of his two fundamental convictions: (a) a realist
understanding of the personal God whose self-disclosure is the ultimate
explanation for the fact of religion; and (b) that God's full and final self-

---

[242] H. H. Farmer, *Revelation and Religion*, p.114.
[243] Ibid., pp.114-5.
[244] Ibid., p.164.

disclosure of his objective being and nature as personal is made through his incarnation in Christ and through the relationship with himself which that revelation makes possible.

The adjectival factors of religion are *adjectival* for two broad reasons: (a) they are concerned with the satisfaction of fundamental human needs. Therefore, propositions describing them "have as their subject term man himself, and can be formulated without any reference to the objective element in religious awareness";[245] (b) such needs, and their satisfaction, can be experienced apart from any apprehension of a religious object, and therefore "apart from the religious consciousness as such". That said, living religion "always enters into the closest relationship with these needs and satisfactions and takes them integrally up into itself. In short, living religion necessarily relates itself to these elements, but they do not necessarily relate themselves to living religion."[246] Farmer is not, of course, wanting to minimise the importance of adjectival elements, his point simply being that they have "no *exclusive* relationship with religion."

This substantival-adjectival distinction he believes to be of considerable importance to the task of classifying religious types. For the very fact that "profound needs and satisfactions of the human spirit...*can* manifest themselves with great power in other contexts than distinctively religious ones"[247] means that two complications arise which need to be taken into account by an interpreter. (a) "[When] these needs and their satisfaction are present, particularly if they are present in an intense form, it is easy to suppose that the reality of living, substantival religion is also present in a correspondingly intense degree: whereas, in fact, it may not be present at all,

---

[245]Ibid., p.163.
[246]Ibid., p.164.
[247]Ibid.

or, if present, only in a quite fleeting and incidental way."[248]   That is to say,
because both the observer and the subject of the experience are aware that
such adjectival states of mind are often associated with substantival religion
they far too readily assume that this is what is in fact being experienced—or at
least that it is evidence of it. (b) Because adjectival elements can arise as a
result of that which is other than living religion, when they are incorporated
into substantival religion they are, he argues, prone "to act as a disturbing or
corrupting or enfeebling factor in it, bringing with them, as it were, an alien
influence from their alien origin."[249] Of course, he maintains that the Christian
apprehension of God, "in so far as it preserves its fullness and balance", keeps
the adjectival elements in the right relation to their substantival counterparts:
"it will discern at once the points where they are taking a form essentially
alien to itself, and will keep their perverting influence in check."[250]

Although there are other thinkers who have produced similar theses, I
would want to argue that (to quote Russell Aldwinckle), "Farmer's
illuminating analysis of the various types of religious worship and
behaviour...[is] a notable contribution which [goes] a long way towards
overcoming the tensions between metaphysics and living religion and between
Christianity and the non-Christian religions in a synthesis which does justice
to all the facts, and above all to the Christian's conviction that God (in Christ)
has acted decisively and once for all for us men and for our salvation."[251]

His second series of lectures (delivered on Wednesdays and Fridays in
February and March 1951, at the University of Glasgow) develop this line of
thought. As he says several times, they are a continuation of his thesis in the

---

[248]Ibid.
[249]Ibid.
[250]Ibid., p.166.
[251]R. F. Aldwinckle, Review of *Revelation and Religion*, in *The Canadian Journal of Theology* 1 (1955), p.124.

first series of lectures and should be read as such. As we have already indicated, they simply seek, as their title suggests, to set forth the uniqueness of the reconciling/unifying/integrating nature of the Christian revelation and faith. Developing his argument in the final chapter of the first series, what Farmer has in mind is not primarily an exposition of the Christian doctrine of the atonement, but rather a discussion of Christianity's ability to produce an integrated worldview, the desire for which, he maintains, is a basic human impulse: "the impulse towards, and the need for, integration constitutes the most deep-going, all-pervasive and significant factor in human experience, and...correspondingly the greatest satisfactions and even joys of which the human spirit is capable are connected with their fulfilment."[252]   This fundamental human need for a unified or holistic understanding of reality is manifested in the human quest for truth, beauty and goodness. As J. C. Smuts pointed out many years ago, "a unitary...conception of the universe...is the immanent ideal of all scientific and philosophic explanation."[253]   The search for truth is "the endeavour to discern intelligible and consistent connections between data which appear to have no such relation with one another, and to order such connections into ever-larger systematic unities."[254]   More specifically, this quest for unification is a basic element evident throughout the history of religions.   This is almost obvious and hardly needs to be substantiated: a religion or worldview, by definition, seeks a unified vision of reality.   Moreover, as Joachim Wach has argued, "that religion is concerned with the whole man and with the whole of human life" is a truth which has "not only been stressed by all great religious teachers throughout the ages, but is also vindicated by modern psychological and psychopathological studies.   It

---

[252]H. H. Farmer, *Revelation and Religion*, p.206.
[253]J. C. Smuts, *Holism and Evolution* (London: Macmillan, 1926), p.108.
[254]H. H. Farmer, *Revelation and Religion*, p.210.

has come as a surprise to many a modern Westerner to realise how significant and indispensable the function of worship can be in preserving or restoring an individual's physical and spiritual health, a fact of which those adept in Yoga or its equivalent in Hinduism and Buddhism have long been conscious."[255] In other words, an integrated worldview is good for our psychological well-being. As Farmer noted, the sense of satisfaction, even elation, which accompanies the discovery of connections and systematic unities is not insignificant.

Although people seek to satisfy the need for unification/reconciliation in a variety of ways, some of which Farmer discusses, his thesis is that the fundamental human need for a *reconciled* worldview is most adequately catered for in the Christian revelation and faith. His second series of Gifford Lectures is thus an exploration and exposition of certain fundamental aspects of the Christian faith, an exploration and exposition which moreover will demonstrate that Christianity meets the need for reconciliation in a uniquely adequate way.

> Of all the variant forms of living religion...at least in effect and by implication...there is none which unites, integrates, "reconciles" man, none which resolves the profoundest dualisms, tensions, conflicts of his being and life with such deep-going and final adequacy as the Christian revelation and faith; on the other hand...in so far as other forms of living religion do meet man's need for unification (and all of them *do* in some measure) they do so in a way that is more or less incomplete, superficial, intermittent, and often productive of new

---

[255]J. Wach, *The Comparative Study of Religions*, ed. by J. Kitagawa (New York: Columbia University Press, 1958), pp.32-3.

conflicts and tensions for which, in the nature of the case, they can offer no solution.[256]

---

[256] Below, p.11.

H. H. FARMER

RECONCILIATION
and
RELIGION

SOME ASPECTS OF
THE UNIQUENESS
OF CHRISTIANITY AS
A RECONCILING FAITH

Gifford Lectures   University of Glasgow   1951

PART ONE
INTRODUCTORY

1

RELIGION AND THEOLOGY

In the earlier volume, *Revelation and Religion*,[1] it was argued that the relation of Christianity to the general religious life of mankind can only be rightly understood if it is held to be, at one and the same time, both in the general class of religions and in a class by itself, unique. The seeming paradox of this assertion disappears if we bring a right doctrine of classification to the enquiry: if, that is to say, we give up trying to work with a *general* concept of religion which shall cover all religions equally, including Christianity, and work rather on the view (which, as Christians, we cannot but hold) that in the Christian revelation and faith there is uniquely given to us the *normative* concept of religion. By saying that in the Christian revelation and faith we have, in a unique way, the normative concept of religion we mean that we have in them, as nowhere else, the full and perfect manifestation of living religion which in other religions is exemplified in varying degrees of rudimentariness, fragmentariness, one-sidedness, distortion or perversion.[2] It was suggested that, working along this line, we are able to bring the multifarious complexity of religious phenomena, or ostensibly religious phenomena, into some sort of order; we are able to classify them into certain broad types, and arrange them

---

[1]*Revelation and Religion: Studies in the Theological Interpretation of Religious Types* (London: Nisbet, 1954).

[2]It may be well to point out that in *Revelation and Religion* an important distinction was drawn between (a) the Christian revelation and faith as normatively defined and exhibited in the New Testament, and (b) Christianity as a religion, as an empirical, historical complex of human and social activities and relationships, persisting and developing throughout the centuries. In the latter, as judged by its own normative concept, there is frequently to be discerned all kinds of weakness, aberration and distortion similar to those found elsewhere. See, p.84.

in a scale of forms under the normative concept of religion given through the Christian revelation and through the personal relation with God which that revelation makes possible.

All this was fully wrought out in the previous work. What we now propose to do is to make some further study of the uniqueness of the Christian revelation and faith, of that which, whilst not taking Christianity out of the general class of religion, sets it apart, puts it in a class by itself, and, in spite of its many failures, weaknesses and perversions, reveals the unique and normative revelation which lies at its heart.

It is obvious, however, that such a theme requires further definition if it is to be brought within manageable limits. I suppose it is true to say that the Christian faith is only fully grasped in its uniqueness when it is grasped as a close-knit unity in which every element is reciprocally determined by every other element as well as by the organic whole which the several elements together constitute and sustain. If we isolate one element or aspect of Christian truth and experience, there is always the danger that, because of that isolation, it will lose some of its distinctive unique quality and become, in corresponding degree, merely something which Christianity appears to have in common with other faiths; this is because, as I have said, the uniqueness attaches to the whole, and attaches to the separate elements, only to the degree that they are still held within the context of, and are interpreted by, that whole. The relation might be compared to that of the separate features of a face to the highly individual character of the face as a whole. Considered in isolation, in abstraction from "whole faces", noses are very much more alike than are the faces to which they belong; the same is true of lips, eyes and ears; but take these members together in the unity of the face and you get something which, by comparison, is highly individual, unique. Even the constituent elements, as the attention focuses upon them within the whole, seem to share in that uniqueness. Bearing this in mind, it would seem to follow from this that the only really adequate way by which to exhibit the uniqueness of Christianity within the general religious life of mankind is to explore and expound Christian truth and experience over their whole range and depth. But that is plainly a task for which a single book, indeed many books, would be insufficient—even if one were otherwise competent to undertake it. We have no option, therefore, but to select and isolate our topic for consideration, and to accept the limitation and loss entailed (whilst seeking all the time to keep these to a minimum). One way of doing this is to select for treatment some aspect of the total organism of the Christian revelation and faith. Such an aspect would of course need to be central and fundamental to Christian belief. The centrality and fundamentality of such a topic will enable us, in our consideration of it, to keep more explicitly in view the whole organism of truth to which it belongs than would otherwise be the case with a topic less central and fundamental.

Furthermore, it will be an added advantage for our thought if we can find an aspect of the whole organism of the Christian revelation and faith which is not only central and fundamental, but also bears directly upon something central and fundamental in the general religious life of mankind; for plainly that will facilitate the drawing out of a comparison, and will help to throw into sharper relief the distinctiveness of Christianity in respect of the aspect under consideration. In other words, it will help to throw into sharper relief what it means to say that, whilst Christianity is in the general class of religion along with other religions, it nevertheless stands apart in a class by itself.

And again, it will be a further advantage if we can find a central and fundamental aspect of the Christian revelation and faith which bears directly, not only, as I have just said, on something central and fundamental in the religious experience of mankind, but also on something central and fundamental, something universal, in general human nature and experience. The advantage of this would be that it might well impart to the argument a point of contact with the general experience of mankind, which, whilst not indispensable to it, would give it at least a potential universality of appeal not without value. If we can relate our central and fundamental aspect of Christianity to some quite fundamental, all-pervasive human need and value, which all men may be expected to feel and appreciate independently of any explicit religious awareness and belief, if we can relate it in such a way that it can be seen to satisfy this need and realise this value with unique profundity and adequacy, then that would at least prepare the way for an understanding, and even an acknowledgement, of the claim of the Christian revelation and faith to truth. It would give the argument a certain apologetic value not to be despised. To say this is not by any means to commit oneself to a purely pragmatic view of truth and of its criterion; it is rather to affirm what I believe to be a fact (though it is not possible to develop the point here), that the validation of the truth of the Christian revelation and faith can never be accomplished by an appeal simply to the intellective, ratiocinative functions of the mind; it must appeal also to the valuational and volitional sides of man's nature, to "reason" in that broader sense of the term which makes it a function of the whole man as a self-conscious person and includes intuitive thinking, imagination, the higher levels of feeling, moral and religious faith.[3]

We seek, then, for some element in, or aspect of, the Christian revelation and faith which is quite central and fundamental in it, which bears directly on something central and fundamental in the general religious life and experience of mankind, in that it is related to some central and fundamental human need and value. We propose to find what we desire in what is broadly indicated by the word "reconciliation". Therefore, what follows is a series of studies of the uniqueness of Christianity as a reconciling faith. That "reconciliation" is a key word in Christian experience and thought, that it represents something central and fundamental in them, hardly needs to be argued, and in any case the course of our thought will sufficiently illumine and substantiate the point. All that needs to be said at this point is that we use the term "reconciliation" to indicate something wider and more comprehensive than the experience and doctrine of the atonement with which it is usually, and rightly, associated in a particularly close way. This also will be made plain in the following pages. It is, however, more important at this point to indicate how this central theme of "reconciliation" is related to the other two desiderata.

---

[3]Cf. W. G. De Burgh, *The Life of Reason* (London: Macdonald & Evans, 1949), p.19. Cf. also Paul Tillich's distinction between "ecstatic" and "technical" reason, *Systematic Theology*, vol.1 (Welwyn: Nisbet, 1953), p.60.

The fundamental human need and value to which we relate Christianity as a reconciling faith, and by which the broad scope of the word "reconciliation" as here used is indicated, is the need for "unification" or "integration". In the earlier volume, to which reference has already been made, it was maintained that the impulse towards and the need for unification constituted one of the most deep-going, all-pervasive and significant factors in human experience, and that correspondingly some of the greatest satisfactions, and even joys, of which the human spirit is capable are bound up with their fulfilment.[4] Leaving on one side the more philosophical analyses of personality or selfhood which find in it the supreme example known to us of an integrative trend which is manifest on different levels throughout all nature,[5] it was pointed out that there is enough empirical evidence to make it quite plain how profound and central in the human person the impulse towards, and need for, unification are. The integrative trend is to be observed, even on the lowest physiological levels. It can be observed in the unconscious organic processes which keep the body in that state of repair and unitary functioning which we experience as good health. At the mental level, it is evident, positively, in the constant building up of the increasing differentiations which mark mental growth into wider and more embracing functional unities and systems. Negatively, it is evident in the disabling consequences of mental conflict, of failure to achieve such unity in face of the complex demands of life. On the highest levels of rational and volitional self-consciousness, the integrative trend can be observed in the pursuit of the ideal values of truth, beauty and goodness, the appreciation and search for which being quite evidently, from one point of view, the appreciation and search for unity in the particular sphere and by the particular methods appropriate to each.[6]

---

[4]See H. H. Farmer, *Revelation and Religion*, pp.206ff. It is because the line of thought we are to follow in this work is a development of the theme opened up in chapter 10, that the two books may be considered to be in a measure continuous with one another. Also, some recapitulation will be necessary.

[5]As, for example, in J. C. Smuts, *Holism and Evolution* (London: Macmillan & Co., 1926).

[6]See H. H. Farmer, *Revelation and Religion*, ch.10. See also *The World and God: A Study in Prayer, Providence and Miracle* (London: Nisbet, 1936), ch.2.—Ed.

The discussion in the first series of lectures also laid an emphasis on the important truth that the unification for which the self consciously or unconsciously yearns cannot be separated from the unification of the world apprehended by the self. The two reciprocally condition one another: unity as inwardly achieved and experienced always depends in some measure on unity as outwardly discerned, and unity as outwardly discerned always depends in some measure on unity as inwardly achieved and experienced.[7]

Turning now to the general religious life of mankind, it almost goes without saying that religion has always entered into the closest connection with the need and impulse of the self towards unification. This point was also fully developed in the previous work.[8] Amongst other things it was pointed out that a strong monotheistic tendency runs throughout all religion, not excluding primitive religion and polytheism, monotheism being, almost by definition, a unifying awareness of God as the one Source of all being and all value, and of the world as a unity under him. Moreover, it was pointed out that central and persistent throughout the history of religion is the idea of man's separation from God and the prescribing of ways in which the separation may be overcome in order for the human person to find peace in a state of final unification with the source of his being. Again, it was pointed out that worship, which is the supreme and distinctive activity of religion, is essentially a unifying activity, an assembling together of the whole being from its distribution and dispersal over a variety of interests and activities and a focusing of them in a unitary way on the one divine reality alone. It was also pointed out how universally and closely associated with religion at all levels has been the finding of satisfaction in, and the endeavour to induce, unified states of consciousness, whether by the use of sacred drugs and intoxicants, or by rhythmic dance and music, or by a technique of mental concentration and withdrawal such as has been elaborated both in the East and in the West.[9]

---

[7]See H. H. Farmer, *Revelation and Religion*, pp.207ff., 220ff.—Ed.
[8]Ibid., pp.213ff.—Ed.
[9]See ibid., pp.187-98; 218-20.—Ed.

Finally, we drew attention to the evidence adduced by Jung and psychologists of his school to show the relation of religion to the deep-seated impulse of the psyche towards its own wholeness.[10]

We have then in "unification" or "integration" a universal and all-pervading human value which all men may be expected to apprehend and, in one form or another, to acknowledge as a value, and which, at the same time, lies in close relationship to the springs of living religion in the soul. And to it that aspect of the Christian revelation and faith referred to under the term "reconciliation" is obviously related. The argument will take the form of exploring and expounding certain fundamental aspects of the Christian faith in such a way that that faith can be seen to meet the need for, to realise the value of, unification in a uniquely adequate way. It will, in short, be uniquely "reconciling" in the comprehensive sense in which we are using that term. Of all the variant forms of living religion, so the argument will run, at least in effect and by implication (for the restrictions of time and space will not allow us always to draw out the comparison explicitly or in detail), there is none which unites, integrates, "reconciles" man, none which resolves the profoundest dualisms, tensions, conflicts of his being and life with such deep-going and final adequacy as the Christian revelation and faith; on the other hand, we shall maintain (or, at least, imply where we do not explicitly argue) that, in so far as other forms of living religion do meet man's need for unification (and all of them *do* in some measure) they do so in a way that is more or less incomplete, superficial, intermittent, and often productive of new conflicts and tensions for which, in the nature of the case, they can offer no solution.

However, before we proceed to our enquiry, I want to consider two preliminary matters.

---

[10]See ibid., pp.215-6.—Ed.

Unification and Mysticism

The first is the question of *mysticism*. This was discussed at some length in the previous volume.[11] Therefore, in order to guard against the appearance of making unwarrantable assumptions, and at the same time to prepare the way for the development of the line of thought we are to follow, we need briefly to indicate the position there adopted.

Although "mysticism" is notoriously a word with an infinite variety of meanings and shades of meaning, I am here using it to indicate a certain powerful trend in religion (or what is widely understood to be religion) towards (a) an impersonalist conception of ultimate reality, and (b) in close relation with this, a certain distinctive method of satisfying man's need for unification. Now, so far as "mysticism" does thus signify an attitude of mind dominated by this dual trend, it stands in complete opposition to the Christian revelation and faith. In its tendency to an impersonalist conception of God, it runs counter to the radical personalism of Christianity and, along with that, to that whole view of the religious life of mankind which was set forth in the previous volume on the basis of the assumption that in the Christian revelation and faith we have the normative concept of religion—the view that living religion in all its forms arises from God's personal self-disclosure to, and encounter with, man.[12] In its method of satisfying the need for unification it runs counter to that distinctively Christian way of satisfying it, some aspects of which it is the purpose of these chapters to explore. I am aware, of course, that something which is usually referred to as Christian mysticism has entered into the Christian tradition, and that, too, in a way that many feel to be an enrichment of it;[13] but that does not impugn what I have just said; it merely means that there are elements in impersonalistic mysticism which can be detached from its impersonalism and incorporated into Christian personalism,

---

[11]Ibid., pp.229ff. [See also H. H. Farmer, *The World and God*, p.31 n., 209; and J. Oman, *The Natural and the Supernatural* (Cambridge: Cambridge University Press, 1931), ch.24; and pp.494-500. This is also discussed in C. H. Partridge, *H. H. Farmer's Theological Interpretation of Religion*, pp.265-72.—Ed.]

[12]See H. H. Farmer, *Revelation and Religion*, pp.24-5.—Ed.

[13]See ibid., pp.235ff.—Ed.

and perhaps also that religious people can sometimes hold two incompatible theological views without realising it and without being religiously a great deal the worse for it! In either case, it remains true that in so far as mysticism does take up an impersonalist view of God, in harmony with which follows its distinctive impersonalist method of satisfying the need for unification, it runs counter to the Christian revelation and faith.

What then is this impersonalist method of satisfying the need for unification. In essence, it is the method of cultivating, usually through highly elaborated techniques of mental withdrawal and concentration, states of consciousness in which the self, or the world apprehended by the self, or both of these together, are emptied of that differentiated content which they have in normal, everyday experience. Indeed, it has even been claimed by some mystics of this type, that, at the highest point of the mystic achievement of unification, even the distinction between the perceiving self and the objective reality it perceives is done away with. Thus, in the mystic state all distinctions in principle disappear, and with them, necessarily, all dualities, oppositions, tensions, so that a completely unified state of consciousness is achieved, which is salvation and peace. The whole experience is claimed to be extraordinarily satisfying and refreshing, and, in view of the centrality and profundity of the impulse towards unification in human personality, we may well suppose that it is. It is obvious, of course, that a technique of mental withdrawal and concentration, issuing in blissful unitary states of consciousness, *might* be associated with almost any view of the nature of ultimate reality and of man's relation to it, or indeed with no explicitly formulated view at all; it might be followed simply as a method of self-culture, or self-management, or mental hygiene by which one achieves a temporary and refreshing escape and detachment from the complexities and pressures of the world and the internal tensions of the mind. But, in point of fact, the use of such a technique has usually, though not always, been associated, as I have already indicated, with a pantheistic, impersonalist worldview. The reason for this is not difficult to find. A psychological technique which aims at expunging from consciousness all the differentiations, dualities and tensions of everyday experience can only be given a philosophical or metaphysical ground and justification (and not many minds could follow a technique so opposed to all the instincts and habits of human nature without seeking some such ground and justification) by a doctrine in which all such differentiations, dualities and tensions are denied a significant place in relation to that ultimate reality with which, in the end, a man must settle accounts. But such a denial necessarily commits you to a fundamentally impersonal view of ultimate reality and of its relation to men. For it is easy to see that if all distinctions and dualities vanish anything in the nature of an ultimate personal order in which man and God, and man and neighbour, are in personal relationship with one another vanishes also.

Thus, to refer only to those basic, comprehensive dualities with which we shall be largely concerned in these pages (the self and God, the self and the world, the world and God), it is obvious that with the expunging of the duality of self and God, the possibility of anything in the nature of a genuine personal I-Thou relation between them is expunged also. Without a real, and not merely an apparent, duality of human person and divine person, the notion of an I-Thou relation is meaningless. The same thing happens if the duality of self and world, and the duality of the world and God, are denied. Empty the world of its teeming multiplicity of persons, events and things, and, along with that, empty the self of all those differentiations of thought, feeling, valuation and choice in which the manifold of the world is reflected, and all possibility of a personal I-Thou relation to God vanishes. For there is now no sphere wherein there can be a real encounter of God's will with man's and a personal relation of freely willed co-operation of man with God achieved.

The mystical way of fulfilling and satisfying the impulse to, and the need for, unification, is, then, fundamentally an impersonal way; it invites man into an impersonal world. In contrast with this, the Christian way of unification stands out in the sharpest possible relief. At no point does it cease to assert the fundamentally personal nature of God and of his dealings with men, and, in accordance with this, at no point does it attempt, in the supposed interest of unification, to eliminate or by-pass the dualities and tensions of human life and human history. This is evident from almost every page of the New Testament.

The note of unification certainly sounds unmistakably throughout the New Testament. Indeed, the unification which God is declared to make possible through Christ is presented as including the whole cosmos in its scope. Christ is the cosmic unifier. Nothing is left out.[14] But it is significant that it is the personal word "reconciliation" which is favoured, and "reconciliation", like all personal words, asserts duality even though in another sense it asserts the overcoming of duality. The whole creation which is waiting to be reconciled to God is waiting for the manifestation of the sons of God; such a manifestation, whatever it may mean, cannot mean—at any rate, when taken in its New Testament context—the absorbing and disappearance of selves into the all-embracing, undifferentiated unity of the absolute One. Rather it means that selves achieve the true end of their being by being brought into trustful and obedient self-commitment to God and brotherly accord with one another—a harmony of persons which is summed up under the category of Love, which again is a term which, in New Testament usage, contains not the slightest hint of the disappearance of duality, but rather presupposes duality. Consistently with this, there is no suggestion at any point that the processes of nature and history, in all their conflict, confusion and impermanence, are opposed to man's quest for unification, and therefore are to be withdrawn from as much as possible if that quest is to succeed. On the contrary, by its central message of the incarnation, of the coming of God as a human person into the world, it asserts both the essentially personal nature of God, and also the significance of the world and history as created by God to be the sphere wherein he is himself at work, meets man in personal encounter and calls him into fellowship and co-operation with himself. This significance of the world and history is also implicitly asserted in the New Testament picture of the final consummation of the divine purpose, when God in Christ shall "reconcile to himself all things".[15] So far removed is this picture from the philosophy of non-duality, and from the setting up of undifferentiated states of consciousness

---

[14]See, for example, Col.1:20 and Eph.1:10.
[15]Col.1:20.

(however conceived) as the highest realisation of God's purpose with and for human persons, that in it the created order is represented, not as passing into nothingness, but as being refashioned into a new heaven and a new earth, and selves are represented as being endowed with new bodies, presumably as organs of self-expression. Such eschatological pictures are extremely difficult to interpret and to express in logically coherent propositions, but as symbols they manifestly arise out of, to some extent draw their meaning from, and are in harmony with, what we have called the "radical personalism" of the Christian revelation and faith.[16]

Christianity then, meets man's profound need for unification not by any form of pantheistic mysticism, but by personalistic monotheism.[17] Pantheistic mysticism seeks to overcome the dualities, contrarieties, oppositions, tensions of man's life in a unification which in effect sponges them away as of no essential or permanent significance; personalistic monotheism seeks to overcome them in a way, which, while retaining their significance to the full, seeks reconcilingly to reinterpret them in terms of the one sovereign will and purpose of God revealed in human history as Love through his own self-giving and self-disclosure in Christ. We may add that the way of unification which Christianity thus opens up is not to be thought of as an *easier* way than the mystic way with its arduous asceticisms and self-discipline. On the contrary, in its insistence on there being no attempt to withdraw and escape from the conflicts and tensions of historical existence (except, maybe, quite temporarily as part of the devotional life), it is a way which runs through a continuous succession of problems and perplexities, whilst at the same time being always a way of victory over them in that life of reconciliation, some fundamental aspects of which we are to explore. On the other hand, the Christian way is an

---

[16]See H. H. Farmer, *The World and God*, pp.210-26; and *God and Men* (London: Nisbet, 1948), pp.163-5.—Ed.

[17]Farmer recognises such a tendency in Schleiermacher's thought: "For Schleiermacher, ultimate reality is the universe conceived (somewhat pantheistically) as an infinite, all-embracing, harmonious unity, and the essence of religion, according to one of his definitions of it, is the soul's intuitive grasp of that unity through a feeling-response which has deeper sources than discursive thought or volitional action" (*Revelation and Religion*, p.27).—Ed.

easier way at least in this respect, that it keeps much closer to the springs of spontaneous, living religion in the human spirit; it keeps closer, because it steadfastly adheres to a personalist understanding of God and of his relation to men and because it grapples with the actual problems and frustrations which men must face if they are to live in the world at all and to which, after all, even the fully trained mystic has to return when his unified states of consciousness have passed.

We may relate this to some remarks made about polytheism in *Revelation and Religion*,[18] thus indicating once again the continuity of our thought here with what is contained in that volume. The point was made that polytheism, at least in its higher forms, for all its shortcomings, did grasp in its own way the two closely related truths about God which, as has just been said above, are from our point of view fundamental—the truth of the personal nature of the divine reality and of man's relation to it, and the truth that the world and history are the sphere in which that divine reality meets man, making his absolute claim upon him and bringing to him the final succour and security of his life. To us, polytheism's belief in different gods to cover all the different interests of man's life seems quite ridiculous, and, indeed, the multiplication of deities in, for example, later Roman religion, reached a pitch which was fantastic and absurd in the extreme; but at least such beliefs asserted, in their own crude way, that all the increasing differentiations and specialisations which marked the emergence of what we are accustomed to call civilisation, are religiously significant. That is to say, they have meaning not only for man but also for his God. The defects and weaknesses of polytheism are, however, obvious enough. They are defects and weaknesses which caused it in due time to vanish from history along with the civilisations with which it was integrally bound up. Among such weaknesses and defects, not the least was undoubtedly its incapacity to meet and satisfy the profound need of, and impulse towards unification, of which we have been speaking.

---

[18]See pp.110ff.

Looking back on the course of the history of religion, we can perhaps now see that there were only two ways out of this bankruptcy of the higher polytheism in respect of the craving for unification. One was to seek to satisfy the craving by, as it were, "toning down" or "blurring" the sharp contrasts and differentiations, the oppositions and tensions, which an increasingly complex civilisation inevitably developed, a process which reaches its climax in a withdrawal into mystical, unitive states of consciousness such as we have been discussing. Such a withdrawal, we may surmise, required a combination of circumstances which only a minority could enjoy. Such thinkers can benefit from a leisurely elevation above the immediate pressures and tasks of the workaday world, a taste and gift for speculative thought, an innate capacity for, and inclination to, mystical states of mind. It tended to be bound up with, what Arnold Toynbee calls, "the philosophies of a dominant minority". There was in it, as we have fully granted, a real satisfaction of the craving for unity, a satisfaction such as polytheism, with its splitting up of divine reality into a multitude of gods, to say nothing of the anthropomorphic absurdities and rational self-contradictions into which it fell, could not supply. But it was at great cost, the cost of surrendering the real religious insights which polytheism, in its own poor and perverted way, expressed, namely, that divine reality is personal and that man's present complex environment of nature and history, and his use and management of it, and the increasing differentiation of his life which that use and management entail, are religiously significant.

The other way was to meet the craving for unity whilst not surrendering the insights to which reference has just been made. This was the way of monotheism, the way of belief in one sovereign, divine personal purpose actively at work in the world and concerned with the individual lives and destiny of human persons. In this, as we have said, there is no attempt to overcome the oppositions and tensions, the dualities, of experience in a unification which, in effect, sponges them away as of no real significance; rather a unification is sought which gives them full significance within and under the one sovereign will and purpose of God. This monotheistic way of seeking and finding unification is, as we have pointed out, much closer to the spontaneous religion of the common man, who is immersed "up to the neck" in the pressures and tasks of managing the world and maintaining a tolerable human life within it. It is, to use another of Toynbee's phrases, the "religion of the internal proletariat", as contrasted with the "philosophies of the dominant minority."

We must guard ourselves here against possible misunderstanding. If we speak of the monotheistic way out of the bankruptcy of polytheism in respect of the need for unification, this must not be taken to imply that progress along this way was the result of an inevitable natural evolution of polytheism itself, whereby, unconsciously impelled by the need for unification, men projected into the universe the idea of one sovereign purpose, picturing it after the analogy of the monarchical constitution of the state. The latter view has often found expression. Thus Toynbee speaks of "the one God being conceived by human minds through analogy from the constitution which a universal state is apt to assume as it gradually crystallises into its final shape. In this process the human ruler, who is originally a king of kings, eliminates the client princes who were once his peers and becomes a monarch in the strict sense of the term. If we now examine what happens simultaneously to the gods of the diverse peoples and lands which the universal state has absorbed we shall find an analogous change. In place of a pantheon in which a High God exercises suzerainty over a community of gods once his peers, who have not lost their divinity in losing their independence, we see emerging a single God, whose uniqueness is his essence." [19] Such a statement needs a good deal of qualification and amplification if it is to be saved from making quite a number of *suggestiones falsi*. (1) It appears to ignore what, from our point of view, is the prime originative factor in all the religious history of mankind, namely, the continuous self-revealing activity of the personal God himself. Thus it may easily mask what is in effect a purely naturalistic theory of religion, according to which man's awareness of God is not the centrally creative factor in his

---

[19] See A. Toynbee, *A Study of History*, abridgement of volumes I-VI by D. C. Somervell (London: Oxford University Press, 1946), pp.473ff.

unfolding life, but rather in the nature of a supernumerary or epiphenomenon which merely reflects processes whose creative sources are elsewhere. (2) It does not take note of, or account for, the burning intensity and intolerance, the religious and prophetic passion, which mark the emergence of monotheistic faith in the midst of polytheism. Polytheism, both in its essential idea, and because of its dominant eudaemonism, is inevitably tolerant, for it is manifestly absurd to exclude any power which might give help to man. Polytheism, as Söderblom says, cannot become really monotheistic except by a violent breach with its own spirit and past, and this remains true even if it be also true that there are monotheistic trends to be discerned in polytheistic religion.[20] (3) It is not in accord with the facts, for, despite the monotheistic tendency just referred to, polytheism never did evolve into monotheism. It had no power of self-transcendence, but tended always to remain fixed and immobilised in a kind of cul-de-sac, or else to sink back into animism and polydaemonism.[21]

Unification and Theology

The second question on which I would like to say something before plunging into the main stream of our thought is the important and difficult question of the relation of the Christian experience of unification/reconciliation, to the reflective working out of a coherent system of theology. Does the power of the Christian revelation and faith to satisfy man's profound need for unification depend on our being able to think that revelation and faith through into a unified scheme of thought from which all oppositions, contradictions, paradoxes have been removed? In short, to what extent, if any, is the Christian experience of unification dependent on unification in the realm of theology?

A possible answer to this question, which has had its representatives in the history of thought, would be to say that it is not so dependent at all. The Christian experience of unification, it is said, does not require a unified

---

[20] See N. Söderblom, *The Living God* (London: Oxford University Press, 1933), pp.264ff.
[21] See A. A. Bowman, *Studies in the Philosophy of Religion*, vol.2, (London: Macmillan & Co., 1938), p.48.

scheme of theology, for the simple reason that living religion does not really require a formulated theology. Christian piety and theology are neutral to one another. The work of the theologian can neither help nor hinder the faith-life of the reconciled man, for this rests on a direct personal encounter and dealing with God, and carries, in itself, its own sufficient sources of conviction. However, I do not suppose that anybody in these days would wish to make quite such a radical separation between religion and theology as this. Even if it be granted that some simple religious souls can get along with extremely little in the way of a formulated theology, it is nevertheless true that when, and to the extent that a man begins to have such a theology, it inevitably works back into and affects his religious experience and life. Piety and theology are not neutral. To suppose that they are would be to deny precisely that deep impulse towards, and need for unification of which I have been speaking. It is quite impossible to split the mind in the way suggested, to separate religion as *erlebt* and religion as seeking expression and clarification in thought, that is, in theology. Reflective thinking is part of the whole man; it belongs to the very ground of our being as persons. Consequently, every experience struggles to express itself in the forms of thought and to submit itself to the norms of thought, and is itself affected by the struggle.[22]

Another possible answer to the question tends towards the opposite extreme, and puts all the emphasis, or at least the major emphasis, on the working out of a rationally coherent theology; it says, in effect, that anything in religious experience (or what claims to be religious experience) which cannot be incorporated in such a rationally coherent system must be rejected or come under grave suspicion as being false, or superstitious, or as being at best a crudely figurative way of expressing a truth of which reasoned reflection knows better how to give an account. Unification/reconciliation in the sphere of thought is therefore a *sine qua non*. Not many today would wish to defend

---

[22]See his important discussions of the "reflective element of conviction" in *Experience of God: A Brief Enquiry into the Grounds of Christian Conviction* (London: SCM, 1929), pp.23ff, 67-80; *Towards Belief in God* (London: SCM, 1942), pp.26-8, chs.7, 8, 11. See also Brandt B. Boeke, "The Knowledge of God in the Theology of H. H. Farmer" (unpublished doctoral dissertation: Princeton Theological Seminary, 1987), pp.184ff. and ch.7.—Ed.

such a completely rationalistic answer to our question since it manifestly fails to do justice to living religious experience. Having said that, (a) there are elements of feeling and volition in living religion which cannot be conceptualised and translated into a scheme of logical connections and (b) Kierkegaard's criticism of Hegel and of the Hegelian theologians still holds, namely, that living religion in general and Christianity in particular requires that there should be *real* dualisms and oppositions—God and man, good and evil, time and eternity. Dissolve these away into some all-comprehending, unitary scheme of thought and, so far from bringing living religion to its highest pinnacle of unification, it is, in principle, destroyed.

This brings us to a third answer which rejects both the two answers just indicated: that is to say, it rejects the view that the Christian experience of reconciliation can be separated from theological reflection. Rather it insists on the inevitability and importance of theological reflection for the Christian experience of reconciliation. It also rejects the view that a completely coherent system of theological truth, from which all contradiction and paradox have been eliminated, is either possible or indispensable in that experience. Theologise you must, but if your theology is not to falsify and, working back into it, to impoverish the experience with which it is dealing, it will necessarily, at one point or another, run out into contradictions and paradoxes which cannot be resolved but must be accepted.

There is much truth in this third answer as thus broadly stated. Indeed it does hardly more than describe the situation in which theologians all down the ages have continually found themselves. They have continually found themselves with contradictions and paradoxes on their hands which they cannot satisfactorily resolve, but which are not felt to be such in the Christian experience of reconciliation/unification itself. An obvious example of this is the apparent contradiction between the Christian man's conviction that divine grace is the *sole* source of his salvation and his conviction, which is inseparable from his awareness of himself as a person personally answerable to God, that he is in some real sense in charge of, and responsible for, his own destiny. It is obvious, however, that this answer calls for some further exploration. For, in the first place, it could easily issue in a contentment with, or acquiescence to, contradiction and paradox, which would be hard to distinguish from sheer irrationalism. In the second place, even if we grant that at *some* point in our theological reflection we must be prepared to run up against irresolvable paradoxes and contradictions, the question remains concerning how we are to know when we have reached that point. Obviously we cannot accept *any* paradox and contradiction which presents itself in the course of our reflection; that would mean the cessation of responsible thinking altogether. If then we have to accept some and not others, how are we to distinguish between them, how are we to distinguish between a contradiction which is just a flat, nonsensical contradiction and one which is the vehicle of profound religious and theological insight.[23] In the third place—and this is important from the point of view of these studies—the answer appears to leave the mind much too divided against itself to be quite satisfactory. It says, in effect, that whilst, on the one hand, there is given through the Christian revelation and faith a unification/reconciliation which is unique in its depth and adequacy, nevertheless, on the other hand, when we theologise the unification must break up again into irreconcilable oppositions. The *final* state would therefore appear to be disunity, for religion, piety, and theology cannot, as I have already said, really be kept separate from one another. They are comprehended within the experience of the one person, and are always in interplay with one another. The situation obviously calls for some further examination.

Donald Baillie[24] has some remarks on these topics in his book *God was in Christ* which are helpful so far as they go, but they do not seem to me to go far

---

[23]An echo of Sidgwick's well-known comment, quoted by H. R. Mackintosh, *Types of Modern Theology: Schleiermacher to Barth*, (London: Collins, Fontana, 1969), p.225: "It was a well-known jest of Sidgwick of Cambridge that he never could distinguish between the kind of contradiction that was just a contradiction and the kind that was a vehicle of the profoundest truth."

[24]He notes in the margin: "Whose recent death has been such a sore loss to us all personally as well as to the world of theological scholarship."—Ed.

enough to be wholly satisfactory.[25] He rightly maintains that there is a higher truth which reconciles our theological paradoxes, and that this higher truth is given in the living religious experience itself: "it is experienced and lived", he says, "in the "I-and-Thou" relationship of faith towards God."[26] It is only when we come to formulate this experience in theological propositions that we inevitably find ourselves with contradictions on our hands. From this it follows, he says, that the only way we have of keeping the contradictions and paradoxes of our theology under control and discriminating between those which are necessary and those which are not necessary is to be continually referring back to the unity of the originating religious experience itself.[27] "No paradox in theology", he writes, "can be justified unless it can be shown to spring directly from what H. R. Mackintosh called "the immediate utterances of faith"; for since a paradox is a self-contradictory statement we simply *do not know what it means or what we mean by it* unless it has that direct connection with the faith which it attempts to express."[28] Of the wisdom of these remarks there can be no question. If they remind us of what is true of thinking in any sphere, namely that it must be kept in close touch with its empirical sources, *and* that the demands of theoretical consistency must never be allowed to override the data supplied by those sources, it is good to be so reminded in relation to the particular point under consideration. Two questions, however, present themselves and call for consideration.

(1) The first question is this: if the "higher truth" which reconciles contradictions is already livingly experienced and apprehended in the relation of faith to God, why must it break up into contradictions and oppositions

---

[25]D. M. Baillie, *God Was In Christ: An Essay on Incarnation and Atonement* (London: Faber & Faber, 1948), pp.106ff.

[26]Ibid., p.109.

[27]Cf. For a good recent discussion of the notion of paradox in Baillie's theology see G. B. Hall, "D. M. Baillie: A Theology of Paradox", in D. Fergusson (ed.), *Christ, Church and Society: Essays on John Baillie and Donald Baillie* (Edinburgh: T. & T. Clark, 1993), pp.65-85. As Hall points out, Baillie "attached a very great importance to paradox not only in his highly regarded *God Was in Christ*, but also in his earlier and less well-known *Faith in God*" (p.65). Cf. *Faith in God and its Christian Consummation* (Edinburgh: T. & T. Clark, 1927; London: Faber & Faber; 1964).—Ed.

[28]D. M. Baillie, *God Was In Christ*, p.110.

directly it is reflected upon? Two reasons are usually given for this: first, it is said that God is infinite reality and our minds are finite. But it does not appear to me to be self-evident that the finitude of our thought about God must necessarily betray itself in irreconcilable paradox and self-contradiction. The emphasis must here be on the word "irreconcilable". It is one thing to say that our thought *must* be inadequate to infinite reality, and that its inadequacy *may* at any point disclose itself in contradictions which we must then seek to overcome, endeavouring thus to make our thought more adequate; but to say that it *must* end in a cul-de-sac of irresolvable contradiction and paradox does not appear to me to be a necessary inference from the premise at all. It should be noted that I am not saying that our theological reflection does not issue in contradiction and paradox, for it obviously does. Rather I only wish to say that I do not find the reason alleged for its so doing convincing. After all, it is the same finite mind which *ex hypothesi* apprehends the infinite God in what is called the higher truth which reconciles. If then, in the one case finitude can apprehend the infinite without splitting it up into irreconcilable opposites, why not in the other case also? In short, is there not here a too easy identification of the inadequacy of thought with necessary and irreconcilable contradiction in thought?

The second reason which is given is that directly we begin to theologise we necessarily withdraw from the living I-Thou relation to God and adopt a spectator attitude to him; we are forced "objectify" him.[29] But God, it is said, since he is the ground and source of all being whatsoever, including our own being and all its powers, and since he is, furthermore, the infinite Person who always and only discloses himself in a personal I-Thou relation which claims our *whole* being as persons, cannot be grasped by making him simply an

---

[29]Farmer is more than likely thinking of Emil Brunner. See E. Brunner, *Revelation and Reason: The Christian Doctrine of Faith and Knowledge*, tr. by O. Wyon (London: SCM, 1947), chs.1 and 24; *Truth as Encounter*, tr. by D. Cairns and A. Loos (London: SCM, 1964), ch.2, pp.134-7. Farmer was very familiar with Brunner's work, particularly the former volume (see *Revelation and Religion*, pp.31ff.). It's also worth noting that Olive Wyon expresses her gratitude to Farmer (and others) for his interest and help in her translation of the work (see *Revelation and Reason*, p.vii).—Ed.

object of thought, standing over against us like other objects about which we think. Such "objectification" of God, inevitable as it is, if we are to *think* about him at all, necessarily falsifies and misrepresents him. This is revealed in the irreconcilable paradoxes and contradictions into which we fall. In regard to this, I can only say once again that the connection between the premises and the conclusion does not appear to me to be quite so luminously clear and self-evident as is suggested. Apart from the fact that there would appear to be, again, a too easy identification of the inadequacy of thought with the irreconcilable contradiction in thought, I am not clear that theology as pursued by a devout Christian theologian (who is doing what Baillie insists he must do, namely, keeping his theology in close touch with its sources in religious experience and faith) need necessarily involve such a complete withdrawal into a merely objectifying, spectator attitude towards God. It would seem to be possible to speak about God in the third person (that is, as "he") whilst being consciously related to him in the first person (i.e. as "Thou") in the very act of so speaking. The first does not exclude the latter, or the latter the former, but each can be an element or "moment" in the other. This appears to be what takes place in preaching as a part of worship, and in serious, reverent religious conversation and discussion.[30] In like manner there appears to be no reason why we should not make God the object of careful and systematic thinking whilst being fully aware, and continually bearing in mind, that he is in his essential nature and in his relation to us (including the relation of being thought about by us) far more than *merely* the object of our thinking. In short, God can be made the object of thought ("objectified" in that sense) within the I-Thou relation itself. Indeed, one might hold that the I-Thou relation is of such a kind that such thinking (such "objectification" of God) is inevitable and appropriate. For it is essential to that relationship that the "I" and the "Thou" should stand over against one another, confront one another, as "objects" to one another, even though they are "objects" with the distinctive quality of being all the time personal "subjects" personally related

---

[30]See H. H. Farmer, *The Servant of the Word*, chs.2-3.—Ed.

to one another. God, by entering into an I-Thou relation with us, chooses to disclose and offer himself as an "object" to our apprehension and thought, and, if our thought keeps within the limits of the extent to which God does thus disclose and offer himself to us, it is not apparent to me why it *must* run out into irreconcilable contradiction. It may in fact do so, but the reason alleged, namely that God is "objectified" by our thinking, does not seem to me to be sufficient.

(2) The second question which presents itself is this: how does it come about that the contradictions, which, on the view we are considering, necessarily disclose themselves in our theology, leave the original experience (the "higher truth which unifies them") unaffected? Why do they not work back into religious life and faith and create there also an unhappy sense of unresolved tension and contrariety? Theology, we have already said, always does tend to work back into the religious experience which is its source, and even comes to determine that experience of which we are capable. To suppose otherwise would be to fall into the error of splitting the human person into two compartments and denying the deep impulse within it towards integration of which we have spoken, an impulse which seeks satisfaction in both "religion" and "theology" and in the unity of both with one another.

The Nature of Thinking and Feeling

Now I want to suggest that if we are to answer these questions we must first grasp certain truths about (a) the nature of *thinking*, and (b) the nature of *feeling* and the relation of thinking to it. To take each of these in turn.

1. The nature of thinking. What we have to realise is that it belongs to the very nature of thinking itself to set up oppositions; we cannot think clearly on any other basis.[31] The reason for this is that we cannot think without forming *concepts*, and we cannot form concepts without the use of opposing ideas. It is

---

[31]Paul Roubiczek has expounded this in his profound and important work *Thinking in Opposites: An Investigation of the Nature of Man as Revealed by the Nature of Thinking* (London: Routledge & Kegan Paul, 1952). My thought here is, at more than one point, indebted to him.

not merely that we need opposed ideas to define a concept—*omnis definitio est negatio*—but also that without them we cannot even form a concept to define. Thus, whilst it is easy to imagine that our minds could *experience* light without ever having experienced darkness, or joy without ever having experienced sorrow, or beauty without having ever experienced ugliness, it is difficult to see how our minds could ever *think* light, ever conceptualise light, without thinking of, conceptualising, its opposite, darkness, at the same time, and similarly with the other instances. This inseparable interconnection of contraries or opposites in our thinking is perhaps evidenced, as Paul Roubiczek suggests, by the fact that when we take words back to their etymological source we sometimes find the *same* root-word doing duty for two opposed ideas; the word needing both opposed ideas to have any standing as a meaningful concept, inevitably tended at first to draw both into consciousness, and so, could, as a purely verbal symbol, indicate either according to context and intonation.[32] Waismann, writing on this *antithetical sense of primal words* in another connection, says:

> There is evidence that in the oldest language opposites such as strong and weak, light and dark, large and small were expressed by the same root word. Thus in ancient Egyptian *keu* stood for both strong and weak. In Latin *altus* means high and deep, *sacer* both sacred and accursed. Compare further *clamare*, to shout, and *clam*, quietly, secretly, or *siccus*, dry, and *succus*, juice. Nor is it only the ancient languages which have retained as relics words capable of meaning either of two opposites. The same applies to present-day languages. "To cleave" means to split, but in the phrase "cleave to" it means to adhere. The word "without", originally carrying with it both a positive and a negative connotation, is used today in the negative sense only. That "with" has not only the sense of "adding to" but

---

[32]See ibid., pp.11, 18.

also that of "depriving of" is clear from the compounds "withdraw" and "withhold".[33]

Bearing this in mind, we are, to some extent, able to understand why, when we begin to theologise, the unity of religious experience *necessarily* tends to break up into irreconcilable antinomies and contradictions. It is not because our finite minds are trying to comprehend the infinite; nor because we are passing from a living I-Thou relation to God to a detached, spectator, objectifying attitude; neither of these reasons, as I have said, seem to be fully adequate. The reason lies in the nature of thinking itself; we cannot think systematically except by the use of concepts which can only be defined by their opposites. This necessity of thinking is no disability and raises no problems when we are thinking about limited sections or spheres of our world. But when we reflect about, and seek to characterise, reality as a whole (which is what we are by implication doing when we think about God), when we try to formulate an all-inclusive, unitary theory about the whole universe, the trouble begins. Because of this law of our thinking by which we are compelled to "think in opposites", by which we are compelled to use concepts which break up unities into dualities and oppositions which oppose and exclude one another, it is evident that we cannot, simply by thinking, transcend inclusively all dualities and oppositions whatsoever, any more than a snake could swallow and digest itself. In other words, the search for an all-inclusive, unitary theory of reality can never in the nature of the case be successful. For if we apply a concept to reality as a whole we must, at the same time, find some point of application within the whole for the opposite concept by which the first concept is defined and in relation to which our minds are able to give it a clear and defined meaning.

We may illustrate this by reference to the fundamental assertion of religious faith that God is wholly good. It is impossible to give precise

---

[33]F. Waismann, "Language Strata", in A. G. N. Flew (ed.), *Essays on Logic and Language*, second series (Oxford: Blackwell, 1953), pp.11-12.

meaning to the term "good" except by an implicit or explicit reference to its opposite, "evil", which in one way or another it negates. This is particularly clear when we apply the term to a personal being. Goodness as applied to a person can only be given meaning, in part at any rate, by thinking of that person's attitude and activity towards evil, whether actual or possible—an attitude and activity of repudiation and exclusion. This is not difficult when we are thinking of finite, limited persons. But when we are thinking of God, we get into difficulties just because, as has been said, a statement about God always implies something about the whole of reality. God, as good, must also be thought of as repudiating and excluding evil; but that means we must have an understanding of evil in reality (an evil for the divine goodness to be opposed to). The problem is, how can this be if the good God is to be thought of also as the ground and source of all reality. We are forced to think of God, in his relation to the whole of reality, as somehow positing and *including* evil, and yet also to think of him, in his goodness, as opposing and *excluding* evil. The problem of the presence of evil in a universe created and sustained by a good God is, of course, a standing one for philosophical theology, and no doubt some illuminating things can be said about it to lighten the burden on religious faith. But the point of what I have been saying, if it is sound, is that the problem in the nature of the case can never be solved theologically (i.e. in the realm of conceptualising theory). In that realm we must have the opposites of good and evil in order to think about good or evil at all, and therefore can never achieve a position where they are finally "ironed out".[34]

Nevertheless, in the realm of religious insight and faith, as distinct from the realm of conceptualising theory, we must say that God is the source of good and good only. The history of thought reflects this situation. In it there has been a perpetual pendulum swing between two positions. On the one hand, there has been a marked tendency towards a monistic pantheism which seeks to eliminate the antithesis of good and evil altogether in its

---

[34]See his discussions in *Experience of God*, 140ff., 161ff.; *The World and God*, chs.6, 13, 14; *Towards Belief in God*, ch.13.—Ed.

characterising of ultimate reality; this gives a certain satisfaction to religious feeling, but considered simply as "theory" usually contrives to give the impression of intellectual *legerdemain*. Moreover, it does violence to the fundamental Christian assertion that the goodness of God is supremely manifest in his redeeming work in relation to evil. On the other hand, there is an equally marked tendency towards a dualism which leaves the antithesis of good and evil intact, but does not know what to make of the fundamental religious assertion that God is the transcendent source of all being.

2. *The nature of feeling and the relation of thought to it.* It is not necessary for our purpose to launch out on a full discussion of the nature of feeling and its relation to other functions of the mind. It is sufficient to state several points briefly and rather dogmatically.

(1) By the term "feeling" I mean, broadly, that way of becoming aware of my world in which it is apprehended through its meaning, its value or disvalue, its "importance" for me as a personal, self-conscious being. If we were to speak of "feeling" as a valuing apprehension of, and active relation to, the realities which constitute my personal world or situation, we should not be far wrong, provided we give a sufficiently broad meaning to the term "valuing" and do not confine it to explicitly formulated value judgements (such as, for example, those which are discussed by ethical writers). Or we might describe "feeling" as *interest* or *concern* in what is presented to us. A situation is of interest or concern to us only in so far as it in some way evokes an affective state of mind (i.e. engages our feelings).

(2) It is a commonplace that feeling in this sense accompanies in some degree all our apprehension of reality and all our activity in relation to it. This includes even the activity of reflective, conceptual thinking. Even the thinker who explores the remote and frigid abstractions of higher mathematics is sustained in his activity by the interest of the subject to himself, by an implicit sense of the value of truth in this sphere and, therefore, of the worthwhileness, the importance, of the enterprise, by the satisfaction, at times the thrill of discovery, and even, so we are told, by an aesthetic delight in form. But not only does feeling thus accompany all our apprehension of reality, it is also and

always an indispensable factor in it. Our mind would not be improved as an organ of knowledge by having feeling eliminated. Indeed, it would not function at all. We are apt to overlook this. Because we are well aware that our feelings can fog and distort reality, we are apt wrongly to infer that if we could eliminate feeling altogether we should have a more secure grasp of reality. But this is like arguing that, because one cannot masticate properly with toothache, one should be able to masticate best without any teeth at all. The fact that feeling can fog and distort reality merely shows that in relation to any given situation there can be wrong, inappropriate or immature feeling, which needs clarification, discipline and development, just as there can be wrong, inappropriate and immature ways of thinking.

(3) This is the important point for our thought here—it is primarily through feeling that the mind keeps a grasp of the unities of its world and of its experience even when the analytic conceptualising intellect is breaking them up into oppositions and contradictions in the manner of which I have already spoken. If thought works always by analysis, by separating and splitting up, it is feeling which synthesises and holds together, which grasps the world as a unity and insists that it is a unity, a unity which conceptual thought itself, in spite of its analytic, breaking-down methods, must constantly bear in mind and at least seek to realise and to formulate, even though it cannot by such methods ever fully do so.[35] I have said that feeling and interest or valuing in the broad sense of the word might be used almost as a correlative term, so inseparably are they bound up with one another. If that is so, it is not difficult to discern what the interest is in which the feeling grasp of unity is rooted. It is rooted in that deep impulse towards, and craving for, unification, of which I have already spoken so much.

In connection with this unifying function of feeling we may take note of some remarks of F. H. Bradley. He too grounds in feeling that apprehension of unity which underlies and persists through the contradictions and

---

[35]Cf. Farmer's discussion of the analytic and synthetic approaches to reality in *The World and God*, pp.32ff.—Ed.

antinomies which emerge in reflection. There is, he says, always a primordial feeling apprehension of the unity of experience. This may contain in it elements of uneasiness and disquiet, but the sense of unity remains dominant. "For however great our uneasiness, however discordant and unstable our condition, whatever comes in feeling must come together and must come somehow in one...Within feeling...and in many cases even within sensuous perception, the discrepant elements were, by virtue of an unknown condition, together in one whole."[36] It is in analytic conceptualising reflection that the discrepant elements are forced into the open and into irreconcilable contradiction. Nevertheless the underlying feeling apprehension of unity abides through the oppositions which are thus produced, for the contradictions themselves have to be held together in a unity of apprehension before they can be seen to collide. "In order to perceive them or to think of them, even as repellent, they must be still before us in a medium in which so far somehow they do not collide. And obviously they and our whole knowledge of their collision must be felt. It must depend on a positive and an immediate awareness within my finite centre."[37]

(4) We have now to ask how these functions of the mind (the apprehension of unities through feeling and the splitting up of unities into oppositions through conceptual thought) are related to one another. We cannot suppose that they operate independently of one another, the mind at one moment grasping and affirming unity feelingly and at another splitting it up conceptually. The mind is fundamentally much too much of a unity, or at least set towards unity, for such dissociation to be possible, except perhaps as a temporary and always perilous makeshift. The answer to the question, I want briefly to suggest, is that so far from reflective thought, with its inevitable contradictions and antinomies, necessarily running counter to the feeling-grasp of unities, it can, and often does, play an important, and indeed indispensable,

---

[36]F. H. Bradley, *Essays on Truth and Reality* (London: Oxford University Press, 1914), pp.269-70.
[37]Ibid., p.271. Cf. J. Macmurray, *Interpreting the Universe* (London: Faber, 1933), ch.1; and also P. Roubiczek, *Thinking in Opposites*, chs. 2 and 3.

part in developing and enlarging it, and so in satisfying the need for unification in which it is rooted. By not running away from the contradictions and oppositions which thinking brings forth, but rather by welcoming them, and seeking always to go as far as thought can take us in the resolution of them, by refusing to take refuge in any sort of forced unification of them through some speculative view which merely cleverly sponges them away, the feeling side of our nature is deepened, disciplined, clarified and made more mature. It is deepened, disciplined, clarified and made more mature because it is now evoked by, and brought continually under the check of, the richer and more complex reality which thought, by wrestling with the difficulties it brings forth, helps to disclose. This, however, does not necessarily imply any loss of the unifying function of feeling, it merely means that it is able to grasp unities in a way that does more justice to the infinite depths and rich differentiations of the world and of our own nature. That said, any attempt to formulate a speculative, unitary worldview, is always in grave danger of impoverishing our world, because we have to omit or ignore or explain away whatever is inconsistent with it. At the same time, it is in danger of impoverishing the feeling life and keeping it immature, for it requires us continually to force our feelings into harmony with artificial unities of theory.

Now to apply this briefly to the problem which led up to our discussion. The oppositions and paradoxes which theological reflection brings forth and often states in the form of logical contradictions which resist any final theoretical solution, do not leave the living religious experience of unification and reconciliation unaffected. To suppose that they could, would be to suppose a fundamental division or departmentalisation of the mind such as we cannot admit. Is then the relation between them one of continuous conflict or tension of a kind to be borne with a sense of frustration and with the desire that it could be otherwise, the underlying assumption being that the deep need for unification could only be satisfied by the complete elimination of the contradictions which theology continually brings forth (as, for example, in withdrawn, mystical states of mind)? All that we have been saying indicates that the answer to this question is clearly negative. On the contrary, the oppositions which theological reflection continually forces us to face, without giving us even the assurance of our ever finding satisfactory resolution of them, have an indispensable part to play in the development of the inward feeling life of the personality through which alone the ultimate unities of existence can be rightly apprehended and rested in. Thus the facing of the paradoxes and contradictions and the continuous, though never in the nature of the case fully successful, attempt to resolve them, helps to clear the mind of merely egotistical, conventional, sentimental, immature feeling-responses which so often pervert religion. It gives it an ever-increasing range and depth of awareness and sensitivity and forces it to realise how much is at stake in the decision for or against the commitment of faith. Above all helps to make possible a feeling insight and discernment which grasps, in and through the very oppositions of thought, a deeper, underlying unity which comprehends them and holds them together.

We might perhaps appropriate Gabriel Marcel's terms "mystery" and "problem",[38] (although using them in a different, but not unrelated, way). "Problems", for our purposes here, might be said to be those contradictions and paradoxes which inevitably disclose themselves in the realm of conceptual thought. "Mysteries", on the other hand, take us more into the realm of underlying feeling, particularly as this is being matured and developed through continuous wrestling with the problems of theological reflection. Mysteries are the paradoxes and oppositions of thought taken up into the sphere of feeling in such a way that they both develop it and are transcended in it. They are transcended through a profound feeling-conviction that in that ultimate mystery of being, which is God, all things are gathered into one. They are not dissolved away into a featureless unity, but are gathered into one.

We are now in a position to proceed to the book's main task. The plan is to select for consideration certain fundamental dualities or oppositions which

---

[38]See G. Marcel, *Metaphysical Journal*, tr. by B. Wall (London: Rockliff, 1952). See also G. Reeves, "The Idea of Mystery in the Philosophy of Gabriel Marcel", in P. A. Schilpp & L. E. Hahn (eds.), *The Philosophy of Gabriel Marcel*, The Library of Living Philosophers, vol.17 (La Salle: Open Court, 1984), pp.245-71; and Marcel's "Reply to Gene Reeves", ibid., pp.272-4.—Ed.

disclose themselves in living religion, particularly as it enters into relation with certain universal factors in the human situation, and to show that through the Christian revelation and faith the opposed elements in these dualities are (a) given full weight over against one another, so that the religious life is deepened, sensitised and enriched, and (b) are, nevertheless, brought together into a felt unity in a way that is true reconciliation and peace.

The dualities and oppositions which I have chosen to consider fall into four main classes, each of which itself requires a dualistic formula to describe it. They are: (1) "God and the World"; (2) "God and the Self"; (3) "The Self and the World"; (4) "The Self and Other Selves". These, therefore, will constitute the four main divisions of our exposition. It may be observed that in making this fourfold division we are already involved, to a certain extent, in that break-up of unities into oppositions which we have said is characteristic of all conceptual thinking and theorising. The reason I mention this is that we are seeking to exhibit a unification/reconciliation, which is claimed to be unique in its inclusiveness and adequacy. Such a unification, therefore, if the claim is justified, will not only unify the separate dualities which can be subsumed under each of the four divisions, but also bring those four divisions themselves into some sort of comprehensive unity with one another. We might, therefore, have a fifth section in which all the other four sections are brought together; but this will not be necessary, for the exposition itself will, in some measure, make evident how closely bound up with one another they all are. For we shall continually find that what we say in one section presupposes or implies what has already been said in another section, or what is yet to be said in a section to come. We shall therefore be describing in effect not four unifications but one. This may lead in some places to some repetition and overlapping, but that may help to emphasise once again the unity of the whole.

PART TWO
GOD
and
THE WORLD

2

IMMANENCE AND TRANSCENDENCE

We begin by considering the familiar opposed concepts of "immanence" and "transcendence" in their non-religious and non-theological use. In so doing, it becomes evident that there is in their meaning and use a core of that spatial imagery which seems unavoidably to enter into so much of our thinking. The primary spatial image here is obviously that of a bounded area, with a space inside the boundary line and a space outside it. The words "immanent" and "transcendent", however, as ordinarily used appear to signify more than merely "*being* inside" and "*being* outside" the bounded area, for these latter phrases suggest something "at rest". Rather the words have in them a suggestion of activity, in accordance with the root verbs *immanere* and *transcendere*. The suggestion is that one either actively remains inside the area instead of moving outside it, or actively moves outside it instead of remaining inside it. It is this underlying suggestion of activity which possibly helps to explain the fact that the concepts of "immanence" and "transcendence" are always used in a sense which breaks away from the primary reference to *physical* space, so that no one would think of speaking of a man at home as being immanent within the house, or, when he goes out or climbs on the roof, as transcending it. The activity to which the terms "immanence" and "transcendence" refer in this usage of them appears to be primarily the activity of thought, and particularly the endeavour of thought to establish connections between, or otherwise explain, phenomena.

Thus one may seek an explanation of a particular fact within a given area of experience by relating it to other facts, or surmised facts, within the same area. The explanation may then be said to be of an immanental kind. On the other hand, the explanation may be sought in facts, or surmised facts, lying outside the area with which one is primarily concerned. The explanation may then be said to be of a transcendental kind. By natural transference the adjectives may then be attached to the facts, or surmised facts invoked in the explanation, the transference being marked, as a rule, by the dropping of the suffix -*al*. If, for example, we seek to explain that aspect of human experience which we broadly designate morality "humanistically", that is, in terms of those purely human facts and forces which are studied by psychology or sociology (as, for example, Freud does), then we may be said to be offering a purely immanental theory of morality or, to transfer the adjective, a theory in terms of purely immanent facts or forces. On the other hand, if we seek to explain morality by going outside the "human" sphere and relating it to the self-revealing will of God (as theists do), or to certain self-subsistent entities called "ideas" or "values" (as, for example, Plato and Nikolai Hartmann[1] do), then we may be said to be offering a transcendental theory or a theory in terms of transcendental factors. Similarly, we may seek to explain the apparently teleological functioning of organisms, as many biologists do, by reference merely to internal, non-teleological processes within the organism itself, in which case we are proposing an immanental theory or theory in terms of immanent factors.[2] On the other hand, we may seek to explain it, as St Thomas Aquinas does, by reference to the divine intention and design, in which case we propose a transcendental theory or a theory in terms of a transcendent reality. Along parallel lines, we have Kant's use of the term "transcendental" to indicate realities which he holds it is necessary to assume in order to explain how it is possible to have experience of an object, but which cannot themselves become objects of experience. They lie beyond the area of the "experienceable". Another example might be found in the use

---

[1]See Farmer's discussion of Hartmann's philosophy of value in *Revelation and Reason*, pp.130ff. "Hartmann...returns to something not unlike the Platonic doctrine of ideal essences, and combines with it both something of religious fervour and faith and also an explicit rejection of theism" (p.130).—Ed.

[2]See his discussion of "immanent teleology", in *The World and God*, pp.39ff.—Ed.

made at one time by some scientists of the concept of force. In so far as this was conceived as an actual entity underlying physical phenomena and only known by its effects in those phenomena, the theory might be said to be a transcendental one in terms of transcendent realities. On the other hand, the more modern use of the concept of force as being simply a convenient way, perhaps unavoidable for our minds, of grasping the "togetherness" or "prehensiveness" of empirical facts, valid only as such and becoming invalid directly it is thought of as referring to an additional reality of some sort, might be thought of as a return to a purely immanental interpretation.[3]

Two things will be evident from all this. First, how fluid the meanings of the terms are, and how much they are determined by the particular interest and point of view of the one using them. What is immanent from one point of view may become transcendent when the point of view is changed, and immanent once more when the point of view is changed again. The deciding factor in each case is how our particular interest at that moment defines and delimits the sphere in relation to which the terms are being used.

Second, it will be evident that the use of the concepts "immanent" and "transcendent" is governed by the necessity for our minds to think in opposites (as discussed in the last chapter). We cannot make clear to ourselves what we mean by immanence without contrasting it with, and opposing it to, what we mean by transcendence (and vice versa) any more than we can define the spatial notions of "inside" and "outside" which lie at the root of the two concepts, except by opposing them to one another in a way that makes it impossible to say of the same thing in respect of the same bounded area that it is both inside and outside at the same time.

God's Relation to the World

Turning now to the religious use of the two terms, we begin by commenting on two points related to the two indicated above.

---

[3]See T. Steinmann, "Religion", in *Religion und Gegenwart*, Bd.3, p.189.

(1) The fluctuation in the meaning of the terms in accordance with the particular interest or point of view, along with the ever present tendency to be led astray by the underlying spatial imagery, is responsible for some of the confusion in which the discussion of the immanence and transcendence of God in relation to the world often seems to get involved. Thus if our interest is concentrated, say, on man's status in the midst of the causal nexus of nature as a free, independent, morally responsible being, we may be led, as James Martineau and F. R. Tennant were, to deny God's immanence in man whilst being prepared to assert it in nature. (If we are thinking only of his independent freedom, it is hard to see how this can be avoided.) On the other hand, if our interest is concentrated at the moment on man as the creative bearer of moral and spiritual values which appear to find little or no place in nature apart from man, we may be led, as F. H. Jacobi was, to assert God's immanence in man and to deny it in nature. If, next, we enlarge our interest and try to grasp man and nature as a single whole, then we shall inevitably think of God as immanent in both man and nature. However, even then we may find it necessary to say that God's immanence in man is one of a kind that is transcendent of his immanence in nature in the sense that it involves activities of his being to which we cannot appeal, in our attempts to understand the working of nature without landing ourselves in error and defeating our purpose. This last point indicates how a similar fluctuation occurs in our sense of divine transcendence as our interest expands or contracts. As our thought takes in wider and wider ranges of existence, so the transcendence of God may easily seem to grow less. That is to say, we have the feeling that we are dealing with areas more commensurate with his greatness, and that therefore more of his being can be incorporated immanently within them as their ground and explanation.

This I believe is one reason (though only one reason) why minds which combine something of genuine piety with philosophic breadth so easily express their religious awareness in a pantheistic form. As the mind surveys the apparently infinite reach and depth of the spatiotemporal system of nature, particularly as this is presented to the imagination by modern astronomical science, it has the feeling[4] that the world is, so to say, big enough to contain God and the notion of his transcendence easily fades away before that of his immanence. Whereas to the Hebrew religious mind, working with the narrow cosmological ideas of the time, it seemed self-evident that "the heavens, even the highest heavens, cannot contain him",[5] to the modern mind it seems self-evident, if it entertains the idea of God at all, that they can.

(2) It will be found that when the terms are applied to God in his relation to the world, that their inevitable spatial associations, along with the necessity of defining each through its contrast with the other, lands us in paradox and contradiction. As indicated in the last chapter, it does this because, when we begin to think conceptually about God and, therefore, by implication, about the whole world we have to find room for both the opposites (through which concepts are defined) at the same time. Ordinarily (that is to say, in respect of limited spaces and finite realities) there is no difficulty in this. We are quite clear that a thing cannot be both inside and outside a bounded area at the same time, and no contradiction arises—a thing being inside means that it is not outside, and vice versa. But, when we conceptualise the religious apprehension of God in his relation to the world, we find ourselves compelled to say of him that he is both transcendent of the world (i.e. in some sense *beyond* and *outside* it) and immanent in the world (i.e. in some sense *within* it) at the same time. And because it is of God and the world that we are speaking, this seems to involve us in contradiction. We are compelled to make the double affirmation because, in living religion, transcendence of the world belongs to God's essential and distinctive being as God, and yet, at the same time, in living religion, God is encountered, in his essential "Godness", within the world where we are, for otherwise it would not be living religion. But how can that be? If transcendence of the world belongs to God's essential being as God, to meet him within the world would be to meet him as so far shorn of his transcendence. It would mean, in other words, not meeting him as God at all.

---

[4] I use the word "feeling" advisedly, for there may be little of clearly formulated theory in it.
[5] 1Ch.2:6. Cf. also 1Ki.8:27; 1Ch.6:18.

To assert, therefore, that we really do encounter and apprehend *within the world* the God who is only God at all by virtue of his *transcendence of the world*, would seem to be asserting a contradiction. Nevertheless, that is precisely what the religious mind does assert, and must assert, for it is confident that it really does encounter and apprehend God in his Godness. Yet, and *qua* religious, it asserts it without any sense of contradiction; the contradiction only appears when the experience is conceptualised in these two opposed notions of transcendence and immanence with their underlying spatial reference and the necessity to define each by its opposition to the other.

It seems obvious that if we are to get clear of these difficulties, and if, in addition, we are to understand the way in which these two concepts are held together in unity with one another in the Christian revelation and experience, we must first try to grasp what corresponds to them in living religion, what gives rise to these concepts in human experience and imparts to them the vitality they seem to have in religious and theological usage. In exploring this area we shall find that we can get rid of a good deal of the implicit spatial reference of the terms which is, to some extent, at the root of our difficulties; though I do not think we can get rid of it altogether.

Divine Transcendence

The element in living religion which corresponds to the concept of the divine transcendence of the world is the apprehension of what I have elsewhere ventured to call the sheer "Godness of God", his essential and radical otherness as God.[6] As discussed in the first series of lectures, there can be distinguished in the human apprehension of God, two elements which cannot be separated from one another. The first we termed his *ontological otherness*, meaning by this that he is the sole and absolute source of all existent things.[7] From him all else receives an utterly dependent and derivative being and nature, so that apart from him it would not exist, or continue to exist, in any

---

[6]See H. H. Farmer, *Revelation and Religion*, pp.50ff.—Ed.
[7] See H. H. Farmer, *Revelation and Religion*, pp.52-4.—Ed.

form or fashion whatsoever. God's being, on the other hand, is in no sense derivative from, or dependent on, anything else. Here, clearly, through whatever symbols, verbal or otherwise, it may be expressed,[8] is a divine "transcendence" of a final and absolute kind. The second we called his *axiological otherness*, meaning by this his incommensurable perfection and glory of being.[9] He is apprehended not only as the sole source of all "good" which characterises, or can characterise, finite existence, but also as comprehending in himself infinite and inexhaustible ranges of "value" which belong exclusively to him as God and cannot belong to finite existence at all. They constitute the unique, unapproachable and "transcendent" (the word becomes necessary and proper) divine glory.[10]

We may now add a third element to the "ontological" and "axiological" otherness of God—though perhaps it only expresses the same elements in "transcendence" in another way, or rather, a certain reaction of the human mind to them. The element I am referring to is the element of "mystery". To the religious mind, God, in his absolute, unconditioned being, and in his unapproachable majesty and glory, is (and must ever be) beyond the comprehension of man. Because he is ontologically and axiologically "transcendent", he is also "epistemologically transcendent", if one may add still another ugly phrase to those already used.

Such, then, is the "transcendence" of God in its fundamental religious meaning, as apprehended, that is to say, in the living encounter with God. It may be observed that in the analysis we have given, the spatial reference of the term "transcendent" has been reduced and pushed into the background, though I do not think it has been got rid of altogether. I doubt whether the three terms we have used to describe the divine otherness could convey their meaning to anybody, or at least to any religious person, without calling up an

---

[8] One such symbol is a doctrine or myth of creation which, in one form or another, is widespread throughout the religions.

[9] See H. H. Farmer, *Revelation and Religion*, pp.54-6.—Ed.

[10] The widespread association throughout the religions of light, or the sky, or the sun with the thought of God might perhaps be taken as a symbolic expression of this element in divine "transcendence".

image of God as "distant" from man and his world, as "high and lifted up" above them.[11] "Distance" or "height" is a much more pictorially spatial word than the quasi-technical term "transcendence", and, as we shall see later, has certain advantages over it.

What we have said, however, does not quite take us to the heart of the matter. Although we have done little more than set forth the meaning or content of the "transcendence" of God as religiously apprehended, for our purpose it is important to understand *how* it is apprehended. That is to say, what is the living root or source of the apprehension of specifically divine reality. Here again I must take up a point made in *Revelation and Religion*.[12] I hold that the living apprehension of God, God in his distinctive otherness as God, is never apart from, but is rather always centred in, and mediated through, the sense of the absolute claim he makes upon man's being and life. The impact of absolute demand, of "sacred value", claiming to override all other desires and preferences, all merely *natural* values, is the central point of God's disclosure of himself as God, as the *supernatural* specifically *divine* reality to man. To use again a somewhat inadequate simile, the sense of absolute demand is the focal point, the *Brennpunkt* (or burning point), around which there is an area of broader, less defined, but not less compelling, *Ahnung* or awareness of the infinite, mysterious divine reality from the depth of whose "transcendent" being there comes forth to meet man this revealing impact, this penetrating (one might also say "pricking") pressure of overriding claim.[13]

---

[11]Cf. E. Bevan, *Symbolism and Belief* (London: Allen & Unwin, 1938), chs.2 and 3.

[12]See H. H. Farmer, *Revelation and Religion*, pp.64-5, 138ff.

[13]In this I follow Oman, and accept, in particular, his rejection of Otto's attempt to separate the primary religious use of the term "holiness" as signifying God's "transcendent" otherness, from the use of it as signifying some sort of "ethical" claim upon man. Against this, Oman insists that it is improper to regard any response of man to his environment as religious which does not contain within it some awareness of the divine, supernatural reality as disclosing itself to man through "sacred value." See J. Oman, *The Natural and the Supernatural* (Cambridge: Cambridge University Press, 1931), pp.60ff. See also J. Oman, "The Idea of the Holy", in *The Journal of Theological Studies* 25 (1924), pp.275-86. [Cf. C. A. Campbell's critique of Oman's criticism of Otto, in *On Selfhood and Godhood* (London: Allen & Unwin, 1957), pp.342-4. See also J. P. Reeder, "The Relation of the Moral and the

This close and inseparable connection of the apprehension of God with the awareness of his absolute claim upon man's whole being and life brings into view another important element which, in living religion, has always entered into, merged with and intensified the apprehension of his transcendent otherness or "distance". That element is the religious man's consciousness of sin, guilt and impurity which touches the innermost core of the self. There is a profound sense of alienation from, opposition to, and remoteness from God. It would be easy to misunderstand what is here intended. This sense of sin which we have in mind penetrates far more deeply into, "reverberates" far more through the whole being than the mere consciousness of having transgressed this or that particular requirement of a moral or ritual code could ever do, even when the code in question is in some way associated in the mind with the idea of God. Such a sense of sin may arise in connection with a particular transgression (it very often does), but it goes far beyond what such a transgression considered by itself could ever explain or justify. It is essentially a profound religious functioning of the human spirit, a functioning of the human spirit in its living encounter with God. If, then, we ask what is the immediate source of the profound sense of sinful separation and distance from God, the answer is that it arises out of the awareness of God's absolute and total claim upon the self and of the self's refusal, indeed incapacity, to yield absolutely and totally to it. And if we ask, next, why does this sense of sinfulness always get taken up into the sense of God's unutterable otherness and transcendence so that it becomes an indispensable "moment" in the living awareness of that otherness and transcendence, the answer is that it is precisely through an *absolute claim* that God mediates his "Godness" to us. That some such linkage as this must be involved becomes evident if we consider that there is, after all, nothing in the thought of God as ontologically and axiologically other (when it is taken non-religiously and in abstraction from anything else) which should evoke in man such self-reproach, such a profound

Numinous in Otto's Notion of the Holy", in G. Outka & J. P. Reeder (eds.), *Religion and Morality: A Collection of Essays* (New York: Anchor Press, 1973), pp.255-92.—Ed.]

sense of personal sinfulness and estrangement, any more than there is a necessary connection between seeing, say, the glory and sublimity of the Himalayas and being conscious of oneself as personally inglorious and mean. There would appear to be no reason why the attitude should not be one of more or less absorbed contemplation from which any vivid self-awareness, still more any vivid awareness of the self as profoundly sinful, is completely absent. But, of course, to consider the apprehension of God's ontological and axiological otherness or transcendence in such abstraction is precisely what we must not do when we are thinking about *living religion*. In living religion such apprehension of God is given in and through the absolute claim he makes upon man's whole being and life, and it is because of this that there so immediately and spontaneously arises in the religious mind the sense of sin and impurity, making a merely contemplative attitude possible.

The close relation and interpenetration of the two elements of which we have been speaking is perhaps most clearly to be seen on the higher levels of biblical, particularly Old Testament, religion. Having said that, it does tend to characterise living religion on all its levels. In the Old Testament the apprehension of God as "high and exalted" in the sublimity and awfulness of his divinity (not infrequently expressed and symbolised through pictures of the sublimity and awfulness of his creation) and the apprehension of him as making such a claim upon men that they are revealed at once as sinful and impure and so for this reason also put at an infinite distance from him, are held in close connection with one another. To use some phrases I have used elsewhere, "the divine voice which condemns iniquity is the voice of him who walks in storm and thunder through hills, and the plumb line set against and revealing the iniquity of man is an infinite perpendicular from the stars." [14]

---

[14]H. H. Farmer, *The World and God*, p.64. Although he doesn't indicate which passage he has in mind, the following is the most likely: "The divine voice which condemns injustice is the voice of him who walks in thunder through the hills, and the plumb line set against the immoralities of Jerusalem is an infinite perpendicular from the stars." Incidentally, John Baillie cites this passage in his *Invitation to Pilgrimage* (Harmondsworth: Penguin, Pelican, 1960), pp.152-3.—Ed.

The clearest and most striking expression of the connection comes in the familiar passage dealing with Isaiah's commission:

> I saw the Lord seated on a throne, high and exalted [observe the inevitable spatial image of remoteness, distance], and the train of his robe [i.e. merely the skirts, one might say the outskirts, of his being] filled the temple. Above him were seraphs...And they were calling to one another: "Holy, holy, holy is the Lord Almighty; the whole earth is full of his glory." At the sound of their voices the doorposts and thresholds shook and the temple was filled with smoke. "Woe to me!" I cried. "I am ruined! For I am a man of unclean lips, and I live among a people of unclean lips, and my eyes have seen the King, the Lord Almighty." [15]

It is hardly possible in this vision to separate from one another the awareness of the transcendent being and glory of God, the awareness of his absolute claim and right to praise and service (symbolised in the praise and service of the seraphim around the throne) and the awareness of the utter impurity and sinfulness of the self as revealed by that glory and that claim.

Divine Immanence

We now consider that element in living religion which corresponds to the concept of the divine immanence in the world. We might borrow a phrase of Paul Tillich's and say that the element in question is the religious man's awareness that God is the one reality with which he is "ultimately concerned". God is not merely "out there", "high and exalted" in his otherness, but is also one with whom the religious man's total being and destiny here and now and everywhere and always is inseparably and fatefully bound up.[16] This,

---

[15]Isa. 6:1-5.
[16]P. Tillich, *Systematic Theology*, vol.1, pp.14ff. Tillich writes: "The religious concern is ultimate; it excludes all other concerns from ultimate significance; it makes them preliminary.

however, is to speak in terms which are much too abstract and general for our purpose. Moreover, they could obviously be made to cover the awareness of God's absolute claim of which we have just spoken in connection with the apprehension of him as transcendent. We come nearer to the central living root of the concept of divine immanence in religious experience if we note how frequently and spontaneously there springs to the lips of religious men such phrases as "my God" or "our God", phrases which, if God be indeed apprehended as wholly other, "transcendent" in his absolute being and glory, might well strike us as very strange indeed. That they do not strike us as strange is because the sense of God as "close" enough for his name to be coupled with a possessive pronoun is as central and inevitable in living religion as is the sense of his "distance". And again, we come nearer to what we are seeking if we note how widespread throughout religion is the thought of God as indwelling, an "immanent" life and power, a creative and sustaining and enabling energy within the depths of the human person itself—God as Spirit.[17] Not even God could contrive to be nearer, more immediately present, than that. Taking these forms of expression (and others that might be cited) as pointers, it becomes clear, I think, that the living root of the apprehension of God as immanent is the consciousness of him as the final succour and security of man's life, not at some distant time or in some distant world, but here and now in this present world. God is of ultimate concern to man and may be thought of as "my/our God", or as an indwelling presence and power, because he is, in all things, man's ultimate refuge and strength, a very *present* help in time of trouble, the one sure helper and saviour of man in all the weakness and dependence, the perils and vicissitudes of his life.

It will be observed that we have already, and almost inevitably, used such terms as "near", "close" and "present" in describing that apprehension of

---

The ultimate concern is unconditional, independent of any conditions of character, desire, or circumstance. The unconditional concern is total: no part of ourselves or of our world is excluded from it; there is no 'place' to flee from it. The total concern is infinite: no moment of relaxation and rest is possible in the face of a religious concern which is ultimate, unconditional, total, and infinite" (p.14).

[17]See H. H. Farmer, *Revelation and Religion*, pp.179-86. Cf. also pp.66ff.—Ed.

God as man's succour and security which is the living root of the conception of his immanence. A God who succours, sustains and redeems is a God apprehended as, so to say, right down on man's level, interested in, concerned with, present within his affairs in this world. We can, then, substitute for the concept of immanence the more pictorially spatial word "nearness". This would correspond with the substitution of the word "distance" for the concept of transcendence which we made earlier. One advantage of this substitution is that the word "nearness" does express and emphasise more clearly than the word "immanence" what we have been saying, namely, that the central living root of the concept of immanence is the awareness of God as man's succour. This also may be illustrated from biblical usage. In the Bible the thought of God's succour frequently finds expression in the spatial image of his nearness. "The Lord is close to the broken-hearted." "You are near, O Lord, and all your commands are true." "The Lord is near to all who call on him." "He who vindicates me is near." "Seek the Lord while he may be found; call on him while he is near" (i.e. while he is offering salvation). "He is not far from each one of us. 'For in him we live and move and have our being.'" [18]

Although it is true that God is also thought of as livingly present and active within human affairs and human history in judgement and retribution, [19] it is significant that, on the whole, this is not expressed through the image of the divine drawing near. This, we may surmise, is because the dominant element in the thought of God's judgement and retribution is the thought of the absolute claim of his righteousness upon men, and it is precisely this, as I have said, which is the focal point of the apprehension of his otherness, his distance, from man.

---

[18]Pss.34:18; 119:151; 145:18; Isa.50:8; 55:6; Acts 17:27-8.
[19]See, for example, Isa.44:28-45:13.—Ed.

The Apprehension of Divine Transcendence and Immanence
in Living Religion

We have, then, these two elements lying alongside one another in religion and giving "life" to what might otherwise be the purely abstract notions of transcendence and immanence: the apprehension of God's *ultimate* otherness or distance centred in and mediated through the apprehension of his absolute claim, the apprehension of his *intimate* nearness centred in and mediated through the apprehension of him as being, in the most immediate and practical way, concerned with men's well-being. It is perhaps almost superfluous now to go on to say that these two elements, just because they thus lie close alongside one another at the heart of living religion, inevitably tend to get in one another's way, to enter into a relation of tension or polarity or even conflict with one another. The history of religion shows a marked tendency toward a kind of pendulum swing from one to the other. It would not be difficult, along the lines followed in *Revelation and Religion*, to classify religious types into those whose tendency is to emphasise the divine transcendence or distance at the expense of his immanence or nearness, and those whose tendency is to emphasise the divine immanence or nearness at the expense of his transcendence or distance. In this connection, we may recall that in *Revelation and Religion* two types of religion (among others) were distinguished and described: the one puts the dominant emphasis on the divine demand, giving us what we call a religion of obligation, as, for example, in the later history of Judaism and to some extent in Islam; the other puts the dominant emphasis on the divine succour, giving us what we call eudaemonistic religion, as, for example, in the *bhakti* cults of India.[20] It may be noted, as an illustration and confirmation of the line of thought we are now pursuing, that in later Judaism and in Islam the thought of the divine distance from man, the divine transcendence, tended to predominate. *Bhakti* religion, on the other hand, is obviously a religion of the divine personal nearness

---

[20]See H. H. Farmer, *Revelation and Religion*, pp.116-25, 149-62. See also the discussion in C. H. Partridge, *H. H. Farmer's Theological Interpretation of Religion*, pp.211ff.—Ed.

arising, in part, as a reaction against the impersonalist, acosmic pantheism of orthodox Hinduism, which, in its understanding of divine reality as the absolute One, necessarily sets that One out of practical relationship to the multifarious complexities of the world and to the immediate pressures and needs of man's life within it.

It is not, however, necessary to go outside the realm of empirical Christianity to illustrate the tension or pendulum swing of which we have been speaking. It would be possible to make a study of various types of Christian liturgy, architecture, polity, theology, ethical emphases etc. from this angle. Perhaps I may be permitted to give one example from the history of Protestantism. Although broad generalisations, of course, always, in some measure, oversimplify and misrepresent, it certainly seems not without truth to say that Luther's religious life and thought were more permeated by the sense of God's drawing very near to man through Christ in gracious and liberating personal love and pardon, and in consequence have a greater intimacy and warmth, than that of Calvin which is dominated much more by the thought of God's transcendent otherness and distance, and so manifests, along with a profoundly abased attitude to God, a certain pervading coolness and austerity. And this initial divergence of the two great reformers has, to a plainly observable degree, set its stamp upon the subsequent history of Lutheranism and Calvinism. On the other hand, Lutheran piety and theology have shown a tendency to emphasise God's entry into, and presence within, the world and history, and, in accordance with this, the principle *finitum capax infiniti*. Whereas, on the other hand, Calvinistic piety and theology have tended to emphasise the distance of God from (his transcendence of) the world and history, and in accordance with this, the principle *finitum non capax infiniti*. In recent times it is possible to see the same two tendencies at work. The so-called liberal-modernist movement in Protestant theology at the end of the last and at the beginning of this century was, at least in part, the result and expression of an increasing dominance, largely due to the influence of German idealism, of the idea of divine immanence; and we may perhaps see some significance in the fact that in the main it arose within and achieved its greatest ascendancy in Lutheran Germany. On the other hand, the counterbalancing protest, which was bound to come, and which found its chief mouthpiece in Karl Barth, sprang from Swiss Reformed circles. It took the form of a so-called neo-orthodox Calvinism, a new and, as many no doubt think, an extreme and one-sided insistence on the characteristic Calvinistic doctrine of the divine transcendence.[21]

The Unification of Divine and Immanence

Yet though we can thus discern in the history of empirical Christianity (as in the history of religion generally) this oscillation between the two poles of transcendence and immanence, it is nevertheless true to say that it is distinctively characteristic of Christian experience and thought always to come back, as it were, to a mid-point where the two apprehensions of God are held together in unity and balance with one another. Indeed, the phrase "unity and balance" is not quite adequate. What we have, through the Christian revelation and faith, is rather a profound unification of the divine "distance-transcendence" and the divine "nearness-immanence", and we have it in such a form that their unity is continuously and livingly "felt" at the heart of the religious life, in spite of any difficulties which may arise when the attempt is made conceptually to formulate and relate to one another the two apprehensions. How is this brought about?

We may first answer the question in abstract terms. The line of thought we have been following might conceivably make it possible to formulate in advance the conditions of such a profound unification. It might conceivably have enabled us to deduce that if the divine distance and transcendence, as mediated through and centred in the divine absolute claim, and the divine

---

[21]A biblical example of the tension between the "nearness" and the "afar-off-ness" of God in the sense on which we have been using these terms might be found in Jer. 23:23. Although the passage is enigmatic, the prophet appears to have in mind false teachers, one mark of whose falsity is that they think too exclusively of God as a help and ally to man's desires and purposes, as One who is at the beck and call of men's need and guarantees that "No harm will come to [them]" (23:17), and not enough in terms of his holiness and judgement upon their sin. The prophet represents God as saying, "Am I only a God nearby...and not a God far away?"

nearness and immanence, as mediated through and centred in the divine succour, are to be unified with one another so that any tendency for them to fall apart is once for all held in check, God must be so apprehended that his absolute claim is seen to be such that it is supremely manifested in his succour, and his succour is itself seen to be the supreme manifestation of his absolute claim. But whether such an a priori formulation might have been possible or not, it is certainly precisely this that *is* accomplished through the Christian revelation and faith as these are set before us in the New Testament.

It is accomplished in and through the central affirmation that God is holy love, *agape*—not incidentally or occasionally or peripherally (if one may so put it), but essentially, unchangingly, in his very being as eternal God. According to the New Testament apprehension of it, God's love, in its relation to man, is (to use a phrase of J. Cullberg's) an utterly pure will to fellowship with man.[22] This pure will to fellowship with man claims man absolutely for love and for trustful obedience in loving, for only on that basis can there be fellowship between man and the God who is love. At the same time, the absolute claim of God necessarily discloses and utterly repudiates man's self-centred lovelessness and disobedience and unbelief, in short, his sinfulness, thus making him poignantly aware of his remoteness or distance from God.[23] This poignant awareness is at once taken up, in the way of which we spoke earlier, into that apprehension of God's transcendent otherness and distance which in any case is mediated through and centred in his absolute demand, giving it a new and searching vividness and power. Thus it becomes possible to say with Isaiah, though now in a new and specifically Christian way, "I saw the Lord...high and exalted...Woe to me!...I am ruined! For I am a man of unclean lips, and I live among a people of unclean lips." But now, also,

---

[22]J. Cullberg, *Das Du und die Wirklichkeit* (Uppsala: Uppsala Universitets ärsskrift, 1933), p.222. [See also Farmer's discussion in *Revelation and Religion*, pp.63-4.—Ed.]

[23]Cf. Farmer's discussions and comments concerning sin and forgiveness in *The World and God*, ch.11; *God and Men*, ch.3; *Things Not Seen: Studies in the Christian Interpretation of Life*, second edition (London: Nisbet, 1929), pp.131-43, 155-60; *The Healing Cross: Further Studies in the Christian Interpretation of Life* (London: Nisbet, 1938), pp.74, 77f, 79f, 105f., 111, 125, 131-2; *The Word of Reconciliation* (Welwyn: Nisbet, 1966), pp.12-19, 62f, 65-7; "What is Sin?", in *The Spectator* 144 (8 March, 1930), pp.357-8.—Ed.

because God is love, because he is this pure will to fellowship with man, he draws very near to man in his alienating lovelessness to save him in spite of it, and to save him from it, into his true life with God. In this way the nearness and immanence of God is brought livingly home to a man in a new and specifically Christian form. Thus the two things—the divine transcendence or distance as disclosed through God's approach to man in absolute claim and the divine immanence or nearness as disclosed through his approach to man in succour—are given together and held in inseparable unity with one another, "tied in a living tether" in the one encounter with God as holy love. Nor can the living sense of that unity be impaired by any difficulties which may arise when the attempt is made conceptually to formulate and explore them.

All this, however, is to speak in very abstract terms. If we ask how in concrete, living experience God makes this disclosure of himself to men, the answer, according to the Christian revelation and faith, is clear. It is that he makes it through his self-revelation and self-giving in the historic person of Jesus Christ. In Christ, God in his utterly holy love encounters man and brings home to him afresh his transcendent being as God. But in Christ also God, in his utterly holy love, comes right into the very midst of human existence, in all its impurity and lovelessness, to save. Such a coming obviously represents and expresses the divine drawing near, the divine saving immanence, in a maximal degree—God taking flesh and being a man among men for their salvation. It is impossible to draw "nearer" than actually to become man for man's salvation. Thus we are brought back once again, as we are usually brought back by anything fundamental and distinctive in the Christian revelation and faith, to the central Christian dogma of the incarnation.[24] It is quite superfluous to say that it would be possible to explore the idea of the

---

[24]Farmer discusses his understanding of incarnation/inhistorisation in: H. H. Farmer, *Revelation and Religion*, pp.195ff.; *God and Men*, pp.100f.; *The Bible and Preaching* (Birmingham: The Berean Press, 1952), pp.11-15; "The Bible: Its Significance and Authority", in G. A. Buttrick et al (eds.), *The Interpreter's Bible*, Vol.1 (New York: Abingdon, 1952), pp.6-7; "Christian Truths in Daily Experience: Of God in Jesus Christ", in *The Presbyterian Messenger* (September 1933), pp.122-4; and (October 1933), pp.150-2.— Ed.

incarnation both theologically and philosophically in a number of directions and almost certainly in a way which would in the end run out into some more antinomies and contradictions. But our interest in these pages is not primarily in theological problems, but in living religion, and in particular in the Christian revelation and faith as making possible a uniquely unifying or reconciling experience of God in which there is a profound unification of opposites.[25] Our endeavour has been to explore this in respect of the apprehension of God as transcendent and immanent and to show how in the Christian revelation and faith these two ways of apprehending God, which in one form or another run right through the religious life of mankind, and are always falling apart from one another, are, as nowhere else, held together in a living apprehension of their unity. They are held together by the doctrine that God is love in his essential nature and being and that he has revealed himself as such through Christ, or if we like so to put it, through the incarnation. We have in fact been trying to trace back to its religious roots the assertion, which has frequently been made, that in the doctrine of the incarnation the ideas of the transcendence and immanence of God are brought together, an assertion which apart from those religious roots has little value and, perhaps, little meaning.

---

[25]Some of the theological implications were addressed later in "Monotheism and the Doctrine of the Trinity", in *Religion in Life* 29 (1959-60), pp.32-41 (see particularly pp.37ff.).—Ed.

3

TIME AND ETERNITY

The second duality or opposition which we take up under our first general heading of "God and the World" is that of time and eternity. This is obviously closely related to the duality of immanence and transcendence discussed in the last chapter, in that God's eternity is usually thought of as an element in his essential otherness, his transcendence, and some of the perplexing problems for thought which centre in the idea of his immanence arise out of the difficulty of conceiving in what sense an eternal reality can be said to be present and operative within a temporal process without ceasing to be eternal, without being shorn of its transcendence. It is obvious, too, that the concepts of time and eternity, the temporal and the eternal, illustrate again the necessity for our minds to "think in opposites". Here as elsewhere, we can only form and define our concepts by their opposition to and negation of one another. The eternal is by definition the non-temporal, and the temporal is the non-eternal. This lands us in irreconcilable contradiction directly we try to think through the relation of the concepts to God (and therefore to the whole realm of being). Thus, we are bound to say that the eternal alone can give the temporal its meaning, for eternity is an attribute of God and from God all things draw their existence and their meaning. On the other hand, it seems equally necessary for us to say that the temporal alone can give meaning to the eternal, for, as far as the human mind is concerned, eternity has no content, it is sheer emptiness, except in so far as we can project into it something from the temporal process in which we are immersed. Thus we are compelled to try to hold together in our minds an eternity which has no meaning apart from time and a time which has no meaning apart from eternity, and at the same time we can only define the two terms by their opposition to one another! Such contrarieties are baffling in the extreme. Indeed, I am bound to confess that nothing more swiftly reduces me to a state of mental vertigo than the endeavour to rationalise "time" and, even more, "timelessness" which we seem bound to ascribe to ultimate reality. They are much more baffling than the analogous problems connected with space. This is probably because time is the form of our inner experience in a way that space is not, so that the attempt to think away time in order to form a concept of the eternal is, in effect, the attempt to think away thinking itself—indeed to think away our very *self*.

Fortunately our purpose here is not to explore theoretically the concepts of time and eternity, even in the hope that we may be able to reduce (though never being able to overcome fully) the difficulties arising from their opposition. Our purpose rather is to try to grasp how this opposition between time and eternity arises in the sphere of living religion, and so to lead up to an understanding of the way it enters into and is overcome in the Christian revelation and faith, in the Christian experience of unification.

The Apprehension of Time and Eternity Within Religion

The contrast and opposition between time and eternity—*time* being thought of as belonging essentially to the world and to human life within it and *eternity* as belonging essentially to the divine—can be traced in one form or another through the whole history of religion, not excluding primitive religion. According to Wilhelm Schmidt and other authorities, the so-called "high gods" of primitive religion always have a "sort of eternity" ascribed to them. The phrase "sort of eternity" is Schmidt's and is obviously imprecise, but at least it is clear that in primitive religion, there is, in so far as our knowledge goes, a well-nigh universal belief, however dim and undeveloped, in a supreme being who existed before all other beings, has always been and always will be, and is not subject to death.[1] But however that may be, it is certain that when we pass out of the misty and debatable sphere of primitive religion on to the higher levels of religion, we find that everywhere the gods (or God) tend to be thought of as "eternal", at least in the sense that they are not subject to the changes and chances of man's life in this world, and, above all, are not subject to death. The gods are the immortals. We may, then, confidently make the generalisation that the apprehension of divine reality as in some sense eternal, as radically other than man and his world (a world in which there is perpetual flux and change, wherein nothing abides, but everything is destined sooner or later to pass into nothingness, in which, above all, man himself is under sentence of extinction in death) is universal in living religion.

From our point of view, this universality must be held to be due to the fact that the ultimate source of the religious experience and history of mankind is the self-disclosing activity of the divine reality itself. The apprehension of God as in some sense eternal arises on all levels of religion primarily because of God's revelation of his "Godness" to men. Eternity is one element in the transcendent otherness which constitutes him distinctively *God*, so that it is impossible to become livingly aware of him without being conscious of it, however dimly and in whatever words or other symbols it may be expressed.

Of course, many would offer a different explanation. They would hold that the religious belief in an eternal realm of divine reality is simply one manifestation of the fact that all religion is but the product of compensatory wishful thinking. Because man feels the burden of the changes and chances of his life and, above all, his transiency and mortality, he projects from within himself an imaginary being and realm which are without these disabilities. It is not to be denied that such wishful thinking can, and often does, operate in religion, particularly in relation to the pictures men form of another world, of a

---

[1]See W. Schmidt, *The Origin and Growth of Religion: Facts and Theories*, tr. by H. J. Rose (London: Methuen, 1931), p.270. See also G. van der Leeuw, *Religion in Essence and Manifestation: A Study in Phenomenology*, tr. by J. E. Turner, (London: Allen & Unwin, 1938/Princeton: Princeton University Press, 1986), ch. 18. On the "high gods" in primitive religion, see my previous volume, *Revelation and Religion*, pp.106ff.

heaven, but the primary apprehension in religion of eternity as distinctively characterising divine reality must have other roots than that.[2] For *merely* to picture another realm with an eternal being or beings inhabiting it is certainly not of itself an alleviation of the lot of man if one is condemned to inhabit a temporal world such as this is and be a wholly temporal creature in it, destined to die. It is only an alleviation if he can assure himself that he can have, or will have a part in such a realm and such an existence. But the evidence is clear that neither in primitive religion nor on higher and more advanced levels is there any *necessary* connection between the apprehension of God or the gods as in some sense eternal and the hope of being able, either in this life or in the life to come, to share in their exalted and blissful state. Indeed, although there is, as a rule, a belief in some sort of survival after death, such survival is not by any means always associated with any thought of some future translation to the eternal realm as such. Rather, on the contrary, it is often thought of as involving diminution of being, so that man *after* death is pictured as being a good deal worse off than he was before. To use some words of John Baillie, the underworld, where the departed dwelt, "was a dismal sunless region; and life in it, far from being a glorious consummation, was an impoverished and enfeebled continuation of our life above ground. There was nothing either exhilarating or consolatory about the prospect of it, but rather much that was depressing."[3] This is true of primitive religion, of Greek and Roman religion, and also there are hints of it in the earlier stages of Old Testament religion. Hence Psalm 39: "Hear my prayer, O Lord, listen to my cry for help; be not deaf to my weeping. For I dwell with you as an alien, a stranger, as all my fathers were. Look away from me, that I may rejoice

---

[2]Cf. his discussion of "wishful thinking" in *God and Men*, pp.28-32. Also relevant, is the thesis presented in his *Towards Belief in God* and *Experience of God*. See particularly his discussions of the "coercive element" of conviction in theistic belief and his critique of sociological and psychological explanations of religion, in *Towards Belief in God*, pp.22-3, 39-60, 145-80; *Experience of God*, pp.19-21, 27-47.—Ed.

[3]J. Baillie, *And the Life Everlasting*, (London: Oxford University Press, 1934), pp.84-5.

again before I depart and am no more."[4] Not much compensatory or wishful thinking about that!

It will be evident from these remarks that to believe that there is a divine reality which is wholly other than man, in that it is eternal and not subject to the transiency and mortality of his life in this world, need not of itself produce an acutely felt tension and contrariety *in the heart of living religion itself*, urgently calling for unification or reconciliation *therein*. Thus, in the religions I have just been mentioning, the essential disparity between God the eternal and man the temporal is obviously accepted; the two realms are simply *there*, and the awareness of them sets up no tension within the religious relationship itself. A man, like the psalmist just quoted, can still pray, and hope for an answer to his prayer, even though he believes that he is, and never can be any other than, merely "a passing stranger", destined "to depart and be no more". And, on a higher level, where the problem of relating the two realms is explicitly faced and brought into relation with religion, the attempt may be made, not so much to unify and reconcile their opposition, as to escape from it by the simple expedient of denying one of its terms entry into the heart of religious experience itself.

What I have in mind may perhaps be made clear by illustrating it from the development of Greek religion. There was, of course, a strong tendency in Greek religious thought to take a two-storey view of time and eternity, as Karl Heim calls it.[5] Down below, on the ground floor, or perhaps it would be more appropriate to say the cellar, are the confusion, frustration, evanescence, the meaningless repetition, the essential mortality of the time-process and man's life within it. Above, on the upper floor or in the roof garden, remote from and unaffected by what goes on in the basement, is the unchanging perfection of the divine, eternal region, the realm of the immortals. To be immersed in time, to be a man, is necessarily to be separated from God. The emergence of

---

[4]Ps.39:12-13. For other Old Testament citations see ibid., pp.88-9.
[5]For Heim's discussion, see *God Transcendent: Foundation for a Christian Metaphysic*, tr. by E. P. Dickie (London: Nisbet, 1935), pp.29-83. See also, E. P. Dickie, *Revelation and Response* (Edinburgh: T. & T. Clark, 1938), ch.10.—Ed.

the Dionysiac and Orphic cults marks an attempt to overcome this separation religiously, but the way proposed is to escape from the lower sphere of the temporal and mortal life by rising into the empyrean of divine eternal existence on the wings of ecstasy and trance, such ecstasy and trance being interpreted as a sort of deification of the soul, i.e. its ceasing to be human. Clearly, there is no acutely felt tension within, essentially bound up with, the religious experience itself, requiring unification.   In the mystic consciousness—the *unio mystica*, which is the consummation of the religious quest—one side of the antithesis of eternity and time has simply disappeared. If then, we ask how the relation of the eternal God to man's temporality becomes a felt opposition and problem within living religion itself, for which some real unification must be found, the answer, in a general way, has already been pointed towards in what has just been said. The kind of mysticism just referred to must be judged to be religiously deficient (if it is properly to be regarded as religious at all[6]) in that it is lacking a living sense of God's immanence or "nearness"; or to put it the opposite way, in that it puts an exclusive emphasis on his transcendence. Because of this, it can hardly do other than prescribe ecstasy—a rising out of this present world as the solution of the problem of time and eternity, a solution which, as indicated above, is not properly a solution at all, for it merely eliminates one of the terms of the problem.

The Tension Between Divine Eternity and Human Temporality

By contrast with the above, the answer we give to the question concerning the relation of eternity to man's temporality, is that it tends to become an acutely felt problem within living religion in proportion to the extent to which awareness of God's immanence or "nearness" enters in; and, very particularly, it does so through the awareness of God as making an absolute

---

[6]For a discussion of this point see our treatment of the meaning and application of the term "religion" throughout the previous volume, *Revelation and Religion*. [See particularly pp.24-5.—Ed.]

claim upon a man and as securing to him his highest life and well-being *here and now in this present world in all its transience and evanescence.*

How does this encounter create an acutely felt tension between God's eternity and man's temporality right at the heart of living religion itself? It does so, because both God's demand and God's succour bear a close relation to the fact of *death*, in which all the evanescence and insecurity of man's life in the world, all that differentiates and separates it from the eternal realm, is summed up.[7] Thus, first, with regard to God's absolute demand, what do we mean here by "absolute"? Obviously the word as applied to the divine demand can only be defined by reference to *death*. In Oman's phraseology, the absolute claim or "sacred value" is a claim or "value" into the balance with which nothing else is to be put, not even life itself, or to put it the other way round, nothing is to stand in the way of serving God's will as he himself discloses it to man, not even death.[8] But this creates in principle, and may at any time create in fact, a situation in which God is encountered as one who enters into man's terrestrial existence and claims his service *in* it by requiring that he should take his departure *from* it into what appears to be sheer non-existence. He should, as it were, antedate in his own person that dissolution which in any case awaits him and everything else in the world. No doubt this is not a logical contrariety: there is nothing logically absurd in the idea of God demanding that a man should serve him in the world by being ready to take his departure from it. However, taken along with the transitoriness and impermanence of all human life and of the world in which it is set, it is inevitably *felt* not to make sense.[9]

---

[7]See his early sermon on "Death", in *Things Not Seen*, pp.213-24.—Ed.

[8]See his discussion of "the sacred" in *Experience of God*, pp.34-47; and *Towards Belief in God*, pp.49-51, 115ff.—Ed.

[9]We may point out that a similar problem is apt to emerge whenever an absolute ethic is recognised. The man who recognises the authority of a categorical moral imperative over him and comes into a situation in which he must surrender his life in order to be obedient to it, can hardly escape some awareness of the question whether, and in what way, it makes sense, and is rational behaviour to surrender voluntarily the only basis on which it is possible to seek any good at all. It is because it has no answer to this question that a purely humanist ethic which divorces the moral life from any kind of metaphysic or world-view and from any kind of religious faith is inadequate to the actual situation into which an absolute moral

Turning now to the apprehension of God as man's succour and security, this also bears a close relation to the fact of death and so raises in an acute form at the heart of the religious life the problem of the relation of man's temporality to God's eternity. For in what way can the *eternal* God be said to draw near to man as the final succour and security of his life, if that man remains, as he certainly does remain, rooted in, and inseparably one with a world process wherein no good thing abides, everything is subject to the corroding tooth of time, and, above all, he himself is doomed to the gradual enfeeblement of age and the final dissolution of death, if indeed God himself does not by absolute demand require him deliberately to antedate his apparently final departure from the scene?

We have then this tension or strain between the eternal God and temporal humanity living in a world where nothing abides. This tension makes itself felt within the living apprehension of God and urgently calls for something to resolve it. How then is it to be resolved? Obviously, for the religious man, one necessary element in the resolution of it must be that this particular "sting" should be taken out of death, namely, that it appears to cut him off from his personal relation to God, whether by annihilating him altogether or by translating him to a shadowy and diminished existence in a remote underworld. In other words, one element in the resolution of the tension must be the attaining of the religious belief in personal immortality after death; by a religious belief in personal immortality we mean, of course, not belief merely in a survival of some sort, which may not be religious at all and in any case is not a solution of the problem,[10] nor belief in some kind of deification whereby the self becomes merged in the divine, but some kind of translation of the human person in undiminished "human-person-ness" from the temporalities of life in this world to the eternal realm where God dwells. Once this religious belief (however vaguely conceived or pictured) is attained, it obviously

---

loyalty may at any moment bring a man. For the same reason, a purely humanist ethic is always apt to lose the sense of there being absolutes in the moral life and to tumble into an ethic of expediency.

[10]See H. H. Farmer, *Revelation and Religion*, pp.201ff.

becomes possible to apprehend the absolute demand of God as a call to serve him both in this present passing world and in the eternal world which lies beyond, death thus becoming, in a sense, only an incident in the relationship—though an important one, as we have seen, in that through it the absoluteness of the divine claim is revealed and defined.[11] Similarly it becomes possible to apprehend the succour of God as fully meeting the challenge of death, in that it is now possible to think of God as establishing man in a personal relationship to himself which death need not annul.[12]

And there, I suppose, you might think we could leave it. Yet though belief in some sort of personal immortality in a form which, in some manner, participates in the eternity of God is an essential element in the resolution of the tension we are discussing, it is not, by itself, the deep reconciliation and unification which the Christian revelation and faith do in fact distinctively provide. That something more is necessary is indicated by the fact that even a religious belief in personal immortality beyond death, a belief, that is to say, arising out of, and closely associated with the religious apprehension of God can easily slip into something very like the Greek "two-storey" view of eternity and time. It is very easy to slip into the view that this present, temporal sphere is in some fundamental and essential way alien and opposed to an eternal, timeless realm which lies above and beyond it, and to which the human soul, if it can in any way achieve belief in its own immortality, may hope to be translated at death; and this even if it is also believed that some sort

---

[11]Cf. H. H. Farmer, *The World and God*, pp.213ff.—Ed.

[12]For Farmer, eternal life must not be conceived in terms simply of the survival of bodily death—that which "comes after". The truth, he says (and this is why he concluded his first volume of studies in the Christian interpretation of life, *Things Not Seen*, with a chapter on "death" rather than "eternal life") is that "we are not much beyond the bare threshold of the Christian interpretation of life, unless we are at least beginning to discern that the eternal world is not a mere addendum to the Christian life, as a beautiful roof garden is to a bustling common-place store, but in some way is its pervading atmosphere, giving every part, from the basement upwards, a dignity and a zest and a blessedness which it would otherwise inevitably lack. To think of eternal life in any other way than as the abidingness (though not without enhancement) of a relationship whose demands and satisfactions are already being experienced here and now, is to be in perpetual danger of corrupting the moral life with the very thing which ought to cleanse and deepen it, namely, religious faith" (*Things Not Seen*, second edition, pp.1-2).—Ed.

of personal fellowship with God within this world is possible.   Death, according to this view, is simply the way of release from, the way "up from" and "out of", this weary, frustrating wilderness of a time-world into the upper sphere of the eternal, even as ecstasy and trance are in the Orphic mysteries or in Neoplatonism. There is, in other words, no deep and real unification of the opposites of time and eternity here and now within this present time-order and our life within it; nor will there ever be such a unification, for at death we are, God be thanked, jerked right out of the time-order into the eternal, which lies on an entirely different level, in an entirely different dimension of being. How much this essentially Greek view has in fact entered into Christian thought on these matters hardly needs pointing out; it is evident, for example, from many Christian hymns.

The Unification of Time and Eternity
This brings us at last to the specifically Christian revelation and faith and the way it resolves the tension between eternity and time. I believe that the unification and reconciliation which Christianity brings, when it is true to its New Testament norm, and does not allow itself to be distorted by the two-storey view to which we have referred, is distinctive and unique. We might sum it up in a preliminary way by saying that the Christian is given a radically new *time-feeling*, without being in any way invited or encouraged to look for an escape from his time-situation, whether by some kind of mystic withdrawal or even by a final exit at death. This radically new time-feeling is centred, as everything else that is distinctive in Christianity is centred, in the incarnation.

If, however, we are to understand how this is so, we must rightly interpret the word "incarnation". We must not interpret it in terms of the two-storey view of the relation between eternity and time, God's entry into the world being thought of as a direct, unmediated descent in an embodied form from the upper storey to the lower. Such an idea of the incarnation is in fact widespread in the history of religion. It can be found in the higher polytheism of Greece and Rome, in Hinduism, in Mahayana Buddhism and elsewhere, and might be called the characteristic non-Christian idea of it.[13] But the Christian belief in the incarnation is radically different from this, and it is precisely with that difference that, what I have called,   the new time-feeling or time-sense which is given through the Christian revelation and faith is bound up. The distinctively biblical and Christian faith in the incarnation might be indicated and emphasised by dropping the word "incarnation", and, to coin another, speaking of the divine "inhistorisation" in Christ.   The Christian faith is faith in the divine "inhistorisation" in Christ. In order to make clear the distinction between incarnation and inhistorisation which is of the highest importance I cannot do better I think than repeat, with but slight verbal alterations, what I have written elsewhere.[14]

Suppose that I am a missionary sent to lift the life of a savage tribe to a higher level. There are two ways in which I might go to work. On the one hand, I might seek to break up and prohibit their degraded traditions, customs, laws, belief, and substitute for them, as it were from above and by *force majeure*, the higher civilised style of life which I represent. It is obvious that, in so far as I succeed in doing this, whilst in one sense I have actively entered into their life, in another sense I have not entered into it at all. I have not acted into their *history*, their very own history. I have not "inhistorised" myself in relation to them. I have sought rather to annihilate and negate their history and to substitute something entirely different in its place; there has been no continuity, only discontinuity; action "into" but not "in and through"; down the vertical but not along the horizontal. On the other hand, instead of thus, in principle, annihilating the tribe's whole manner of life, I may seek to make myself one with it, to "get inside" and work from within, to recreate it by building on what is already there. In that case my action will be not merely vertical "into" their existence, but also horizontal "in and through" their history: there will be continuity. For what takes place will still, in a very real

---

[13]Cf. H. H. Farmer, *Revelation and Religion*, pp.157ff.—Ed.
[14]See my article, "The Significance and Authority of the Bible", pp.11ff. See also, *The Bible and Preaching*, pp.11ff. In *Revelation and Religion*, pp.195-6, the same main point is more briefly made in relation to a different problem.

sense, be *their* history, yet also there will be discontinuity in that my coming to them, and the new style of life which I bring, constitute something which nothing in their previous history could of itself have brought forth.

Broadly speaking, non-Christian incarnations correspond to the first of the two alternative lines of action. The divine being drops into the human scene in an embodied form from the upper realm of the immortals, unheralded, unprepared for, without roots in what has gone before in history, or results in what comes after. The New Testament understanding, on the other hand, is in line with the second alternative. It affirms that the divine action in Christ is *both* action "in and through" *and* action "into", both horizontal and vertical at one and the same time. There is both continuity and discontinuity. There is *dis*continuity in that the advent of Christ marks a divine saving entry into history which is new and unique, an event which could not have happened without God's deliberate will so to act at that particular point in the historical process, that *kairos*, in that particular way. But there is continuity in that Christ is, nevertheless, a fully historic, individuated human person, a Jew whose whole being and life are rooted in, derivative from, incomprehensible except in the light of, the previous history of the Jewish people.

Now, it is evident that if full weight is given to both the "in and through" and the "into" aspects which the Christian faith thus predicates of the divine action in Christ, then it is necessary to include in the scope of that action much more than the history of Christ in the days of his flesh, though that, of course, will stand out in its unique significance. It is necessary to include, as the New Testament does, the previous history of Israel which prepared the way for Christ, with which his whole life and ministry, his whole understanding of his vocation, were bound up, and apart from which he could not have been a truly historical person. Moreover, a truly historical life can no more be cut off from what comes after it than it can from what comes before it. Hence the New Testament includes within the scope of the divine saving action in Christ that stream of events which flowed directly from his unique historic life, from his own express purpose and intention and from his creative, saving impact on those to whom that purpose and intention were imparted. In other words, there must be included in the coming into being and the continuing life of the Church, the new Israel. Thus the divine saving action in Christ comprehends within it, according to the New Testament faith, a prolonged stretch of time, beginning away back in the calling into existence of the covenant people of Israel, reaching its centre and climax in Christ (who illumines and interprets the whole), and passing on into an as yet uncompleted future through the Church. In other words, the Christian faith in the incarnation involves the crucial and highly distinctive Christian concept of saving history, redemptive history. The phrase *Heilsgeschichte* sums up this distinctive Christian understanding of incarnation as "inhistorisation", for which, as I have insisted, there is no parallel elsewhere.

But, further, this distinctive biblical faith in the incarnation as "inhistorisation", because it does not rest in merely theoretical speculation, but is part of a living and profoundly monotheistic apprehension of, and faith in the one God in all the transcendence of his being, it is necessarily impelled to extend the scope of the divine saving action in history through Christ to include even more than the particular stretch of the time-process which we call "saving history". This in two ways:

(1) It is impelled to extend it longitudinally or lengthwise. One can observe in the New Testament how that the divine saving purpose in Christ, being the purpose of the one God, inevitably comes to be thought of as "running back",[15] not merely throughout the history of Israel, which led up to the coming of Christ, but beyond it into what is thought of as the creation of the world, and through and beyond that again into the ultimate, unfathomable mystery of God's transcendent being. Similarly, and by a like necessity, it is thought of as "running forward" through the history of the new Israel, the Church, to some sort of end of the world process (corresponding to its beginning at creation), and beyond that again into the unfathomable mystery of God's transcendent being and of his finally consummated kingdom or rule.

---

[15]This is, of course, a metaphorical expression which does not exactly fit the noun "purpose". Purpose is more naturally thought of as looking and moving *forward*, but the meaning intended is, I think, sufficiently clear.

Only by such a lengthening of the perspective in both directions from the central fact of Christ can the full religious sense of God find expression and, *along with this*, the faith that in Christ God himself acted "into" and "in and through" history in a unique, final and saving self-disclosure and self-giving.

(2) It is impelled for the same reason to extend the scope of the divine saving action in history latitudinally or breadthwise. If God is effectively active for the redemption of men through saving history, through the *Heilsgeschichte* of which Christ is the centre, then he must hold in the control of his saving purpose a much wider band of history, so to say, than the relatively narrow band which constitutes the history of the old and new Israels. For the history of the old Israel and of the Church and of the life of Christ, just because it is *real* history, is all the time set within the context of, and conditioned by, the natural, social, political, economic, international factors and forces which play upon human life and in large measure control the course of events. In other words, saving history under the control of God's saving purpose obviously cannot be thought of as simply "piped through" secular history, or through the world-process, or through the complex conditions which universally govern human life, these *not* being under the control of that purpose. Such a "piped through" saving history would not, of course, be history at all, nor would Christ be at its centre as the real "inhistorisation" of God, nor would God be the God of monotheistic faith, who is "over all, and through all, and in all".[16] The whole course of history, universal history, indeed, the whole course of nature, must therefore be brought within the scope of the divine purpose, without however in the least diminishing, but rather enhancing, the central and unique significance of the narrower strip of the *Heilsgeschichte*.[17]

---

[16]Eph. 4:6.

[17]Cf. C. H. Dodd, *History and the Gospel* (London: Nisbet, 1938), pp.168ff. For New Testament references confirming and illustrating the statements made in the last two paragraphs, the reader may be referred to Oscar Cullmann's *Christ and Time: The Primitive Christian Perception of Time and History*, tr. By F. V. Filson (London: SCM, 1951), *passim*.

It is in the light of all this that we can in some measure understand why the biblical writers apparently never come within sight of the Greek two-storey view of eternity and time, never give even a hint of thinking of God's eternity in such a way as to exclude completely from it anything and everything in the nature of temporality. The notion of a timeless eternity simply has no place in biblical thought, still less anything that might be taken even distantly to suggest the Scholastic and Neo-platonic view of God's eternity as simultaneity, as a *totum simul* or a *nunc stans*, without distinction of past, present and future. The biblical writers, of course, do not think of God's time as being of the same nature as the time we know and experience. Time as a mode of the divine being and life is for them other than time as a mode of terrestrial life because God is *God*—but it is time and not sheer timelessness. This otherness is expressed and emphasised in three ways: (a) by the notion of endless duration, without any limit in a backward or forward direction: "from everlasting to everlasting you are God";[18] God is he which was, which is, and which is to come. (b) By the insistence that human standards of measurement must not be applied to God's time: with God "a day is like a thousand years, and a thousand years are like a day." [19] (c) By the insistence that God's time is not to be thought of as in any way a limitation of his absolute being as God: he is, as men are not, if one may so put it, the absolute master of his own temporality even in its unthinkable everlastingness, just as he is of that temporality, with its beginnings and endings and perpetual passings away, which characterises the existence of this world and of men. He is the Lord of time in all its modes; he holds all "ages" in the grasp of his infinite power and wisdom and unchanging constancy of will.[20]

The notion of time as a mode of divine being no doubt raises many problems for thought, but not more so than the notion of divine timelessness. The latter notion has to carry the added fatal difficulty of cutting right across

---

[18]Ps.90:2.
[19]2Pet.3:8.
[20]See Isa.40:12-31.

the distinctive content of the Christian revelation and faith as normatively
defined in the New Testament. It is not our purpose here to discuss these
problems.[21] Rather, as we have said, we want to understand why the biblical
writers never present a two-storey view of time and eternity with its corollary
of an eternal "timelessness". It would be easy to regard the ascription of
some sort of time-succession to God as the somewhat naïve, poetical imagery
of minds which, whatever they might possess by way of religious insight and
fervour, had little aptitude for abstract philosophical thought and criticism (an
example of what Hegel called the religious *Vorstellung*, in contrast with the
philosophic *Begriff*). But that would be superficial. Paul had a profound,
indeed speculative mind, and one may surmise that he was not unaware that
there were quite different notions of eternity current in Greek thought and
religion. The same is true of the writers of the fourth Gospel and of the
Epistle to the Hebrews. It is true that the human mind has to use inadequate
images and metaphors in thinking and speaking about God, but an image or
metaphor must at least hint at something which is sufficiently definite and
graspable to exclude other meanings, and what is definitely not hinted at by
the New Testament writers is timelessness. Again we ask why? The reason, I
suggest, is that their thoughts about God spring right out of the heart of the
basic and central belief in the saving "inhistorisation" of God in Christ, as this
is taken up into monotheistic faith. Everything, every attribute of God as
known through his own self-disclosure to man, including his eternity—his
transcendence of specifically human temporality—is seen, as it were, through
the medium, along the perspective, of history. It is seen from the perspective-
centre of Christ, and the perspective runs (as indicated above) through and
beyond the *Heilsgeschichte* in both directions. It runs backward through the

---

[21]I know of no better discussion of them, along with the firm insistence on the necessity, laid
upon us by the Christian revelation and experience to retain "time" as a mode of the divine
being and to reject the idea of divine "timelessness", than that by Edwyn Bevan in his
Gifford lectures, *Symbolism and Belief* (London: Allen & Unwin, 1938), chs. 4 and 5. I find
myself in agreement with everything he says there. Since Bevan's book, we have had
Cullman's *Christus und die Zeit* (referred to above) and its insistence on the point that the
biblical writers say nothing that even distantly supports the notion of divine "timelessness".

history of the old Israel and forward through the history of the new Israel. Then it passes beyond these to the world-beginning and to the world-end, and then beyond these again into the unfathomable mystery of the transcendent being of God. But it is *one* perspective line throughout, with God just as much living, personal purpose in its furthermost reaches as he is known to be in and through his saving activity in the person of Christ in the midst of the temporality of the world. If I may so put it, the perspective of the New Testament writers, as they look out from the perspective-centre of Christ, is not suddenly and completely blocked-off in both directions by a vast, impenetrable rock face which their vision can only pass beyond if they leap out of temporality on to an entirely different, upper level, and there look along an entirely different perspective from another centre. Inevitably, therefore, the eternity of God is thought of as containing a perspective of successiveness, though one, no doubt, not subject to human limitations and time measurements. It is " from everlasting to everlasting" and it is at all points in the grasp of, and under the control of, the infinite wisdom, knowledge, power and love of God.

We now return to the question which launched us on this discussion. Our purpose is to try to grasp what the new " time-feeling" is and how it arises— the " time feeling" which the Christian revelation and faith make possible, and through which the duality and opposition of God's eternity and man's temporality (inevitably and acutely felt at the heart of living religion) are continuously overcome.

The answer, as it may be drawn from the pages of the New Testament, is that the saved man, by virtue of the new relation to God in which, because he is a saved man, he is established through Christ, is himself aware of being taken up into, and united with, the whole course of saving history as centred in Christ. To put it slightly differently, the saving purpose of God, as this is wrought out through saving history, achieves its end in relation to individual men and women by incorporating them into the age-long saving process itself. Put simply, the Christian becomes a member of the Church, the new Israel, which, as we have seen, is itself part of saving history. But that, though true, is not very satisfactory, because "becoming a member of the Church" has become, in common parlance, such a flat and jejune phrase that it hardly takes us to the heart of the matter. In the New Testament, membership of the Church means being one with Christ in some real, if indefinable, way; being "in Christ", incorporate in his body which is the Church. "Union with Christ" is an idea, or rather a reality, which is not easily described in precise terms. But so far as this new time-feeling of which we are speaking is concerned, the Christian is taken up into saving history in such a way that he is enabled to stand at the perspective-centre with Christ and, as it were, look both backwards and forwards along the perspective of it from Christ, which means *from himself as united with Christ*. This finds supreme realisation and expression in the life of the Church and of its members in the communion service. In the communion rite the Church deliberately, individually, collectively and repeatedly stands with Christ at the centre of saving history and looks backwards and forwards along the perspective of it. That is why "remembrance" is basic in the rite, particularly remembrance of his death and resurrection in which his saving work was consummated, but is very far indeed from exhausting the meaning of it.[22]

It is obvious, however, in the light of what was said earlier, that this does not fully state the matter. We said that because the New Testament faith is a monotheistic faith in the God who is maker and ruler of all, the perspective of the stretch of history which we call saving history is, for the Christian, necessarily extended both lengthwise and breadthwise. We take each point in turn.

Its extension lengthwise, we said, means that it runs beyond Israel to the creation, and through the creation into the mysterious counsels of God, and forwards beyond the new Israel to some sort of world-end, and beyond that again into the mystery of a final consummation when God "shall be all in all". Because the saved person is standing at the centre with Christ and in Christ, these extended perspectives become his also. This constitutes the deep

---

[22]Cf. C. H. Dodd, *History and the Gospel*, p.163.

religious root of the New Testament doctrine of election and predestination. A doctrine of predestination has, of course, appeared in other religions, notably Islam. And in Christian theology it has been developed in a purely speculative theory—first making its appearance in the teaching of Augustine and reaching its sharpest and most ruthlessly logical expression in Calvin's doctrine of the double decree that goes far beyond anything in the New Testament. The New Testament teaching is not speculative, it is rather deeply religious and springs out of the heart of the distinctive Christian experience of being saved by Christ and being united with Christ. It is bound up with the sense of having been made one with, incorporated into, saving history, and in particular with the lengthened perspectives which we have been discussing. The saved man is conscious that his salvation in Christ, like the *Heilsgeschichte* of which Christ is the centre, can be causally traced back beyond the creation of the world into the mysterious depths of the transcendent mind and purpose, the "determinate counsel and foreknowledge", of God, and it can be proleptically traced forward beyond the end of the world into the mystery of the final consummation.[23]

The extension of saving history breadthwise means, we said, that the whole process of the world and of history is brought within the control and under the direction of the same divine saving purpose which is manifested in the saving history and has its centre in Christ. From this it follows that the redeemed man as he stands at this centre in Christ is enabled to look out over the whole temporal process of nature and history, including his own temporal existence as conditioned by the process and to see them in a new light. Everything, no matter how evil, no matter how apparently fortuitous and meaningless, no matter how frustrating and disappointing, no matter how subject to the tragic transiency of man's natural life in the world ("all men are

---

[23]That this does underlie the New Testament ideas of election and predestination is evidenced by the fact that they are applied to the old Israel (Rom. 9.11), to the new Israel and to the individual members of it (1 Pet. 1:2; Eph. 1:4; Rom. 8:28-30) and to Christ himself (Jn. 17:24; 1 Pet. 1:20). See Cullman, *Christ and Time*, p.220.

like grass, and all their glory is like the flowers of the field"[24]), no matter what obediences unto death may be called for by the divine absolute demand itself, everything is taken up into the majestic sweep of the divine saving purpose of love which has manifested itself in history in Christ.

It might be thought that all this is but an elaborate and roundabout way of saying that the Christian believes in providence. But to think that would be to miss the point. The important thing is what the sources of belief in providence are and what sustains that belief. Belief in providence can have a number of different sources and its bearing upon the testing actualities of man's historical existence will differ accordingly. Thus it may be proposed as a necessary element in a general theistic worldview, partly perhaps as a somewhat precarious induction from such teleological patterns as can be observed in the world, and partly perhaps as a postulate which we are bound to make when we set out to interpret the world in terms of a single divine will. Or it may be proposed, as it was by the Stoics, as a necessary corollary of belief in an all-pervading Reason or Logos. Or it may have its roots only in the soil of passing feelings which express hardly more than a genial temperamental optimism that has never been put to any really severe test; or in a cheerful belief in progress, born of prosperous times; or in a subconsciously felt need to whistle a song in order to keep one's courage in the dark. Or it may be simply a way of expressing, in objective, quasi-religious terms, what is subjectively hardly more than a resigned acquiescence in what cannot be altered. Belief in providence with such sources is likely to have as little staying power, when put to the test, as the plant in the parable which sprang up luxuriantly in shallow soil, but withered away when the hot sun beat down upon it, or the house built on sand which collapsed when winds and floods of unusual violence smote it. And this is likely to be so, even when there is in such belief, as I would not care to deny there sometimes is, and possibly always is, some genuinely religious apprehension of God.

---

[24]Isa.40:6; 1Pet.1:24.

Obviously the distinctive Christian faith in the divine providence (the belief, that is to say, which is rooted in and sustained by that distinctive Christian faith in the divine saving action of God in history—the divine "inhistorisation" in Christ—and all that that carries with it) *is* very different, alike in its inward sources of conviction and in its power to meet the challenges which are continually flung in its face by the facts, or apparent facts, of man's life in the world. It is in fact unique. There is, so far as I know, nothing in the other religions even distantly suggestive of it. And not the least important element in its uniqueness is the new time-sense which we have been seeking to describe and analyse. The time-process of the world, and of my being and life in the world, and all the evanescence, decay and death (not to speak of other evils) which characterise it, has an entirely different "feel" when I find myself in it in union with the incarnate, the "inhistorised", divine redeemer; when I stand, with him, at the centre of the saving history (being now myself incorporated in it) and look out from that centre, lengthwise along its infinite perspectives into the ultimate mystery of God's being, and breadthwise to the outmost rim of the world. Any inclination to find an *irreconcilable* conflict and opposition between the temporality of life in this world and the eternity of God (a conflict and opposition only to be resolved by escape from the former by mystic ecstasy or by the longed for release of death) is continually rebuked and overcome by the sense that there is an unbroken continuity between the two, that God is not "timeless" but has temporality within his own being, a temporality which both transcends our temporality, and includes it within itself. We come from God, go to God and travel with God, and it is, so to say, one journey throughout.

I am very conscious that these statements are very inadequate and that they could hardly stand up to rigorous logical analysis and criticism. But that is certainly, in part, due to the fact that they are an attempt to describe in abstract terms that which lies more in the realm of feeling-apprehension, involving the whole man, than in the realm of the intellective processes of the mind. Perhaps, therefore, we cannot do better, in conclusion, than turn once again to the pages of the New Testament where the writings spring from a new, immediate and wonderful experience and have the flow of the experience upon them; and in particular to that chapter which is not only concerned with those things of which we have been speaking but also stands out, even in the New Testament, because of its elevated passion and power. I refer to the eighth chapter of Paul's epistle to the Romans.

We observe, first, that there is in Paul's mind an acute sense of what he calls "the groaning as in the pains of childbirth" of "the whole creation".[25] His vision thus takes in the whole temporal order of the world, and he is profoundly conscious of the transience and evanescence which characterise it. "For the creation was subjected to frustration", in "bondage to decay".[26] Moreover (and this is the important thing for it is surely this which has prompted him to write the whole passage), this consciousness penetrates into the experience of even the Christian believer who has a new and living experience of God in what he calls "the firstfruits of the Spirit". It reveals itself there in the sense of a contrariety between man's temporality, as summed up and symbolised in the mortality of the body and the working of the eternal Spirit of God in him.[27] The Christian, therefore, has to live by hope.[28] But it is plain that Paul is not here using the word "hope" in the sense in which it is often used, namely, to express the absence, rather than the presence, of conviction and assurance—"I am not sure", we say, "but I rather hope so." "Hope" for Paul here means complete assurance about the future, about a future wherein the antithesis between the weakness and the transiency of his life in this world and the eternal purpose of God (with which he has fellowship now through the Spirit) will be overcome. What then is the source of this assurance? The source is God's great act of redemptive, self-giving love in Christ. "He who did not spare his own Son, but gave him up for us

---

[25]Rom. 8:22.
[26]Rom. 8:20, 21.
[27]Rom. 8:23.
[28]Rom. 8:24.

all—how will he not also, along with him, graciously give us all things?"[29] But observe how from this centre Paul's thought is not only moving forward to the final consummation, as you would expect it to do seeing that it is a question of hope, but it is also moving in the reverse direction past the mystery of God's creation of the world subject to vanity, beyond "time" as we know it in that world, into the unfathomable depths of the determinate counsel and foreknowledge of God. "For those God foreknew he also predestined to be conformed to the likeness of his Son, that he might be the firstborn among many brothers. And those he predestined, he also called; those he called, he also justified; those he justified, he also glorified."[30] Thus Paul is conscious of being personally taken up into the majestic sweep of the purpose of God as it comes forth from the infinite mystery of his being before the foundation of the world, and passes through the world, and after that returns again to the mystery of the final consummation. And this purpose he knows to be, throughout its whole course, a purpose of saving love, the saving love which was manifested in the "giving up of his Son for us all", the saving love which binds the saved man inseparably to himself. Being thus taken up into the ongoing movement of the divine saving purpose of love, its infinite perspectives being now his perspectives, Paul finds that his life in this world, with all its "groaning as in the pains of childbirth", all its "bondage to decay", all its "frustration", is now radically transformed. The "feel" of them is different; all their power to defeat and overwhelm has gone. "Who shall separate us from the love of Christ. Shall trouble or hardship or persecution or famine or nakedness or danger or sword?...No, in all these things we are more than conquerors through him who loved us. For I am convinced that neither death nor life, neither angels nor demons, neither the present nor the future, nor any powers, neither height nor depth, nor anything

---

[29]Rom. 8:32.
[30]Rom. 8:29-30

else in all creation, will be able to separate us from the love of God that is in Christ Jesus our Lord." [31]

31Rom. 8:35-39.

PART THREE

GOD

and

THE SELF

4

GOD'S DEMAND AND GOD'S SUCCOUR

We come now to the second of our main classes of duality, namely, *God and the Self*. Under this heading, we begin by considering a deep-going conflict or opposition which discloses itself in some degree in all living religion, but which becomes increasingly acute and evident the more something approaching a full ethical monotheism is achieved. It is a conflict or opposition between those two elements which have already entered so very much into our thought—the apprehension of God as making an absolute claim or demand upon man and the apprehension of him as man's final succour and security.

I am conscious that by this time I must have spoken of these two things almost to the point of exhaustion; but it is the facts which are to blame. We have maintained again and again, both in the previous volume[1] and in this, that these two elements are right at the centre of the living awareness of God, and the fact that we are always encountering them, no matter from what angle we approach and explore religious experience and thought, is but a verification of that assertion. It may be pointed out, however, that hitherto we have principally spoken of the two elements in separation from one another, or else we have thought of them as not in harmonious interaction with one another. We have not so far seen them in, so to say, head-on collision with one another, and therefore as posing a special problem for religion. We have also not explored the uniqueness of the Christian revelation and faith as a unifying power in this regard.

---

[1]See, for example, H. H. Farmer, *Revelation and Religion*, pp.63ff, 138ff, 149ff, 152ff.—Ed.

It is not difficult to see how in a general way conflict between these two elements almost inevitably arises at the heart of living religion. The absolute claim of God in its primary impact can only define itself and obtain meaning and content by its relation (implicit or explicit) to the goods and values of man's immediate, practical life in this world, to what might be called natural values. Only through the surrender of such goods and values can a man, in any realistic way, give meaning to and acknowledge an overriding divine claim upon him. That is, no doubt, one reason why sacrificial rites, usually taking the form of an actual or symbolic offering of man's dearest possessions, are so universal throughout religion.[2] They are in part an expression, in concrete imagery, of the impact of the divine claim upon man and man's acknowledgement of it.[3] On the other hand, it is precisely in respect of the goods and values of his immediate natural life in this world, or rather in respect of the lack (or threatened lack) of them, that man feels in the most immediate and acute way the need for divine help and succour. If the divine demand is primarily defined in terms of the surrender of such goods and values, the divine succour tends to be primarily defined in terms of their provision and guarantee. This remains true even when the things that men desire come to include values which we might prefer to call cultural or even spiritual, rather than natural; for it is here and now in this present world that man yearns to enjoy such values, and in any case they rest upon and presuppose the provision of such natural necessities as food, clothing, shelter, children, etc. Living religion therefore inevitably tends to present itself under this dual guise which results in the following tension at its heart. On the one hand, the demand for the giving up of the good things of life, and on the other hand, the guaranteeing of the good things of life. It has within it a powerful impulse to negate and deny the world—what might be called the ascetic impulse—and at the same time a powerful impulse to affirm it—what might

---

[2]See ibid., pp.153-4.—Ed.
[3]I remarked in the last chapter how that the word "absolute" in the phrase "absolute demand" can only be defined with reference to death, which is to all appearance the surrender of *all* the goods and values of man's life.

be called the eudaemonistic impulse. That is why it is possible for two opposed descriptions of the essence of religion to be given, such as those of, for example, Salomon Reinach and Harald Höffding. The former speaks of it as, " A sum of scruples which impede the free exercise of our faculties",[4] and the latter speaks of it as "the valuation of existence"—and of religious ideas as the expression of "the relation in which actual existence...stands to that which, for us, invests life with its highest value."[5] This explains why some criticise religion for being negative and restrictive, whilst others criticise it for being nothing more than an example of wishful thinking.

It is not difficult to see that in any religion where these two elements are given full and equal weight, neither being allowed to overwhelm and submerge the other, the conflict between them will become very acute, as a result of which some way of adjusting them to one another will be consciously or unconsciously sought.[6] It is evident too that if our claim for the uniqueness of Christianity as a reconciling faith is to be justified, its uniqueness will be manifested in the way in which it resolves this contrariety.

Divine Demand and Succour in the History of Religions

We may best grasp the uniqueness of the way in which the Christian revelation and faith deal with this problem by contrasting it with the way in which some other advanced religions have sought to deal with it.

The way they have sought to overcome the problem might be broadly described as keeping the divine demand and the divine succour in a kind of balance or counterpoise with one another by separating their spheres of operation, but at the same time providing an essential link between them. You obey the demands of God at certain sacred times and places, yielding up your

---

[4]S. Reinach, *Orpheus: A History of Religions*, revised edition, tr. by F. Simmonds (London: George Routledge & Sons, 1931), p.3.

[5]H. Höffding, *The Philosophy of Religion*, tr. by B. E. Meyer (London: Macmillan and Co., 1906), p.6. [Cf. J. Oman, *The Church and the Divine Order* (London: Hodder and Stoughton, 1911), pp.15ff.—Ed.]

[6]For a discussion of types of religion in which one or other of the two elements is dominant see *Revelation and Religion*, ch.7.

dearest heart's desires, if need be, at the divine behest. But you are bidden to expect that, as a result, God will grant your heart's desires at other times and places as a reward for your obedience; or, to put it negatively, you expect that if you do not obey the divine demand, you will not receive the positive reward of happiness and prosperity, but rather, on the contrary, may expect to receive the negative reward, the penalty of misery and loss. The linking together, as I have already indicated, is through the idea of reward. The God who makes his claim upon you in the sacred sphere rewards you in the secular sphere. If we want a single broad name for this way of relating the two elements, we might call it the "legalistic" way, not only because it tends, for reasons I shall explain later, to formulate the divine claim in a strict code to be obeyed, but also because it works with the idea of a divine, distributive justice which bestows rewards and penalties in proportion to obedience. The outstanding illustrations of this way of relating the two elements are to be found in Zoroastrianism, Pharisaic Judaism, and Islam; but, of course, it can be illustrated many times from the history of Christianity which, in this matter, has often fallen below the level of its own highest insights and standards.

This legalistic type of religion is of great interest for three reasons. (1) In its outstanding historic manifestations (with the exception of perhaps Zoroastrianism) it succeeded in retaining a clear and definite monotheism, an apprehension of God as the one holy, sovereign personal will concerned with man and with meeting him in the actualities of his everyday life in the world. In this connection we may note the significance of the fact that all these religions took their rise from, or found their inspiration and renewal in, great prophetic individuals—in Zoroastrianism Zarathustra, in Islam Muhammad, in Pharisaic Judaism Moses and the prophets—who rose up in passionate protest against the prevailing polytheism of the time. We can discern a necessity in this. For it is difficult to see how a new and living apprehension of God as one, indivisible, holy, personal will encountering man (an apprehension which shears right through the confusion and often crude eudaemonism of polytheistic belief) could have been given except by a direct confrontational meeting of the will of a single, sensitive and responsive individual with the will of the self-revealing God. It could hardly have been mediated through the elaborate communal religious observances of state-polytheism in which group consciousness so easily submerged the individual in mass-feeling and mass-behaviour.

(2) The second reason the legalistic type of religion is of interest to us is because it has such a vivid awareness of the one holy and perfect will of God in its absolute demand, and, because of that, is, at the same time, as vividly aware that the divine succour cannot be had cheaply. Only as man obeys the demand is it capable (in favourable circumstances and within its inevitable limitations) of rising to considerable heights of devoted and disciplined living, of moral austerity, of faith in the overruling sovereignty of God, as, for example, it often did in Pharisaic Judaism.

(3) Finally, this type of religion because of its strong and vigorous monotheism and its vivid sense of both the demand and succour of God, advances a long way towards what is given in the Christian revelation and faith. Nevertheless it falls short of it, and must do so, in spite of the heights to which it can rise. This is why the understanding of it is important for our purpose. On the background of such religion the distinctiveness of Christianity as a reconciling faith is thrown into sharp relief. As is so often the case, the most useful clue to the appreciation of the best is the second-best.

Wherein then does this type of religion, in spite of its often high achievement, fall short? The root of failure is that it does not rise above a predominantly eudaemonistic interpretation of the divine succour, an interpretation of it, that is to say, in terms of the natural values of man's life. The rewards which are confidently promised and expected for obedience to the divine demands are the prosperity and happiness for which the natural man craves, and to the winning of which the bulk of his activities are directed. We might say that, whilst this type of religion achieves a relatively high and pure level of awareness of God as demand, it remains on a relatively low and immature level of awareness of the divine succour. The result is a disproportion, an imbalance, in the religious life, a maturity at one fundamental point and an immaturity at another, which is bound, in face of the facts of experience, to break up the unity of the inner life into conflicts and oppositions. Of course, solutions are found, but they are solutions which bring forth fresh conflicts, and thus, in the final analysis, never provide a permanent unification and peace.

The fundamental fact of experience which reveals the weakness and inadequacy of the attempt to unite the divine demand and the divine succour legalistically through the link of rewards eudaemonistically interpreted is, of course, vividly brought before us in the Book of Job. Rather than righteousness and prosperity keeping pace with one another, the reverse is true. The promised goods are not delivered. Suffering and loss fall upon the righteous man, whilst the unrighteous man seems "to get away with it". Now, at this point of contradiction between expectancy and fact, two ways are open. One is to continue to adhere to the eudaemonistic interpretation of the divine succour and the fundamentally legalist interpretation of its relation to the divine demand, and to seek a solution on that basis; the other is radically to transform the whole idea of the divine succour and its relation to the divine demand. The former is exemplified in Zoroastrianism, Islam and Pharisaic Judaism; the latter is the way taken in the Christian revelation and experience. We consider each way in turn.

In their search for a solution to the problem, Zoroastrianism, Islam and Pharisaic Judaism exhibit a strong tendency to move along three lines. First, there is a movement towards a dualistic interpretation of the world; in this there is to some extent a departure from the original monotheism. Second, there is a movement towards a compensatory eschatological hope. Third, there is a movement towards an increasingly elaborated ceremonial legalism. The meaning of these statements can best be made plain by illustrating them from the rise and history of Zoroastrianism.[7]

Zarathustra emerged in the midst of the Iranian people at a date which is, we are told, impossible to fix with anything approaching precision, but which can hardly have been later than during the first two or three centuries of the

---

[7]Cf. Oman's discussion: *The Natural and the Supernatural*, ch.25.—Ed.

first millennium before Christ.[8] Dates are, however, of little importance. The significant thing is that if the sacred writings of Zarathustra, the Gathas, in any measure take us back to the original teaching of the prophet, and it is at least not impossible that they do, then we can discern lying alongside one another right at the very beginning the two elements of a eudaemonistic conception of the succour of the one God in terms of the natural values of man's life and an austere conception of his absolute demand. Given the social and economic circumstances in the midst of which Zarathustra appeared, it was perhaps inevitable that the eudaemonistic element should have been so prominent. The prophet's soul was stirred apparently by the misery and insecurity of the peasantry in their continuous wrestling with the forces of nature, a wrestling rendered trebly hard by the depredations of oppressive overlords and pillaging banditry. By a curious transference of thought (though it really bears witness to the intensely practical context in which the prophet's thought moves) he personifies the cattle and speaks of their cry, along with that of their owners, going up to God for help.[9] But how does Zarathustra think of God, and of the succour he gives to the peasants and their cattle in their need? At this point the other strand of his teaching enters in. For Zarathustra rises up, not only as the champion of the peasantry in their poverty and distress, but also as the teacher of a noble ethical monotheism which fiercely repudiates and calls men from the traditional nature gods of the Iranian peoples. There is only one, all-supreme deity, Ahura Mazdah, creator of all things in heaven and earth, the Lord of light, wisdom, purity and truth, whose holy will is utterly antagonistic to all that is evil, destructive, impure and false. In his relation to men, he is not merely their creator and Lord, but also he who challenges their will, judges their actions, searches their hearts, from whom none can hide. He claims all men whether exalted or lowly, powerful or weak, for his service which is the

---

[8]See R. C. Zaehner, *The Dawn and Twilight of Zoroastrianism* (London: Wiedenfeld & Nicolson, 1961), p.33; N. Söderblom, *The Living God: Basal Forms of Living Religion* (London: Oxford University Press, 1933), p.230.—Ed.

[9]See, for example, Yasna 29: *The Gathas of Zarathustra*, tr. by S. Insler, Acta Iranica 8 (Leiden: E. J. Brill, 1975), p.29. See also R. C. Zaehner, *The Dawn and Twilight of Zoroastrianism*, pp.34f.; and N. Söderblom, *The Living God*, p.178.—Ed.

service of the good and the right; he demands their enlistment on his side in his age-long warfare with evil in all its forms. How then is this connected with the succour of the peasantry and their cattle? After all, it would not appear that a demand for an arduously pure and pious life is much alleviation of the lot of a people already burdened and oppressed. The answer is, of course, that obedience to this demand is set forth as the condition precedent of the divine succour and protection. God certainly answers the cry of the needy husbandman by sending his prophet, but the prophet's first duty is to call men to a more orderly, honourable, industrious and obedient daily life. To those who obey the call, the Lord's succour is available as reward, and succour means principally the bestowing and preserving of the natural goods of an agricultural community, particularly cattle.

Here then is clearly that combination of a high and mature sense of God's absolute demand and a naïve and immature sense of his succour, the two linked together by the notion of reward, to which we have referred. Nathan Söderblom, who has the highest admiration for the pure ethical monotheism of Zarathustra, and who asserts that the emergence of Zarathustra in the midst of Iranian polytheism is "a rare and fateful phenomenon in the history of religion",[10] is, nevertheless, constrained also to emphasise this unredeemed eudaemonism. "Zarathustra", he says, "worships and serves the Lord, Ahura, the all-wise Mazdah, for the sake of farmers and the cattle."[11] "The spiritual atmosphere of the Gathas is wholesome and bracing, but...earthbound. The natural lust of life had not yet begun to abate in him and in his contemporaries. His attitude to the good things of life is yet naïve."[12] And again, "the conceptions as well as the divine intercourse of Zarathustra are by no means profound...But the air is pure and wholesome. Labour, truth, right, obedience, the inexorable struggle against the powers of evil, against barbarism and destruction, the untiring endeavour to gain new ground for civilisation and

---

[10]N. Söderblom, *The Living God*, p.206.
[11]Ibid., p.183.
[12]Ibid., pp.210-11.

orderly settlement for men; peace, and comfort under good rulers, and the certainty that the struggle is not dubious, but will be carried to victory. Assurance of the support of Mazdah...for the faithful labourer, the assurance of prosperity, immortality and bliss beyond the bridge of decision in the dwelling of the Lord...such is the world of ideas in which Zarathustra moves."[13] "Happiness and riches will be the lot of true piety."[14]

The test of this pure and bracing, but naïve faith, as Söderblom calls it, comes when it is realised that these standards of the divine succour with which the believer sets out on his way of obedience to the one, holy will of God are found not to accord with the facts, when it becomes evident that prosperity and righteousness do *not* march together. At this point of contradiction between promise and fulfilment, Zoroastrianism, still bound to its eudaemonistic ideas, begins to move down the three tracks I have mentioned.

(1) Zoroastrianism moves along the line of an increasingly thoroughgoing dualistic interpretation of the world. The problem of the untoward event which overtakes even the righteous man who obeys the demand of God is solved, or at least lightened, by, in effect, removing it from the control of God and ascribing it to some evil power or powers. The one righteous, holy will of God, in other words, although it has achieved sovereignty over the pious man's heart and life, has not yet achieved it fully over the pious man's world. God, in fact, is rather like a contractor, who, although he accepts full legal liability, has to inform his client that he is no longer able to fulfil the contract on the stipulated date "owing to circumstances beyond his control". There are indeed manifest signs of a dualistic tendency in Zarathustra's original teaching, or what, in the Gathas, purports to be such. Over against Ahura Mazdah there is set a host of evil powers, whose dwelling place is the abyss and who come forth and wrestle with the purpose of the Most High in the arena of this world. In this battle every man is called to take part through the

---

[13]Ibid., pp.197-8.
[14]Ibid., p.217.

purity and virtue and labour of his daily life.[15] It is possible, however, that this teaching was hardly more than a naïve, dramatic expression of what was fundamentally an intense religio-ethical dualism, of that profound sense of the irreconcilable opposition of good and evil, that refusal to follow the pantheistic way of denying positive reality to evil by merging it in the incomprehensible unity of the absolute One, which always characterises prophetic monotheism. But however that may be, it is certain that later in the history of Zoroastrianism, when we may suppose the contradiction offered by the facts and events to the alleged equivalence of righteousness and reward became increasingly an established fact of experience too obvious to be glossed over, the original dualism, whatever it was, hardened into something approaching a metaphysical dualism, and the head of all the evil powers was elevated to a position almost, if never quite equal to that of Ahura Mazdah himself. Angra Mainyu comes to be thought of as not only *not* owing his existence to the Creator of good, but as himself a creator who calls into existence creatures opposed to the will of the latter. The right interpretation of Zoroastrian dualism has been much debated, and it has been denied by some that Zoroastrianism is properly to be called a dualism at all. But whatever terms we use, there can be little doubt that the movement of thought we have described is there and that one religious root of it is what I have suggested. Oman describes Zoroastrianism as "monotheistic in tendency but dualistic in outcome."[16] And Casartelli calls it "a monotheism severely limited and modified by dualism."[17]

No living faith, however, can really rest content in a quite unrelieved dualism of good and evil, destined never to be resolved; for what then becomes of the apprehension of God as the final succour and security of man's life? It is bound to assert an ultimate victory of the good purpose of God

---

[15]See, for example, Yasna 50:7-9; and 51: *The Gathas of Zarathustra*, tr. by S. Insler, pp.101; 103. See also Insler's commentary: pp.302, 308-9; 310-21.—Ed.

[16]See J. Oman, *The Natural and the Supernatural*, pp.432-40.

[17]L. C. Casartelli, "Dualism (Iranian)", in J. Hastings (ed.), *Encyclopædia of Religion and Ethics*, vol.5 (Edinburgh: T. & T. Clark, 1912), pp.111-2.

when the reward of the righteous will at last be actualised. But being forced by the facts to an unresolved dualism in respect of this world, there is only one way of making such an assertion, and that is to project the victory and the reward beyond this world. This is what Zoroastrianism did. Having lost its monotheism, so far as this world is concerned, it seeks to recover it, to restore the balance, by reference to a world to come. So we come to the second of the three ways in which this type of religion seeks to overcome the contradiction of events.

(2) The eschatological hope insists that there will come a day when the domination of evil powers will cease. The prince of darkness and lies and all his hosts will be finally and utterly destroyed, and the full reign of Ahura Mazdah over a renewed and transfigured creation will begin, the spirits of righteous men entering at last into the reward of bliss which has been denied them here. This last statement must be taken primarily in a literal sense. No doubt we ought always to be on our guard against interpreting men's pictures of the heavenly state too literally; by so doing we may do them an injustice, for in the nature of the case they have only earthly images with which to represent what they may well agree, when the point is put to them, transcends such images. Nevertheless, whether or not much more spiritual ideas may conceivably be lurking in the background and seeking some sort of expression, it cannot be questioned that the eudaemonistic thought of God's succour which lies unredeemed at the heart of Zoroastrianism determines to a large extent its thought of the reward of the righteous in the life to come. It is largely a question of emphasis and still more perhaps a question of reticence. The mind which is not dominated by the notion of eudaemonistic reward is content, as the New Testament writers are content, to say little more about the blessed state hereafter than the final triumph of God's holy will, and that God will be all in all. On the other hand, where there is a wealth of imagery, and where that imagery is mainly in terms of the natural values of this world, one may suspect that the eudaemonistic motive is strongly at work. Whatever may have been true of the original eschatological teaching of the prophet, later Zoroastrian eschatological pictures are detailed and marked by an

unmistakable "creature-comfort" character, if one may so put it: "fine carpets, rich cushions, gorgeous raiment, fragrant perfume, butter made in the height of spring, men and women restored to a state comparable to their earthly prime, husbands and wives restored to one another, and even those who had not the joys of married life here will find a partner." [18]

(3) Finally, we turn to the way of an increasing ceremonial legalism. If you start from the position that the succours of God are rewards conceived in terms of the good things of life, and if, at the same time, you take the absolute demands of God with that religious seriousness which a monotheistic faith by its very nature (in contrast with polytheism) tends to foster, then the failure of the rewards to materialise is susceptible of another explanation in addition to that of the machinations of the evil power or powers. It is an explanation which is both obvious and adequate. It is that you have not been obedient enough. You must try harder. But what if, trying harder, you are still denied the rewards, and you are increasingly left only with the hope of their realisation in a world to come? Plainly under such circumstances the door is opened to some very unpleasant doubts. Not having the succours of God in this present life to confirm that you have done your duty, what guarantee have you that you have done it sufficiently to earn them in the next? Obviously,

---

[18]Source not traced. However, Zaehner makes the point that, "Unlike Muhammad, Zoroaster does not describe the joys of heaven in physical terms; the blessed attain to "long life", that is, presumably, eternal life and the Kingdom of the Good Mind; they will be blessed with ease and benefit and will be possessed of Wholeness and Immortality, God's supreme gifts to the faithful." Yet, in, for example, the Sassanian period, during which there was an attempt to return to a strict orthodoxy, which included—significantly for Farmer's thesis—a highly dualistic interpretation of Zoroaster's message, both heaven and hell "are thought of in material forms and the pure contemplation of God is rarely mentioned. Manushchihr [an influential high priest] almost goes out of his way to emphasise that the joys of heaven are exactly like the joys of earth except that there can be no real comparison between an infinite and a finite form of existence...Moreover, it is very definitely a place, not a state. It is "above"..."most brilliant, fragrant, pure and beautiful, most desirable and good, the place and abode of the gods. In it is all ease and pleasure, joy and bliss, a state of welfare greater and better than the greatest and highest welfare and pleasure on earth. In it there is neither need nor pain, nor misery, nor discomfort"...The soul will also enjoy the company of learned and pious friends and of wives who are fair and modest, devoted to their husbands and thrifty" (R. C. Zaehner, *The Dawn and Twilight of Zoroastrianism*, pp.57, 306-7). Cf. also the fragment of the Avesta concerning "The Soul's Fate at Death", quoted by Zaehner (pp.302-5); and R. C. Zaehner, *The Teachings of the Magi: A Compendium of Zoroastrian Beliefs* (London: Sheldon Press, 1975), p.144.—Ed.

there is no guarantee other than your own still more intensified efforts to obey the divine commandments, particularly as set forth in the teaching of the prophet who first called men to such obedience. And the more keenly sensitive you are to the absoluteness of the demands of God, and the more at the same time you crave for those personal rewards which, not having in this life, you are promised in the life to come, the more facile will be your mind, by a process familiar to the psychologist, in devising ways of, so to say, putting the screw on yourself and so firmly establishing your title to those rewards. But you will put it on in the form of demands which, although highly rigorous and exacting, are not beyond your power to perform. For example, what was originally a high demand for moral purity becomes gradually and unconsciously transformed into a demand for ritual and ceremonial purity. So there develops that familiar type of religion which finds its security in an exact and punctilious conformity to a code of behaviour and of ceremonial observance wrought out, supposedly on the basis of the original prophetic teaching, by subtle, earnest, casuistical minds.

This kind of thing increasingly characterised Iranian religion in the course of the centuries. It became a mass of legal and ceremonial requirements, formulated through finicky, casuistical debates. The purity of which the prophet Zoroaster had spoken in genuinely ethical terms, making fire its symbol, was transformed into a matter of precise external conformities and of ritual cleanness and uncleanness. A tariff of expiatory penalties, covering every offence, was elaborated, the penalties, as one perhaps might have expected on psychological grounds, being often of the severest kind. One should perhaps emphasise again that we are speaking of a *dominant* religious tendency. That there were other aspects of Zoroastrianism, that the strictness of its ethic contributed something, and even much, to the building up of a stable cultural and political life in Persia cannot be questioned; but it remains true that over the whole there is spread the blight of legalism, the perpetual strain of effort to conform to detailed prescriptions of conduct, and all the hardness and externalism and anxious self-righteousness which these bring;

and the religious root of all this is the unredeemed eudaemonism of which we have been speaking.[19]

So much for Zoroastrianism. It is not necessary to spend much time pointing out that the same three tendencies, though in a less clear and unqualified form, can be discerned in later Judaism and Islam. The main difference is that in Judaism and Islam the tendency towards a metaphysical dualism is kept in check by a much more explicitly realised and jealously guarded monotheistic belief. This is particularly true of Islam, of course. In later Judaism the tendency to dualism is much more clearly marked (probably because of the exposure of Judaism to Zoroastrian influence during the Captivity[20]), but here also it is kept in check by the dominant monotheistic tradition which comes down from before the exile and prevents any approach to the extremes reached in Zoroastrian belief. Satan and his angels in later Judaism are essentially creatures, subordinate to God. But if dualism as a theology is thus avoided, dualism as a problem for faith remains, as it must do if the succour of God is still thought of primarily in terms of the happiness

---

[19]E. Lehmann speaks in this connection of "an abstract rigidity, which will not adapt itself to life (and, indeed, in its senseless consequences, often runs counter to it) and a hardness that often amounts to brutality. Just as the administration of justice by the Persians was generally marked by cruelty, so there is to be discerned a certain crudity in the reckless way in which in their ethic they distinguished only between good and bad, leaving no room for the individual and spontaneous. Disinterested feelings counted for little; even in the religious feelings one misses the lyrical note, and feels the heavy pressure of legalism. It is significant that in the Avesta "religion" is called "the law"." Of the Zoroastrian doctrine of God, Lehmann writes: "There is no suggestion of mercy or grace in God; he is the world-judge and under compulsion to abide strictly by his own law; if the constitutive principle of the world is moral, the governing of it is strictly juristic" (Chantepie de la Saussaye, *Lehrbuch der Religionsgeschichte* bd.2, 4th edition, ed. by E. Lehmann & A. Bertholet [Tübingen: J. C. B. Mohr, 1924-5], pp.246, 221). Söderblom, in the passage already quoted from, has some sentences which suggest that this external, legalistic moralism, with its lack of an interior life, can be traced back to Zarathustra himself. "Zarathustra never perceived the opposition (of good and evil) within his own bosom...He never penetrated to the problems of the soul...Neither the corruptibility and vanity of existence nor distress of soul had brought him to the critical point when self-confidence and the natural man are slain, and man is born, if it be so, to a new existence...The conquest of self never entered into his ethical programme. The art of overcoming evil with good remained unknown to him. He declared, on the contrary: that he who is good to an evil person becomes evil himself and worthy of punishment...Man must learn discipline, order, and labour. But we hear little of any renewal of the heart" (*The Living God*, pp.210-11).
[20]Cf. R. C. Zaehner, *The Dawn and Twilight of Zoroastrianism*, pp.51-2.—Ed.

bestowed on the good man as an equivalent reward for his behaviour.[21] There is no way out of the problem of the suffering of the righteous on that basis. The two other tendencies, however, appear quite clearly in Islam and in later Judaism, namely, first, the postponement and projection of the rewards of the righteous to another world or another age, second, the elaboration of a ceremonial legalism. This latter is an outstanding character of both Islam and Pharisaic Judaism. Despite other noble elements in them, especially in later Judaism, they are both legalistic religions, requiring the punctilious performance of religious and moral duties and promising rewards to those who fulfil them if not in this world then in the next.

The Unification of Absolute Demand and Final Succour
In contrast with all this, we now turn to the way taken by the Christian revelation and faith—although it must be admitted that it is not always taken by empirical Christianity. Here the relation of the divine demand to the divine succour is reinterpreted in the light of a single profound truth, with the result that, instead of being set over against one another and kept in a kind of counterpoise by the balance-arm of reward, they are fused with one another in an inseparable unity. That truth is that the approach of God to the human spirit in an absolute claim upon him is at one and the same time his approach in a final succour. The supreme final blessedness of man is not something different from and added to his obedience, but it is merged in, is one with, that obedience. In the words of Christ, "my food is to do the will of him who sent me."[22] It is not something added to the doing of his will as a reward.

The statement just made, however, can serve only as a preliminary indication of the contrast with the kind of legalistic religion we have just been discussing. It does not carry us quite to the heart of the matter, though it points directly to it. Such a formula as "the fusion of the divine demand and succour" might be used to describe that austere type of religion described in

[21]Cf. J. Oman, *The Natural and the Supernatural*, pp.432-3.—Ed.
[22]Jn.4:34.

Revelation and Religion as "the religion of obligation",[23] wherein the tension between the divine demand and the divine succour is reduced by putting all the emphasis on obeying the divine will, with no favours asked or expected, and letting the idea of succour fall into the background. Such a formula might even be taken by some to be more or less identical to the doctrine that virtue is its own reward, a statement which, taken as it stands, always seems to me, in spite of its air of nobility, to be untrue, out of touch with the actual complexities of human nature and with the situations which confront it, and, in addition, as neat an expression of humanistic self-confidence and irreligion as one could devise. What we need to add, if we are to do fuller justice to the distinctive Christian view, is that the final blessedness of man is not in the doing of the divine will, but in the personal fellowship with God which the doing of it presupposes, expresses and fosters. Yet even this does not carry us far enough. We must ask what is the character of the personal fellowship made possible by the divine "drawing near" and self-disclosure as love, holy and saving in the midst of human life through Jesus Christ. It is only in such a relationship that the two elements of demand and succour really unite with one another without either being in any degree submerged in the other. Because God is love, his absolute demand is *for* love, and this means that man's sinful lovelessness is continuously exposed and condemned. God's goodness is thus extremely austere. But because he is love, the demand is not only the demand *for* love; it is also the demand *of* love. That is to say, it is not a matter of God laying his high requirements upon man, marking his obediences and disobediences with an awful all-seeing eye and meeting out equivalent rewards and penalties; rather, it is a matter of God approaching him with the sole intention of drawing him, here and now, into his highest life, which is the life of fellowship with God and with other men in God. Everything is thus brought within the one curve of God's holy purpose of love towards man. In all his approaches to men God is seeking to draw them within that curve. For men to be within it, within it in yielding to his absolute claim, within it in

---

[23]H. H. Farmer, *Revelation and Religion*, pp.139ff.

receiving his pardon for every failure so to yield, within it in knowing that they are within it and that nothing can take them out of it, *that* is their final succour, their final blessedness and peace. Thus in the apprehension of God as love through the revelation in Christ, the demand and succour become one. Obedience and trust merge with one another into a single personal relationship which has within it, even in the harshest circumstances, a distinctive blessedness and peace. A striking expression and illustration of this is to be found in the fourteenth chapter of John's Gospel. There is a continuous transition of thought between the divine commandments and the divine comfort and blessing, without any apparent sense of opposition or tension between the two ideas. This is possible because they are held together in a personal relationship of love, the love of God to the disciple and the disciple's answering love to God.

These statements may well sound, because of their brevity, somewhat pietistic. The only way wholly to obviate that would be to give them that fuller exposition which it is the task of a Christian dogmatic to provide. It will help, however, if we follow the line of thought we have pursued in this chapter, and observe how the unification of the two elements of the divine demand and succour in the Christian revelation and faith (which we have described) sets the religious life on a new line of development in respect of the three ways in which "legalistic religion" seeks to overcome its difficulties.

(1) In respect of dualism, we have said that in Islam and Judaism the tendency to a metaphysical dualism, which went to such lengths in Zoroastrianism, was held in check by a more explicitly realised and passionately held monotheistic faith. As noted above, even in Judaism (which probably owed something to Zoroastrian influence) Satan and all the powers of evil remain essentially creaturely, subordinate to God and destined, of course, to final ruin and defeat. Now it would appear that the New Testament writers, and more particularly Paul, share these beliefs in Satan and the powers of evil. Such powers are even regarded as the causes, or part-causes, of the

evils which overtake men, including physical disease and suffering.[24] However, it would seriously misrepresent the New Testament faith to suppose that this belief was in essence the same as that of contemporary Judaism. There is at least one vital difference, namely, whereas Judaism looked forward to the defeat of evil powers as lying wholly in the future (so that the world was thought of as lying to that extent outside the full divine succour now), the New Testament writers believed that that defeat had already been accomplished by God's saving action in Christ. The powers are already defeated once and for all in what can only be described as an act of cosmic redemption. Religiously, this amounts to the surrender of dualism in the very act of seeming to concede it. There is undoubtedly much that is puzzling in this whole range of New Testament belief. For example, what exactly is meant by "Satan", by the "rulers, authorities and powers of this dark world", "the spiritual forces of evil",[25] etc.? How exactly was the victory over them accomplished by Christ, especially in view of the fact that the victory already gained was regarded as somehow also not yet fully accomplished, but only to be so accomplished in some final consummation? These are matters into which we cannot here enter.[26] The important thing for the line of thought we are following emerges when we ask ourselves this question: What was the religious source of this confidence that the victory over the powers of evil had already been won, even though it was fully apparent that they were still operative in the world, and indeed in the life of the Christian himself? There is no doubt that it lay in part in that entirely new range of living, personal fellowship with God into which Paul and the other New Testament writers had entered through the revelation in Christ and of which we have been speaking. When once it begins to be grasped, however falteringly, that fellowship with the personal God in the doing of his will of love in obedience and trust is the highest blessedness of

---

[24]It is hardly necessary to give references; there are so many passages scattered throughout the epistles. For references and discussion, see A. D. Galloway, *The Cosmic Christ* (London: Nisbet, 1951), ch.4.

[25]Eph.6:12.

[26]Cf. H. H. Farmer, *The Word of Reconciliation*, pp.96ff.—Ed.

man, then it becomes possible livingly to know, and to have peace (that "peace of God which passes all understanding") in the knowledge that the most untoward happening, no matter what its cause, is no contradiction of, or barrier to the good purpose of God as it reaches out to the individual and offers itself to him in a present "I-Thou" relation of love. In other words, the conquest of Christ over "the powers", however difficult to conceive or to picture, is made apparent and continually verified in the fact that Christians are themselves "more than conquerors through him who loved us". Nothing, not even "the spiritual forces of evil" when they do their worst, can separate us from the love of God which is in Jesus Christ. What cannot any longer disrupt the soul's fellowship with God has already quite clearly been defeated. And if we ask why this profound and transforming experience should be so connected with the crucifixion of Christ, so that, as Paul says, it was through the cross that Christ "disarmed the powers and authorities, [and] made a public spectacle of them, triumphing over them",[27] the answer is surely in part that the love of God is there disclosed as coming and offering itself to man precisely through those evil events which the dualist view takes to indicate at least the temporary impotence and withdrawal of God's rule.

(2) Secondly, we turn to the eschatological hope. It is hardly necessary to say that this also has a central place in the Christian revelation and faith, as set before us in the New Testament. But the Christian revelation and faith set their own stamp upon it in accordance with the fundamental insight with which we are concerned. This is done in two ways. (a) Firstly, the Christian faith, while looking forward to the full realisation and consummation of the divine saving purpose beyond this world, does not, when it is true to the New Testament revelation, drive the contrast between this present world and the world to come so deep that the present world becomes, by contrast, a patch of almost atheistic wilderness to be got through as quickly as may be with no true

---

[27]Col.2:15.

present joy or victory of peace. Once again dualism is avoided.[28] The will of
God which is to be fully consummated in the hereafter can be known, served,
trusted and celebrated, in an immediate, present, personal fellowship with God
through Christ, even in the midst of the worst frustrations and sufferings. The
victory has already been won, though it is not yet complete. The divine
kingdom is here and now, though it is also yet to be; it is yet to be, yet also
here and now. This is, of course, the "realised eschatology" of the New
Testament, as C. H. Dodd has taught us to call it,[29] and there is no doubt that
it is something highly distinctive of the Christian faith. What we want to
emphasise particularly here is that in the New Testament experience the two
aspects, the now and the not yet, are not split from one another, but
interpenetrate and support one another. It is because the New Testament
writers can set the changes and the chances, the tribulations and the distresses
of this world in the context of the divine kingdom which lies beyond the limits
of this world, that, whilst in the midst of such evils, they could experience a
present blessedness and peace in their fellowship with God. Yet it is equally
true that it is only because they were thus able to have fellowship with God in
the midst of their sufferings that the consummation yet to be was a sustainable
certainty to them and not merely a vague intermittent aspiration or an excited
imagination of a compensatory good time to come.

(b) This has brought us to the second way in which the Christian
revelation sets its stamp upon the eschatological hope. Putting the legalistic
idea of an equation between righteousness and reward on one side and the life
of fellowship with God having already begun, the Christian hope, as
normatively set forth in the New Testament, is free from the eudaemonistic
and egotistic otherworldliness which has so often disfigured empirical
Christianity. What is looked forward to with such ardour of hope by the

---

[28]Dualism has, of course, often entered into Christian thought at this point, but it has come in
very largely from alien sources—for example, from the Hellenistic view of time and eternity
as opposed to one another in an "absolute qualitative difference". Indeed, what we are
saying is obviously closely related to the discussion of time and eternity in the last chapter
and should be read in that context.

[29] It might perhaps be better named "inaugurated eschatology".

reconciled man is not primarily his own reward, but rather the complete fulfilment of the divine will of holy love. No doubt his own highest life and blessedness, far exceeding anything that he now enjoys, is included in that fulfilment, but that is not at the centre of the picture, even though, in certain circumstances he may not improperly dwell upon it. The centre of the picture is the consummation of the divine will and victory. This is so because the transforming truth has been grasped that man's blessedness and joy is in the doing of the divine will in obedience and trust, and the fellowship with God that that involves. Hence, he can forget his own blessedness and joy and think only of that will and that victory. Thus it becomes possible for Paul to write that he could have wished himself "cursed and cut off from Christ for the sake of his brothers, those of my own race, the people of Israel",[30] in order that God's saving purpose of love towards them might be accomplished—a thought which is beyond the reach of legalistic religion.

(3) Finally, in respect of ceremonial legalism, this whole line of thought is cut off from its roots directly the eudaemonistic idea of the divine succour and the linking of it with the divine demand through reward are surrendered. God's demand and God's succour are made one in that fellowship with him which he himself brings into being by his own revelation of himself as holy love. No other assurance of participation in the blessedness of the realised divine kingdom than what is contained in the blessedness of that fellowship is required. To seek further assurance by trying to build up a claim through the punctilious observance of an increasingly elaborated code of duties would be to contradict and annul the whole relationship. And in any case, as we have seen, there is no assurance that way, but only the strain of perpetual effort to attain it; or, if it is attained, it is by means of a self-righteousness and self-complacency which is continually bringing down the divine demand to the level of man's own attainment, and so making him increasingly insensitive to its ever new and searching claims. On the other hand, and in contrast with this, there is, through the personal fellowship with God, which the revelation

---

[30]Rom. 9:3.

in Christ makes possible, a great increase in sensitivity to the divine claim, the sort of sensitivity which can neither be expressed through, nor fostered by, any kind of external code of behaviour, however casuistically elaborate, for it touches the innermost dispositions and impulses of the heart. Hence, there runs through the whole of his relationship with God the constant and unaffected sense that even the best righteousness of a man is but "filthy rags", that even when he has done that which it is his duty to do, he is still an unprofitable servant; wherefore his only hope and assurance is in the divine forgiveness which has already made itself known to him in Christ, a forgiveness which, taking no account whatever of earning or merit, is freely given and must be daily sought and humbly received.

All this brings us to the verge of deep matters which it is beyond our purpose here to discuss. I will only point out, without developing the thought, that we can discern in the central New Testament experience of forgiveness that profound unification of the elements of the divine demand and the divine succour in a new personal relation with God which is so uniquely characteristic of the Christian revelation. Whatever be our reflective formulation of the experience in a theology of the atonement, there is no question that at the heart of it is the encounter, through the cross of Christ, with a divine will of holy love, which, in its absolute claim upon man, utterly condemns him in his lovelessness, and, in its infinitely costing self-giving, draws him in forgiveness to itself. Thus the whole realm of rewards and penalties disappears from view. Each element is essential to the full impact of the other, and both together, in their mutual, inseparable implication are essential to the whole revelation and to the new relationship of man to himself which God, through it, calls into being. For it is only in the light of God's infinite claim that the full need for, and wonder of his forgiveness can be apprehended; and it is equally true that it is only through the cost and wonder of the proffered forgiveness that the "breadth, and length, and depth, and height" of the divine love, and, therefore, of its infinite claim, can be apprehended. Here our concepts and propositions once again break up and disjoin that which, in the unity of the personal encounter with God, are inseparably one.

5

MORALITY AND RELIGION

The second duality or opposition to be examined under the more general heading of "God and the Self" is that of morality and religion. The relation between morality and religion has, of course, been much discussed from a number of different angles. In accordance with our general plan in this work, our purpose is the limited one of considering certain tensions or oppositions which are apt to arise at the point where morality and religion interpenetrate one another, and, further, to consider the relation of the Christian revelation and faith to them.

The phrase just used ("at the point where morality and religion interpenetrate one another") might be taken to imply that I regard it as in some degree accidental and adventitious whether they do or do not interpenetrate one another. But that is by no means intended. On the contrary, I hold that there is an inevitable and profound interconnection between them. The truth of this statement is not impugned by the fact that they have apparently sometimes shown a tendency to fall apart from one another. Thus, on the one hand, men have sometimes professed and defended a purely secular, humanist morality, and, on the other hand, they have sometimes cultivated and enjoyed states of mind which they have claimed to be religious, but which, apparently, bear no direct or central relation to moral requirements and standards. But even so, I think that this tendency to separate must not be taken at its face value, for certainly morality and religion have had a much more powerful tendency to come together and interpenetrate one another. The association of religion with morality all down the ages of man's history—an association much more immediate, close, continuous and universal than its association with any other major function of man's life—bears witness that there *is* something inherent in them which continually brings and binds them together.

It might be said that the question is simply one of the definition of terms, that it all depends on how we define religion and how we define morality. And that, in a sense, is true. But definitions, though they may legitimately depend in some degree upon choice, cannot be purely arbitrary; they must bear some relation to the facts of the field under discussion. Religion, no doubt, can be so understood and defined that it follows, by definition, that it can function without even an implicit reference to, still less any close, integral connection with morality. But, in that case, it would be legitimate to ask whether it is rightly so understood and defined, whether it *is* religion which is being talked about, essential, substantival religion as it livingly and spontaneously wells up in the human spirit, and not something which merely looks like religion, or is in frequent association with it.[1] Similarly, morality can be so understood and defined that it follows by definition that there is nothing in it which has any affinity with, or in any way points towards, or predisposes it to religion. But then again, in that case, we may properly ask whether such an understanding and definition has really explored and grasped the full range and depth of the moral consciousness of man. In what follows we will develop this line of thought.

The Moral Consciousness and High Morality

We begin by looking briefly at the moral consciousness. The first thing we need to note is that the words "moral" and "morality" are by no means clearly defined in the ordinary man's mind. In common usage the words refer in the main to the obligations and responsibilities which arise out of living in a group. The group prescribes, through its traditions, customs or codes of conduct, certain kinds of behaviour in the interest of group harmony, and the man who lives in accordance with what is thus required is generally

---

[1]See his comments on the importance of distinguishing between "substantival" and "adjectival" religion, in *Revelation and Religion*, pp.163ff.—Ed.

recognised as a "moral" person. Now, if morality be so understood, it is certainly easy enough to think that there is no inherent or necessary connection between morality and religion. For, the facts show that it is possible to be at least an averagely decent member of one's group, loyal and co-operative in one's social relationships, without being a religious person at all. The facts show that such qualities can be the result merely of being well-trained in youth, and even of congenital gifts of temperament, of sympathy and imagination, not to speak of a congenital lack of "devil". Nor do they receive any the less moral approval from men because that is their origin. Indeed, the question of their origin and source is not usually raised at all. It is enough that the person concerned fulfils his group obligations and so is constituted what everybody thinks of as a morally respectable individual. Having said that, I would wish to maintain that there is *latent* in most men's minds, and ready, in appropriate circumstances and under appropriate stimulus, to come to the surface, a much deeper and more discriminating sense of morality, and what it means to be a morally good person, as distinct from being merely one who "measures up" tolerably well, for whatever reason, to social standards and requirements. In saying this, one must not over-idealise the ordinary man. It is possible that for some, and even many people the appropriate occasion and stimuli never occur, or, if they do occur, the resultant sense of a morality which goes beyond, and is deeper and fuller, than mere social pressures and conformities is extremely weak and transient. Possibly for many, such a sense only emerges in their minds, and then but momentarily, when they encounter some great moral personality who does unmistakably embody a *higher* morality than one of merely social conformity, and for whom they cannot but feel admiration and even reverence. Something within them says, in effect if not in so many words, "Now that is a *truly* moral person, that is the sort of person I ought to be", and this although they may make no effort, and have no intention of making any effort, to be like him or her. Thus another range of morality than that of social conformity momentarily discloses itself to them and they feel its authority over them.[2] It is this further range of morality, this higher morality, which goes beyond the primary morality of group requirements and conformities, that we must examine, seeking to make explicit what is implicit in it, if we are to see the deep interconnection between morality and religion, and are to understand the way in which they do inevitably tend to interpenetrate one another.

If then we examine this higher morality, this morality which is pre-eminently exemplified in serious and sensitive moral personalities, but which also finds some echo and endorsement in varying degrees in the moral consciousness of the plain man, we find, I suggest, the following elements more or less clearly present within it.[3] I shall state them briefly and somewhat dogmatically without taking up any further problems and questions which they raise.[4]

(1) The morally sensitive man is conscious that he is confronted by, and is apprehending (however imperfectly) an objective moral order of some sort which stands over against, and is independent of, not only his *own* desires and preferences, but also those of all other persons whatsoever. When he judges this or that to be " good" or "right" in the pre-eminently moral sense of those two terms, he emphatically does not mean that he happens at that moment to like it or desire it or approve it, simply because he happens to have a particular kind of temperament or taste, or has had a certain kind of upbringing, or is in a particular mood; rather he intends to say that goodness or rightness does in fact characterise it whether or not he or anybody else, now or at any other time, likes, desires or approves of it. The fact that serious moral persons are prepared to discuss moral questions with great earnestness, whereas they would regard disputes over preferences and tastes as a waste of time, or at best a diversion, has rightly been regarded as an indication of this implicit claim of

---

[2]Cf. H. Bergson, *The Two Sources of Morality and Religion*, tr. by R. A. Audra and C. Brereton (Westport, Connecticut: Greenwood Press, 1974), pp.23f.

[3]He notes in the margin: " This is not to say, of course, that the moral subject should himself be able to formulate them and bring them before his mind."—Ed.

[4]Some of what follows is a repetition of points made in *Revelation and Religion*.—Ed.

the moral judgement to objectivity. Differences in moral judgement are felt to be significant, so that there is a duty to try to resolve them, and failure to do so leaves a sense of disquietude and frustration. How this claim of moral judgement to report an objective order is to be interpreted, whether it can be validated against a purely "subjectivist" interpretation of it, are of course questions which have been, and are, very much under discussion—but it is beside our purpose to pursue them. We are interested in what has been called the phenomenology of morality, and from that point of view, it can hardly be questioned that the claim is implicitly there.

(2) The awareness of the moral person that when he makes a specifically moral value-judgement he is apprehending an objective order is not done full justice merely by saying that he feels that contradictions between moral value judgements ought to be discussed and if possible resolved, that it is not a futile waste of time to argue about their truth or falsity, though to say that may be a very good way of bringing this home to the mind. Such a way of putting it is much too abstract to be adequate. After all a similar statement could be used to describe the awareness of objective truth in respect of the most abstruse conclusions of pure mathematics. But in any really crucially significant life-situation the objective reference of the moral judgement is *not*, I think, apprehended in the same way as that of a judgement in pure mathematics. However, as soon as a moral value is discerned in a situation, that situation is not apprehended as having merely disclosed just one more factor in addition to others in it, but as having now changed radically as a whole, so that it is now in its relation to the self a new situation. There are three elements in this radical change. First, the moral value is apprehended, however dimly, as revealing a deeper stratum, so to speak, of the environing world than that which presents itself apart from it. Second, it is apprehended as speaking to, and calling into action, a deeper, more central, more permanently significant element in the personal life than that which is involved in the ordinary utilities and routines of living. Finally, it is apprehended as entering into a certain finite distinctive relation to the will, the relation of "*unconditional* oughtness" or "obligation". Hence when the morally sensitive person makes a

specifically moral value-judgement he becomes conscious of a certain quality of crisis. As unconditional, or in Kant's phrase "categorical", it cuts, in principle, and may at any time cut in fact, right across even the most settled habits and adjustments of life, across what are otherwise perfectly legitimate desires and satisfactions. The sensitive man is implicitly aware of this, even if he does not formulate it to himself in explicit terms. The categorical nature of the moral imperative has, of course, been widely discussed since Kant insisted on it and hardly needs to be developed. All we are concerned to maintain is simply that Kant, in his assertion of it, was doing no more than reporting or describing something which is a fact characteristic of any sensitive man's moral experience.

There are, however, one or two things implicit in the unconditional "oughtness" of the moral value-judgement which are perhaps not so evident. To these we now turn.

(3) The awareness of the unconditionality of the moral obligation involves the awareness of being bound by it, independently of anything that any external, empirical authority claiming to direct conduct may say. Even if family, group, state, or church enjoin the contrary, your own moral judgement, still binds you. In other words, it is an essential part of man's being a moral subject that he is called in the last resort to walk by his own insight, by his own internal perception of obligation, however crude and undeveloped and even perverted this may be. In short, to use some phrases of Oman's, it means that he is subject to his own self-legislation in his own self-conscious world.[5] Unconditionality, internality, independence are in this sphere correlative terms. So stated, this may seem to be the product of the deductive theorising of the philosopher, but our point is that it is in fact a deliverance of the highest moral experience from Socrates onwards; yet such experience is not so high as to be remote from, or to find no echo in, the mind of the plain man. The latter is no stranger to the feeling, however vague, that an Athanasius who stands out *contra mundum* for conscience sake is, in so standing out (that is, apart

---

[5]See J. Oman, *Grace and Personality* (London: Collins, Fontana, 1960), ch.5.

from any judgement which may be made upon the rightness or wrongness of what he is standing out for) morally admirable; and he feels this not less strongly, but rather more strongly, if he suspects that he would not himself have the courage to make such a stand in like circumstances.

(4) The awareness of the unconditionality of the moral judgement involves the awareness of being bound by it *independently of one's feelings and desires*, no matter how strong and clamant they may be. This does not mean, of course, that a moral judgement, simply because it is a *moral* judgement, must be apprehended as necessarily cutting across such feelings and desires; the point is simply that, if and when it does so, they have no further standing in the matter and must be set on one side. It is this collision of the moral "ought", because of its unconditionality, with the life of natural instinct and feeling which, perhaps more vividly than anything else, evokes in the moral subject the sense of having both the task and, at least in some degree, the capacity to *rule himself.* He becomes aware of himself as a being who is not under compulsion to act merely as a result of impulse and desire, but has an inward power of control which can, in some measure, inhibit, resist and direct the flow of the instinctive life and determine behaviour as the moral ought requires. This is why a vow enters so intimately into any high moral conduct of life. In a vow the serious moral nature acknowledges and endorses the call to the self implicit in the unconditional imperative to govern, to stand, so to say, upright in the midst of the flux of its interior life. In a vow a man promulgates an edict to the kingdom of his soul and to every unruly element that dwells therein.[6]

I have purposefully not used the word "freedom" in describing this aspect of the moral awareness because of the many theoretical problems which that term is apt to raise in the mind, problems which it is beyond our purpose here to discuss. We are interested only in the "phenomenology" of the moral consciousness, and we want simply to insist that, certainly in the high moral consciousness, and also, though perhaps less vividly and consistently, in the

---

[6]Cf. H. H. Farmer, *The Healing Cross*, ch.3.—Ed.

moral consciousness of the plain man, the "ought" does carry with it a strong sense of "can", of both a call and some capacity for self-control and self-direction in the face of the most clamant feelings and desires. Furthermore, it does so, not through the analysis of concepts, nor through a merely traditional and induced association of ideas, but through something much deeper and more immediate, namely, the profound implication in one another of the awareness of "unconditional oughtness" and the awareness of being a responsible self who is, in some degree, in charge of his own destiny.

(5) The awareness of the unconditionality of the moral judgement involves an awareness of being bound by it independently, not only of impulse and desire, but also of all other deliberately planned and willed ends. The importance of this point is that it brings into view the fact that there is in the serious moral life, in "high morality", always a strong tendency to seek inward unification. A man may school and discipline the flow of moment to moment impulses and desires in the interest of some end he is pursuing *without* any specifically moral valuation entering in. He may forego delights and live laborious days to make money, or to pass an examination, or to win a race, or simply because a disciplinary and punitive authority requires it. His life may have within it at any one time, or at different times, several such purposive structures or patterns, and, in so far as he resolutely follows them, his life may at quite a number of points take on a quasi-moral quality which evokes admiration. But when a specifically moral end enters in, it presents itself, because of the unconditional "oughtness" which attaches to it, as something exclusive and tyrannical, as claiming that all other willed ends must be adjusted to it, even if this should involve something like a revolution in the whole structure of a person's life. And this is so even if the other willed ends have been in some measure morally evaluated. In the latter case, a conflict of moral loyalties may develop, and when that happens the need to achieve some unity of plans and ends under the moral "ought" or "oughts" can be very acutely felt by a serious moral nature; for *prima facie*, unconditional "oughts" cannot compromise with one another.

It is for this reason that the endeavour of moral philosophers to bring moral ends into a systematic unity, ranging them perhaps in ordered subordination under a supreme end or *summum bonum*, must be judged to have a far more than merely theoretical interest even though it may be pursued in a very abstract and theoretical way. As Hartmann says, unity of principles is in many spheres merely a postulate of thought, whereas unity of moral ends is a postulate of life and conduct. The more a man consciously and seriously realises himself to be a morally responsible self under the unconditional authority of moral norms, the more vividly he becomes aware of the need for unification, for internal coherence and stability, and the more painfully burdensome he feels the lack of such unification to be.

It will be evident from this analysis of "high morality", if we may so call it—morality, that is to say, which rises above social requirements and conformities—how great an affinity it has with living religion, and how inevitable, therefore, has been their interpenetration in human history.[7] In high morality there is the awareness of some sort of objective moral order which is deeper and more ultimate in itself, and also speaks to a deeper and more ultimate element in the self, than anything involved in the more immediate, routine adjustments of man to his world; in religion there is the awareness of the encounter with God and of the crucial significance of that encounter for a man's whole life and being and destiny; in high morality there is the recognition of the unconditional authority of the moral "ought"; in religion there is the apprehension of the absolute claim or demand of God.[8] In high morality there is the awareness of the call, inherent in the unconditional "ought", to walk by one's own insight independently of all external authorities; in religion there is the strong sense that in all circumstances one "must obey God rather than men!"[9] In high morality there is the awareness of the call to, and the capacity within man to rule the life of natural instinct

---

[7]See H. H. Farmer, *The World and God*, pp.46ff.—Ed.
[8]See ibid., pp.13ff.; *God and Men*, pp.51ff.; *Towards Belief in God*, pp.50f., 148.—Ed.
[9]Acts 5:29. Cf. the Apostles' answer to the Jewish authorities in Acts 4:19: "*Judge for yourselves* whether it is right in God's sight to obey you rather than God."

and desire; in religion there is a like awareness of the call and the capacity to bring everything into obedience to God; in both, this awareness often finds expression in the making of vows. Just as in high morality there is the strongly felt need for inner unification, so also the same need is felt in living religion.[10]

I propose now to consider three oppositions or tensions which are apt to disclose themselves in "high morality". We shall observe that in each case morality comes as it were to the very threshold of religion, perhaps closer than at any other point, but that so long as it remains at the threshold, and does not pass right over into it, there is no reconciliation of opposites, no resolution of the tension. We shall then briefly indicate the way in which the Christian revelation and faith provides such a reconciliation or resolution. Each of the three tensions has to do with fundamental points in the analysis of the moral consciousness which we have made. The three are: the tension between the "good" and the "right"; the tension between "risk" and "security"; the tension between "being" and "doing".

The Tension Between the Good and the Right

We begin with the tension between the "good" and the "right".[11] Students of ethics have of course been long familiar with the distinction between the categories of the "good" and the "right" and with the cognate distinction between a utilitarian or calculative ethic in which the "good" operates as the dominant category and a duty ethic in which the "right" operates as the dominant category. Broadly speaking, according to a utilitarian or calculative view of the moral life there are certain ends which the moral judgement

---

[10]See his discussion in *Revelation and Religion*, ch.10.—Ed.

[11](a) Because Farmer indicates his dissatisfaction with the argument concerning the "good" and the "right" in the Gifford lectures, (b) because there are sections of the argument which have been removed or crossed out, and (c) because he produced a fully revised version for his 1957 Alex Wood Memorial Lecture, *The Christian Person and Morality*, which he was happy to publish, sections of the latter lecture have simply been reproduced here. To understand Farmer's thought on the issues discussed, readers should consult both *The Christian Person and Morality* and "The 'Good' and the 'Right'", in A. Sampson (ed.), *This War and Christian Ethics* (Oxford: Blackwell, 1940), pp.59-79.—Ed.

declares to be intrinsically valuable or good. The decision as to what ought to be done in any given situation is reached or should be reached, according to this view, by assessing the probable consequences of different possible lines of relevant action and choosing that which seems likely to produce the greatest amount of good or the least amount of evil. The action which, so far as can be calculated will produce the greatest good or the least evil is morally obligatory upon us, is the "right" action for us. The "right" thus becomes the category subordinate to, derivative from, the category of the "good". The other view tends to move in the opposite direction. It puts the emphasis on the capacity of the moral judgement to discern intuitively, though not necessarily without reflection, that a certain way of acting in relation to a given situation is right and binding or wrong and prohibited independently of what the consequences may appear likely to be. Often there is implicitly in this a belief that the consequences of such right action cannot finally be evil, but such belief is a matter of faith not of clear prevision and calculation, and does not enter as a determining factor into the decision between the alternatives of action which are open. It is not the envisaged good results which make right action, as on the utilitarian view, but rather the rightness of the action which ensures that the results will be good in spite of all appearance to the contrary.

There is no doubt that a purely calculative or utilitarian ethic can give a good account of itself. It covers a good deal of everyday morality, and the moral life can apparently attain a commendable level of loyalty and seriousness with such an ethic as its only declared basis. But I want to suggest that it inevitably encounters certain difficulties, and reveals in consequence certain weaknesses, which cannot be overcome so long as it adheres strictly to its utilitarian premises and definitions.

Thus, in all but relatively narrow and simple situations—"closed" situations we might call them—there is the immense difficulty of estimating with any accuracy and confidence what are likely to be the results of various possible lines of action. In complex "open" situations such an estimate seems to require a knowledge of causal connections, both immediate and remote, which we do not and cannot possess. This incapacity is due not only to the immense complexity of the situations in relation to which many of our most difficult and fateful moral decisions have to be taken, but also to the fact that the sphere of moral decision is largely the sphere of personal relations in which the unpredictable reactions and choices of an immense number of other free persons will play a large part. It might be said that, true as this is, it cannot be helped; probability is the guide of life, and therefore we must be content, here as elsewhere, to make the best, if admittedly precarious, estimate of probabilities that the meagreness of our knowledge and the urgency of the situation permits and act accordingly. But such comment and advice will hardly allay the burden and anxiety, even anguish, of moral decision in situations which are fraught with destiny for other persons and in which our action will clearly be a, perhaps the, crucially deciding factor. A purely utilitarian and calculative account of the moral life has nothing to say to a serious and sensitive moral nature in that sort of situation.

Again, suppose a man sets out on a course of action exclusively on the basis of a rational estimate of probable good or evil consequences, and suppose that, as he pursues it, events seem to show that his estimate was wrong, what is to save him from a continuous and serious loss of moral tenacity and energy in pursuing the course in question?—if, that is, he remains strictly within the bounds of a purely calculative approach. It may be said in reply to this that a man should not after all pursue any course of action too obstinately; he should be ready to acknowledge and learn from his miscalculations as he goes along and shift course accordingly. But the matter is not so simple as that. Just because the estimation of consequences can be so precarious, and ought to take into account more remote and delayed results as well as those which are more immediate and obvious, there is always the possibility that the more immediate and obvious results of a man's action are deceptive and that he ought in fact to keep on course in spite of them; but then we must ask from what source are the conviction, courage and tenacity to be drawn to do this, if the whole thing is kept strictly within the limits of the argument, within the limits, that is to say, of a purely human assessment of probable results? My point is that there is a certain disparity between the courage and tenacity which characterise high and serious moral purpose and the basing of morality exclusively on the calculation of results.

Finally, an ethic based exclusively on the estimation of consequences seems necessarily to imply the principle that ends justify the means; no sort of action is ruled out on that basis. But this is a principle which, I venture to say, a sensitive moral nature cannot but recoil from and repudiate, both in its general statement and in those concrete exemplifications of it which are almost certainly sooner or later to occur in any attempt to put such a purely calculative ethic consistently into practice. Sooner or later such an ethic will prescribe actions from which the whole moral being recoils, and if the actions are carried through, as in consistency with an exclusively calculative viewpoint they ought to be, there is left in a serious and sensitive moral nature a distressing and paralysing feeling of moral failure, and even degradation and guilt, which nothing can allay except perhaps an increasing moral insensitisation of the mind. The obvious illustration of this is the horrible things which war, even when it is waged for relatively good ends, requires men to do; the destruction of Hiroshima and Nagasaki, for example, was justified by those who ordered it, as well as later by others, on the ground of the balance of good or least evil consequence which it was calculated it would produce.[12] Nor was there anything morally unsound in this position if such calculation is in fact the only proper basis of action. On such a basis the only relevant criticism is that the calculation was wrong, but that is not so much a matter of morals as of intelligence.

How then are these weaknesses to be overcome? The answer I give is that they can be overcome only as the other category, the category of "right", not defined in terms of "conduciveness to the good", asserts itself in, and makes its distinctive impact upon, the moral consciousness. And this, I suspect, is how in fact they are overcome in serious minds, even when such minds try to interpret their moral experience in purely calculative terms.

---

[12]Cf. H. H. Farmer, "The 'Good' and the 'Right'", pp.61ff.—Ed.

We may see how this is so by taking note of three elements in the impact which the category of right makes upon the mind when it asserts itself in the moral consciousness. (a) First, it expresses and conveys to the mind, as part of its essential meaning, a peculiarly binding sense of the absolute, unconditional obligation resting upon the will, an obligation whose magisterial authority transcends and cannot be construed merely in terms of conduciveness to good results. Indeed, by its arrival it seems to put the very notion of calculating consequences out of countenance. I think that anyone who examines his own consciousness will perceive that the word "right" does not simply signify "conducive to the good", which is what it can mean in a purely calculative ethic; it carries with it this strange, deep, ultimate relation of binding "oughtness" to the deepest and most ultimate thing in the human person which is his will.

(b) This brings me to the second element which is that, in W. G. de Burgh's words, "people are much more profoundly influenced by the plea to do what will promote good."[13] Such a plea seems to penetrate to the springs of moral enthusiasm, energy and tenacity. It evokes *feeling* in a way that an invitation or exhortation to make a reasoned assessment of probable good or bad consequences does not.[14] There is implicit in it more of the sense of a call coming from a deeper and more ultimate reality and speaking to a deeper level of the self than anything involved in the ordinary choices, adjustments and prudences of life. It is in accordance with this that the apprehension of "right" always tends to carry with it a sense of what has been called "the higher expediency", the faith that the results of doing what is right must in the long run be good, even though it is impossible at the moment to see how.

(c) The third element in the awareness of right or wrong is the element of intuitive immediacy. In the making of a moral decision you come to a point where you just know, it is "borne in upon you", as the saying is, that this is the right action for you which you are under obligation to do. This point may

---

[13]W. G. de Burgh, *From Morality to Religion* (London: Macdonald and Evans, 1938), p.122.
[14]Cf. H. H. Farmer, "The 'Good' and the 'Right'", pp.63ff.—Ed.

be illustrated and emphasised by taking note of the fact that, whilst the consideration of consequences ought to enter into the making of a moral decision, nevertheless it is the sense of right that is usually left in possession of the field. Into the making up of your mind there enter a forecasting and assessing of the probable results of different possible lines of action or inaction, an awareness of certain goods or values to be pursued by appropriate means; on the other hand, there is also an awareness that certain acts or relationships, or types of act or relationship, are intrinsically right or binding or intrinsically wrong and forbidden, regardless of consequences. And out of the interplay of these two kinds of awareness there emerges an intuitive judgement of what is right for you; but you cannot justify this judgement, or the strength of the obligation with which it is felt to bind you, merely by reciting the various considerations which have in fact entered into the process of its formation: the decision could not have been reached without such considerations, but when it is reached it seems to contain something of which they fall short. "Here stand I, I can do not other, so help me God."

It is this triple impact of the idea of right which in practice saves a calculative ethic from the weaknesses indicated earlier. Thus it offers a check upon the principle that the ends justify the means, which otherwise cannot be kept out of such an ethic and from which, as I have said, a morally sensitive nature recoils. Again, it provides a source of moral energy and drive, of persistency in a moral enterprise, even when the anticipated and hoped for results are proving meagre and disappointing. In exacting moral enterprises the people who count most are often those who have a strong sense of right and of the unconditional claim upon the will which it carries. No doubt such people can have their own peculiar faults: an unteachable and egotistically obstinate fanaticism sometimes masquerades as moral tenacity; but that does not affect the point. Finally, the burden of moral decision in "open" and complex situations in which action is bound profoundly to affect the course of events and the lives and destinies of men, but in which some action must be taken without any clear vision or certainty as to its results, is at least lightened when the category of right enters in, for that, as I have said, calls into play the faith in the "higher expediency".

That a calculative ethic has to move over into an ethic or right which cannot be construed in purely calculative terms, if it is to be rescued from its otherwise unavoidable weaknesses, is, I think, in accord with the general sense of mankind. Most people would agree, partly from their own experience and partly from the observations of others, that, amidst all the complexities and perplexities of the practical moral life and the clear obligation not to act blindly but always to weigh the consequences of what they do, there may confront them at any time, and almost certainly there will confront them at some time, an intuitively apprehended obligation of right. Moreover, most, I think, would feel, when they meet an instance of a man acting in costing loyalty to such an obligation, that they are in the presence of a very high, perhaps the highest, manifestation of the man's moral nature—the deeps of moral feeling would be in some measure stirred in them also, even though their own moral judgement did not endorse the action in question and even though they were conscious that if, in like circumstances, it did, they themselves would probably not prove capable of a like steadfastness or moral purpose. A vivid illustration of what we have in mind may be found in the frightful moral decision and choice which Hugo depicts in *Les Misérables*, whereby Jean Valjean deliberately goes back to the hell of the galleys rather than allow an old, half-witted tramp, on whom none depend, whom none would mourn, a burden to his fellows, and with only a few useless years to live, be sent there in his place through a false identification; and this even though doing so will mean the collapse of the industry he has built up and on which the whole town depends; will mean, that is to say, want, unemployment, hunger and suffering for men, women and children; will mean the leaving of his little orphan ward uncared for and undefended in the midst of unscrupulous enemies. On any sane estimate of consequences, to "lie low" and say nothing would be productive of least evil, for not even justice was involved, inasmuch as Valjean's own original sentence to the galleys was bitterly unjust. Yet the compelling sense of the utter and absolute wrongness of so doing obstinately remains, and in the end Valjean bows to it, goes back to the galleys and leaves the doddering half-wit to potter along the roads and hedges a little longer. The story is fictional, but most people will feel that it does throw into high relief the sort of thing that may happen at any time in real life, namely, that an inescapable sense of right or wrong may emerge and cut across considerations of consequence, binding the will; they will feel also that it gives vivid expression, as Hugo plainly intends it to do, to their feeling that in such a decision and deed a person attains a moral stature and dignity not otherwise possible.[15]

We must now turn to consider the relation of religion, and in particular of the Christian revelation and faith, to these matters. I want to suggest that a distinctive contribution of the Christian person as such to moral matters, a contribution which is independent of the views he holds on particular problems, lies in the strong sense of right which he continuously introduces into them, thus helping to lift them above the purely utilitarian level, with all its attendant weaknesses, into which everyday morality so easily lapses. But the contribution does not end there. That it does not end there becomes apparent when we ask why the Christian person brings with him this strong sense of right, when we ask what is its source. We may best approach the answer to this question and so take our exploration a step further by now taking note of the fact that an ethic of right, taken by itself, also reveals difficulties which so long as they are not met can be a source of weakness in the moral life.

Thus, first, to pursue a course of action in defiance of consequences, despite its manifest heroism, inevitably takes on to a thoughtful mind a disturbing appearance of sheer unreason. It might seem indeed to be almost the definition of rational behaviour to assess in advance the results of different courses of action and to choose accordingly, adjusting one's actions if and so far as the anticipated results do not materialise. That no doubt is one reason why on the whole a utilitarian ethic of good has always had a strong attraction

---

[15]See ibid., pp.63ff.; Cf. also H. H. Farmer, *The Healing Cross*, pp.109ff—Ed.

for moral philosophers, and why Greeks for example on the whole adhered to it. Second, the recognition of an absolute obligation if need should arise to act contrary to the common moral judgements and sanctions of one's group, to resist every empirical authority which enjoins a different course, to be in short a Socrates or an Athanasius *contra mundum*. Now I do not think it is possible, or right, for a sensitive moral nature not to feel that thus to isolate oneself from one's fellows and their ethical judgements is both morally suspect and spiritually perilous. Certainly to anyone wanting to be a reasonable person, to live in the light of the universalities of reason and not to be at the mercy of merely private impulses or unconscious anti-herd compulsions, such a position is a very uncomfortable one. Third, an ethic of right taken by itself seems to contain an implicit contradiction, for it seems at one and the same time to assert and deny the significance of the individual human person. It asserts it because it insists, as we have just said, that the moral subject should, if need be, stand out alone in the midst of his group, an Athanasius *contra mundum*, and that is obviously to attribute to the individual a very high significance indeed in human affairs and in the process of history. But it seems also to deny it in that a readiness to disregard all calculable consequences involves in principle a readiness to plunge both the self and other selves, if need be, to death and destruction, from which, for all that the ethic of right taken in isolation can say, there is no resurrection.

If these difficulties are not being continually overcome they are bound to be a potential source of weakness in the moral life. How are they to be overcome? I want now to suggest that they can only be really adequately met by the moral life passing over into, and becoming dynamically one with, a religious faith, and more particularly a theistic religious faith. Such a faith, if it is to meet these difficulties, would need to include at least three corresponding beliefs.

First, it would need to include a belief in a divine mind and will of righteousness overshadowing, and dynamically participant in, human history and guaranteeing that the ultimate consequences of obedience to the right will be good. To act on any other basis than that of a reasoned estimate of probable results seems to be a surrender of one of the prime uses of reason, and that too at a point where one's whole being as a rational person is so to say focalising and unifying itself in a responsible act of the will. That being so, I do not think that the sense of acting reasonably and responsibly in obeying the right whatever the consequences can be fully restored except by interpreting such obedience as obedience to and faith in an intelligent will of a higher order which is at work in history and sees the end from the beginning, i.e. as obedience to and faith in God.

Second, it would need to include a belief that this divine will, thus active in history, may, in pursuit of its ends, disclose itself in a call to an individual, or a small group of individuals, to break away from the majority of their contemporaries. In other words, the readiness to go counter to the common moral judgements of one's community, which is in principle required by an ethic of right, can only be made tolerable to a sensitive mind by a sense of religious vocation, by the faith, that is to say, that a minority of a few, or even one, is sometimes the chosen and called agent of a divine will of righteousness which is seeking thus to serve the good of all. Such a faith does not lack empirical evidence in its support. It is almost a truism that the agent of moral and spiritual progress in human affairs has very often been an individual who in the first instance stands alone in the midst of mankind—the solitary prophet—and draws strength so to do from the sense of being under call from God. It would appear, therefore, to have been a sound instinct which led those tribunals of World War II which were given the impossible task of adjudging the genuineness of conscientious refusal of military service to propose, as one test, the question whether the refusal of the individual concerned was part of a religious outlook. That is to say, the tribunal sought to ascertain whether or not a person's refusal to participate in war was imbued with a sense of religious obligation.[16]

---

[16]It should be noted that Farmer was, since the breakout of war in 1914, "among those who [had] decided that henceforth they [would] under no circumstances participate in war." He tells us that he was a pacifist "in the face of heavy pressure both from within one's own mind and without from one's friends" (*The Christian Person and Morality*, p.5). See also "The

Third, the implicit contrariety in an ethic of right of seeming both to assert and deny the significance of the individual can only be overcome by the belief that the divine will which calls to the individual for his absolute obedience at any cost to himself and to others, does not, in so doing, treat human persons as mere instruments or vehicles of its ongoing purpose, even if very important instruments or vehicles, but does in fact also value them in and for themselves as persons. This belief obviously requires the further belief that the divine purpose which is thus at work in this world nevertheless transcends this world in its ultimate fulfilment and consummation, for, if it does not do so, it is impossible to see how human selves can be of intrinsic value to God and not mere instruments and vehicles which are used and then cast on one side. I feel sure that only such faith in a divine will which values men in and for themselves and which transcends this world in its ultimate consummation can permanently preserve an ethic of right from sooner or later losing heart and then perhaps, as a defence against such loss of heart, developing a certain hard indifference to the fate of individual men and women. I have, I think, seen this illustrated in the personal history of certain idealistic but secularly-minded young communists.

An ethic of right, then, overcomes its difficulties and so gains in consistency and power if it is taken up into a theistic faith, some of the elements of which I have just indicated. I want now to go on to say something which will take us one step farther along the line of our thought and bring us in sight of its conclusion. It is that an ethic of right gains even more in consistency and power when it is taken up into a specifically Christian type of theistic belief, or rather let us say when it is taken up into the specifically Christian life of faith and discipleship. For that faith and discipleship has at its heart the conviction that God has acted, and indeed is still acting, in history with unique and critical decisiveness through Jesus Christ and through those whom he calls to the unique vocation of discipleship to Christ in the midst of

---

Christian and War", in *Religion in Life* 4 (1935), pp.250-58; "The Revelation in Christ and the Christian's Vocation", in N. Ehrenstrom (et. al.), *The Christian Faith and the Common Life*, (London: Allen & Unwin, 1938), pp.160ff.—Ed.

their ·fellows. Through that call and that discipleship they are bound together into a new community, the Church, and there is made available for them amidst all the perplexities and complexities of moral behaviour the illumination of the Spirit as to what God wills them to do, as to what is right. Furthermore, the Christian discerns in Christ the revelation of the divine *agape*, the divine love, which, one might also say "by definition", confers an absolute and indefeasible value on every individual person as such. And with this there goes the conviction that the divine purpose of righteousness and love revealed in Christ will be realised in a finally consummated Kingdom which lies beyond history—and so on. I say "and so on" because one might continue the exposition until one had covered practically the whole content of the Christian revelation and faith. But the main point I want to make is I hope sufficiently evident, namely, that theistic faith when it takes the specifically Christian form and is nourished and sustained by the life of the Christian community, the Church, achieves, or at least can achieve, a unique steadiness, and weight, and power to shape and transform, so that it continually shines through, the whole being of man.

To sum up the course of our thought, the argument has had a sort of mounting trajectory. We began with the calculative, utilitarian ethic, the sort of ethic which governs, and up to a point rightly governs, so much of ordinary, everyday morality. I suggested that this has in it certain weaknesses and inadequacies which can only be overcome by moving over into an ethic of right. I then suggested that an ethic of right also has in it certain weaknesses and inadequacies, and these can be overcome if it moves over into some sort of theistic belief. Lastly, I suggested that theistic belief itself gains immensely in power and adequacy and formative influence over a man's life as it moves over into the specifically Christian life of faith. The Christian man is as it were at the top of this trajectory, and because he is there he has a distinctive contribution to make to moral discussion on whatever level it may be conducted. Simply by being present and being present in his "Christian-ness" he can do much to keep men on all levels true to their own best insights. He braces and tautens and tightens the whole moral atmosphere, if that is not an outrageously mixed metaphor. He keeps the air tingling. On the Utilitarian level he keeps it tingling by his sense of right; on the level of right he keeps it tingling by his sense of God; on the theistic level he keeps it tingling by his faith in God as revealed in Christ.

The Perceived Difference Between Religion and Morality[17]

Before turning to the second problem or contrariety which arises out of the interpenetration of morality and religion something needs to be said about the notion that there is a certain essential difference between morality and religion; for, on the basis of this notion, it is sometimes said that the contrariety confronts religion alone.[18] Hence, it is to this alleged difference that we now turn.

In the concluding remarks of F. H. Bradley's *Ethical Studies* there are the following two statements:

Religion is more than morality. In the religious consciousness we find the belief, however vague and indistinct, in an object, a not-myself; an object, further, which is real. An ideal which is not real, which is only in our heads, can not be the object of religion: and in particular the ideal self, as the "is to be" which is real only so far as we put it forth by our wills, and which, as an ideal, we can not put forth, is not a real object, and so not the object for religion. Hence, because it is unreal, the ideal of personal morality is not enough for religion...For the religious consciousness, that object is real; and it is not to be found in the mere moral sphere.[19]

The main difference [between morality and religion] is that what in

---

[17]This short discussion was Farmer's Introduction to his second lecture on "Morality and Religion".—Ed.

[18]See A. A. Bowman, *Studies in the Philosophy of Religion*, vol.2, pp.99ff.

[19]F. H. Bradley, *Ethical Studies*, second edition (London: Oxford University Press, 1962), p.316.

morality only is to be, in religion somehow and somewhere really is, and what we are to do is done. Whether it is thought of as what is done now, or what will be done hereafter, makes in this respect no practical difference. They are different ways of looking at the same thing: and, whether present or future, the reality is equally certain. The importance for practice of the religious point of view is that what is done is approached, not with the knowledge of a doubtful success [as in morality], but with the fore-felt certainty of already accomplished victory.[20]

I do not myself regard these statements—parallels of which can be quoted from other writers—as satisfactory. They seem to suggest a far too radical distinction between morality and religion. In contrast with the first quotation, the moral consciousness, particularly at moments of critical decision and choice, is not only aware of dealing with an objectively real order of values, but also aware, however vaguely and indistinctly, that that order has a certain metaphysical or ontological depth and ultimateness (to use Bradley's phrase concerning religion). And in contrast to the second quotation, I want to maintain that in moral experience, again particularly at moments of critical choice and decision, there is to be discerned an implicit, and sometimes quite explicit, faith in the sovereignty and ultimate victory of the good. In support of this one might cite the insistence of Hartmann, who has a very realistic approach to moral experience (unbiased by anything in the nature of explicit religious belief) that "a deep and mighty faith" *is* a basic element in ethical idealism; I am sure that in this Hartmann is not remote from the moral experience of ordinary people. Hence, I think Bernard Bosanquet brings us nearer to the truth than Bradley, when he draws a distinction between what he calls "sheer or reflective morality" and "concrete morality". "In reflective morality", he says, "the contradiction of what is and what ought to be is brought to an extreme...one might say, it rests on the conviction that evil is

---

[20]Ibid., p.334.

real and good is a mere thought. In the concrete morality of social observance the good is at least partially realised, and ethical faith takes the shape of holding the good to be a reality in which the individual finds himself sustained and affirmed against the evil which is less real. In religion the attitude of abstract [reflective] morality is reversed, and that of concrete morality is intensified."[21] If we take Bosanquet's phrase "concrete morality" to signify the moral consciousness under the pressure of real life situations and not as pondering hypothetical problems in the moral philosophy classroom, which corresponds, I suppose, to his abstract or reflective morality, then I think his statement is quite acceptable. It corresponds with the position I have been maintaining that morality and religion lie very close to one another in concrete experience and that to set them in sharp opposition to one another in respect of belief in the reality of ideal values and of the certainty of their victory is not adequate to the facts.

The Tension Between Risk and Security

This brings us to the second tension which I have in mind, namely that between "risk" and "security". The point is that this tension is related to the latter of the above beliefs, and in accordance with what I have just been saying, its presence can be discerned in moral as well as in religious experience. In moral experience, however, it is present in a latent form, lying as it were beneath the surface—in the mind but not explicitly before it. Religion, on the other hand, makes it both more explicit and more acute, partly because, as Bosanquet says, religion intensifies concrete morality. We will look at the tension first from the angle of experience.

The tension or contrariety is that between, on the one hand, a vivid sense of the reality and power of evil and, derivative from that, the crucial importance of human choice in regard to it; and, on the other hand, the conviction that good is rooted in ultimate reality and that its final victory is

---

[21]B. Bosanquet, *The Value and Destiny of the Individual* (London: Macmillan & Co., 1913), pp.241-2. Cf. Bowman's distinction between "theoretical" and "practical" morality, in *Studies in the Philosophy of Religion*, vol.2, pp.105-6.

secure. Both these awarenesses seem to be implicit in the ordinary man's sense of the significance of the moral struggle, of the dignity of man as a responsible agent in it, and of the worthwhileness of that strenuousness of moral endeavour which the paramount authority of moral values and the actual facts and challenges of human existence plainly require. Deny the full reality of evil and its power to increase and spread in so far as it is not checked by the moral energies of men, and all that the moral struggle seems to be in experience is falsified; it becomes a mockery, hardly more than play-acting. On the other hand, deny that the ultimate victory of the good is assured, and assert, on the contrary, that the final enthronement of evil is a *real* possibility, and again the intense sense of the significance of the moral struggle is challenged; the costly sacrifices which the ideal in its absolute authority in principle requires begin to look hardly worthwhile. Clearly, these two implicit convictions, when thus drawn out and stated in explicit propositions, get in each other's way. We may put it like this: the serious moral life must assert the apparent contradiction of the victory of the good being both assured and not assured at the same time; it must ask for both a real and ultimate risk, and a real and ultimate security. The adjective "ultimate" is important. We are familiar enough in other spheres of our life with a hunger both for risk and security. But in other spheres it raises no problem, for the risk we crave is never one which touches the ultimate securities of our life. The risk and adventure we normally crave for (if it is to give us satisfaction) must be in a context of stable circumstances on which reliance can be put. Thus there is an adventurous thrill in being at sea in a rising storm in a seaworthy boat; there is none in being in such circumstances in a sieve. It is the difference between incidental and relative insecurity, between say a burst pipe and an earthquake. We do not grasp the tension or contrariety of risk and security that lies at the heart of moral experience until we realise that both are concerned with an ultimate basis of human life. Moral experience seems to require not an incidental risk along with an ultimate security, but an ultimate risk and an ultimate security at the same time.

I must, however, here guard myself against possible misunderstanding.

Some might be inclined to say that the question of the ultimate victory, or the ultimate defeat of the good, really has nothing to do with the authority of the moral imperative over me and my obligation to obey it. It may be said that even if the final defeat of the good is thought of as a real possibility, it still remains my duty at all times and at all costs to do what I can, little as it may seem to be, to prevent the possibility from becoming an actuality. But even if the final defeat of good should be thought of as a certainty, it would still be my duty to serve the ideal meanwhile, preserving my integrity as a moral person, and bringing into being in the world, so far as I can, pockets or enclaves of good, or relative good, and preserving them as long as possible before they are finally engulfed. But such statements (to which I do not demur) do not really affect the point I am making. For I have not been speaking about the authority of the moral imperative over us, but about the sense of the reasonableness—one might say the sanity—of making the most costing and strenuous efforts to fulfil it in a world which *ex hypothesi* we are unable to think of as supporting them. I am not speaking of immediate obligations but of ultimate sanctions. If we abstract ethics from its actual embeddedness, so to say, in the whole person and in his *Sitz im Leben*, if (to use Bosanquet's phrase) we talk of sheer or reflective ethics, then we must, I suppose, maintain that it is a man's duty to seek the good even if he is fully aware that there is no assurance of its victory, and, indeed, even if he is sure of its defeat. We must, I suppose, maintain that he ought to do his duty in any case and at any cost, simply because *it is his duty*. But if we are not being thus abstract, but are thinking rather in terms of concrete morality, then I can only say that it seems clear to me that the recognition and fulfilment of duty under such circumstances, particularly when it comes to the point of making the final sacrifice, would begin to be penetrated by a feeling of sheer unreasonableness; it would not make sense. And this would inevitably bring with it, sooner or later, an enfeeblement of the moral energies and a diminution in moral certitude and devotion. Nor could this be regarded as evidence of moral weakness, for among our duties there is surely the duty to act reasonably. My point is that no man can feel it to be reasonable to yield up his whole being in a way which leaves him both divided from his world and divided against himself.

However, to reiterate the point, the contrariety of which we are speaking tends to be latent in, beneath the surface of, moral experience. This is certainly so at moments of concrete moral decision and feeling. At such moments the moral consciousness draws energy and inspiration from both elements in the paradox—both from the sense of being able to make, or withhold, a really significant contribution to some ultimate and abiding victory of good over evil, and from the sense that there certainly is, or will be, such a victory in any case, i.e. independently of whether men make or withhold their contribution in this or that particular instance. It is only when the two elements are explicitly and reflectively formulated that their contrariety is apprehended. Such reflective formulation will usually take place at times other than those of intense moral experience itself and will not in fact vitally influence the latter. The moral life at its high moments will probably still function pretty much as it did before, continuing to draw its strength and inspiration from both sides of the paradox, without any sense of their opposition. It is this, I suggest, that explains the fact that it appears to be possible for reflective minds to reject theories which attempt to resolve the contrariety by diminishing one or other of the two opposed elements in it, either the element of the ultimate risk or the element of the ultimate security, without, however, any diminution of the high tone and temper of the concrete moral life being evident. What happens in such cases, I suggest, is that in the concrete moral life the theory is tacitly discarded and both sides of the paradox are once again implicitly affirmed. Thus some thinkers have sought to lighten the paradox by, in effect, putting the major emphasis on the element of risk and correspondingly less emphasis on the element of security. They have proposed the theory of a finite, struggling God, a personal being immensely more good, powerful and resourceful than man, but one who nevertheless stands in real and critical need of man's assistance in his wrestling with evil, which help man is free to give or to withhold. Thus the reality and potency of evil and the cruciality of man's moral choices are preserved, *but* any full assurance of the ultimate victory of the good is removed: all that remains is the added confidence that comes from the belief that there is for the normally earnest man a powerful ally in the unseen. Such a theory may certainly go with a concrete moral life which does not lack earnestness and vigour. Two reasons can be given for this. Firstly, if, in serious moral situations, we do turn our minds to the "ought" of an ultimate personal reality, concerned in and relevant to our immediate task, there is probably, as A. E. Taylor says, no more effective way of doing it than by "allowing ourselves to imagine such ultimate reality as struggling against a hostile power and standing in need of our assistance." Secondly, in so far as we do permit ourselves to use such an image in such a situation, we do not in fact bring explicitly before the mind the thought that such an ultimate power might, in spite of all his resources, be defeated. Rather there is an obscure feeling that he will not be, and cannot be; a feeling that if God, even a God theoretically defined as limited and struggling, be for us who can be against us? Again, a similar emphasis on the element of risk as against the element of security may be achieved by a doctrine of an ultimate life-force, which is pictured as creatively bringing forth, in spite of a certain resistance in things, ever new values. The future, however, is still always open, nothing is settled, nothing assured, there is no telling what will be the outcome, and indeed all that man now judges to be of value may be swept away. Still it is Creativity with a capital C, and man with his sense of values is but a localised manifestation of it, playing a part, through his moral endeavours, in the bringing forth of whatever will be brought forth. I do not myself think that such an apotheosis of the indeterminate and the haphazard can be made to be even philosophically respectable. Nevertheless, it does appear to be able to go with a fine spirit of moral earnestness and vigour, and this I suggest again is partly due to the fact that in the concrete moral life there is still the implicit sense that in point of fact the future is not so completely open as the theoretical view asserts. Rather, the life-force is obscurely felt, even in its free and unpredictable creativity, to be of such a nature that the final triumph of the good is assured. In short, indeterminate Creativity with a capital C becomes transformed into assured Progress with a capital P.

Another theoretical way of lightening the paradox is to move in the opposite direction to the one just indicated and put the major emphasis on the element of security, allowing the element of risk to fall into the background. This is broadly characteristic of pantheistic philosophies of the type advocated by Bradley and Bosanquet which teach that the absolute is already a fully realised perfection in which all value is comprehended in such wise that the antithesis of good and evil as it confronts the struggling finite wills of men is done away with. Here indeed is the stability and security of value *in excelsis*. But what becomes of the concrete moral life on this basis? If reality already comprehends the fullness of good, there would appear to be no place left within it for the intense sense of the reality of evil and of the risk of its triumph which is inherent in the concrete moral experience. It is significant that both Bradley and Bosanquet declare that there is, in the insistence of the moral and religious life on both real risk and real security, an element of "make-believe".[22] Although the use of such a term as "make-believe" might suggest that neither of these two great thinkers takes either morality or religion very seriously, nothing could be further from the truth. Rather one cannot resist the impression that their use of the term "make-believe" reveals a certain awareness that the philosophy which is being propounded will not in fact make any difference at all to concrete moral-religious experience in its insistence on both risk and security, but lies entirely apart from it. Or in other words, what is being said, in effect, is that in proportion as we achieve philosophic truth the more we shall need to forget it in the moral and religious life, and the more we are seriously engaged in the moral and religious life, the more we shall need to forget the philosophic truth we have achieved. Each will in fact be a kind of make-believe to the other.

We turn now to look at these things from the angle of the Christian revelation and faith. Living religion, particularly, in its mature monotheistic

---

[22]See F. H. Bradley, *Appearance and Reality: A Metaphysical Essay* (London: Swan, Sonnenschein & Co., 1893), p.443.

form, as we have it in Christianity, tends at once to make the opposition of which we have been speaking explicit instead of implicit, and at the same time to make both sides of the opposition more intense. That this is its effect is apparent from much that has already been said about the essence of living religion as defined by its normative expression in the Christian revelation.[23] Thus, on the one hand, there is all that has been said about the apprehension of what we have called the Godness of God, and about the centrality in that apprehension of the thought of God as being the ultimate source and Lord of all being and value, and, therefore, the absolute security and guarantee of the realisation of all good and the final defeat of all evil. To a living monotheistic faith, a God who is not this is simply not *God*. That is why the mature religious mind instantly and almost instinctively rejects the notion of a finite, struggling God as soon as it passes from being merely a vague mental picture and receives explicit statement. Then, on the other hand, we have emphasised that this apprehension of God as *God* is given in and through an encounter with him in which his holy, personal will is apprehended as claiming *absolutely* the obedience of man as a personal being. Such a claim, because it is claim and not compulsion, man can reject.[24] It is at this point that the religious consciousness takes up into itself the sense of personal freedom and responsibility which we saw is inherent in the moral experience of men, but at the same time it makes it more explicit by investing it with immensely greater significance and seriousness. The religious man cannot think of his moral failures as merely incidental and passing manifestations of his life, which it will be wise for him not to dwell on overmuch; nor as merely transgressions or infringements of a static and aloof moral order, or law, to which he can make a readjustment at any time by his own volition, seeing that it is always unchangeably and aloofly there for him to make readjustment to. Rather he apprehends that his moral failures concern the deepest roots and ultimate destiny of his personal being, for they constitute a self-willed alienation from,

---

[23]See H. H. Farmer, *Revelation and Religion*, pp.2ff.; ch.3.– Ed.
[24]See H. H. Farmer, *God and Men*, pp.48-59.—Ed.

and antagonism to, the utterly pure personal will of God. Moreover, being such an opposition of two personal wills, clearly man is unable to rectify the situation simply by his own volition. All of which comes to expression in the distinctive and characteristic religious concept of "sin", which appears throughout the whole history of religion. The concept of sin and the concept of moral failure are not the same, though they are, of course, related. Sin is moral failure as taken up into, and purposively reinterpreted by the specifically religious context of encounter with, and answerability to, God as holy personal will. This is why, along with the concept of sin, the concept of the wrath of God appears, wrath being a personal term which has no meaning in relation to an impersonal moral order, law or ideal.[25]

Does then religion, and in particular Christianity, leave us with this contrariety on our hands? Is the man in whom moral experience is informed and transformed by the sense of a living encounter with God condemned to be perpetually torn between the two poles of ultimate security and ultimate risk, between a serene confidence in the ultimate victory of the good and an oppressed sense of the reality of evil and of the awful responsibility and cruciality of human choice in relation to it? At first sight it might appear so. In Christianity itself it is possible to see this contrariety appearing again and again in the unresolved tension between divine sovereignty and human freedom, or between the concepts of heaven and hell—heaven symbolising the final and complete victory of the good through and in God, hell symbolising the possibility of human choice leaving as it were a residuum of unredeemed and unredeemable evil in the universe. This, in other words, is the tension between a universalist view of the ultimate consummation, which maintains that all will in the end be saved, and a view which is non-universalistic precisely because it wants to preserve the reality of human choice and

---

[25]Cf. G. van der Leeuw, *Religion in Essence and Manifestation*, ch.78.

responsibility.[26]

Now I do not believe that there is any general theoretical solution of this tension and contrariety, partly because of that characteristic of all conceptual thinking of which we spoke in the first chapter, whereby we can only think at all through conceptual opposites. Nevertheless, I do not think it is satisfactory to leave it at that and say no more. There is, I believe, a unification of these two opposed elements within the experience of the individual Christian himself, a unification which is an important element in the uniqueness of Christianity as a reconciling faith and experience. It is a unification achieved within the religious relationship of the individual as a moral person to God. The unification has to do with the central New Testament experience of, and teaching about, the divine forgiveness, and more particularly about what is called justification by faith.

I can only state very briefly what I have in mind. The basic thing is once more the central Christian affirmation of God's self-disclosure in Jesus Christ, and within that particularly his self-disclosure as forgiving love which, at infinite cost, brings the sinner, in spite of his sin and whilst he still remains a sinner, into personal fellowship with himself.[27] This central truth of the Christian revelation and faith which in its central statement is familiar enough, carries with it something which, though perhaps easy to overlook, is related to our problem. It carries with it a new understanding of the divine victory over evil so far as this is concerned with God's relationship to man as moral personality—the main point with which we are here concerned. This new understanding arises out of two truths. First, as we have seen, the supreme good of man is to be found in fellowship with God. Second, particularly relevant to our problem is that God, through his self-disclosure in Christ, has

---

[26]For Farmer's own universalist thesis, see *The World and God*, pp.255ff.; *God and Men*, pp.143-51. "...it seems necessary for the Christian consciousness to affirm...that not only is God seeking to reconcile every individual to himself, but also that he will in the end succeed in so doing. For only on that basis can we speak of the ultimate victory of a God who is love" (*The World and God*, p.255). A critical discussion of Farmer's universalism can be found in C. H. Partridge, *H. H. Farmer's Theological Interpretation of Religion*, pp.171-80—Ed.

[27]See H. H. Farmer, *The World and God*, ch.11.—Ed.

made, and makes, this fellowship possible for man, *sin and all*, if I may so put it. I must emphasise the words "sin and all". God's supreme victory in relation to the human person is to bring him into fellowship with himself, *but*, and this is the point, because it is won and continually renewed through an atoning and costing forgiveness, it is a victory in which moral failure (or as we ought to call it in this context, "sin"), without ceasing to be real positive evil involving real diminution of good, so that it would have been better had it never been, makes no difference. Rather indeed it is taken up into it and becomes part of the basis on which the victory is built. I am conscious of expressing this very inadequately. That may be due to the fact that I am trying to state in a sentence or two that profound, yet at the same time, simple and direct encounter with God through Christ, which deep and experiencing natures have sought to formulate and explore in doctrines of forgiveness, atonement, imputation of righteousness and justification by faith. In these doctrines, or rather in the living experience which lies behind them, there is a reconciliation of the contrariety we have been discussing, without either element in it being minimised or ignored. The fellowship which God thus establishes and maintains with the sinful man in his sin is the only relationship between them concerning which, it is not meaningless to say, evil is really annihilated without ceasing to be evil, to be known as evil, to be still deeply regretted and repudiated as evil. And again, it is the only relationship between them concerning which it is not nonsense to say that the loss and impairment of the good due to sin remains real loss, known and always to be regretted and deeply repented of as such, and yet in another sense is no longer real loss, for in the relation of restored and re-established fellowship with God through his forgiving and atoning love, man's being, even as impaired and diminished by his sin, is made complete and his true end is achieved. In the presence of God the forgiven man deeply repents of and hates all the sin that is in him and all the evil choices that it has brought forth and still brings forth, but he is at peace about them because being forgiven he is one with God *even as a sinner*. And again, in the presence of God the forgiven man knows that he stands there and must continue to stand there as a very diminished and defaced human being because of his sin. Nevertheless, he is content and at peace because, even as so diminished and defaced, he is at one with God through his atoning and forgiving love and in that God's victory has already been won. On the other hand, because the whole thing is within the new life of fellowship with God it is impossible that the Christian man will exploit the divine forgiveness by becoming less strenuous in his moral life and in his wrestling with evil and in his seeking of the good. On the contrary, the sense of the cruciality of his choices and decisions and of the possibilities of real evil, real loss, in such choices and decisions will be intensified. The idea of the divine atoning love making sin less significant, or of "doing evil that grace may abound" is so utterly contradictory to the whole relationship as to be meaningless, almost as meaningless and nonsensical as to speak of being inside and outside a closed circle at the same time.

The Tension Between Doing and Being

Having discussed the tension between the good and the right and the tension between risk and security, we turn now to the third and final tension which we consider under the general head of morality and religion, namely that between "doing" and "being". It is once again one which declares itself in some measure in moral experience independently of religion, but which religion tends to make more explicit and acute.

We may approach it through a certain duality in the meaning of the concept of freedom which has often been noted and of which probably most serious moral natures become in some measure aware, even though they are not able to formulate it in precise terms. On the one hand, there is the freedom which consists in the power to evaluate different ends, to choose between them in accordance with such valuations, and to direct behaviour accordingly—we spoke of this in our examination of the moral consciousness and said that man's awareness of himself as a responsible moral subject carries with it the awareness of himself as having this freedom of choice. Nor can any of the admitted theoretical difficulties which attach to the notion of freedom destroy this conviction of being in this sense free at moments of actual decision in the concrete moral life. At such moments the moral subject knows that the option between the higher and the lower course is a real option, a live option; he can follow the one *or* the other. Yet, on the other hand, men are not unaware of another sort of freedom, the freedom, that is to say, of the spontaneous and immediate determination of a man's will by the thought of duty and the good. Here, apparently, there is no open alternative; the lower course, though he can contemplate it, completely lacks any "psychological pull" to the sort of man he is; it is in fact not for him a live option.[28] This dual meaning of freedom may be illustrated by the dilemma of moral judgement people are apt to feel themselves to be faced with if they are confronted at one and the same time by a man who has continually to fight, even if successfully, lustful impulses and on the other hand by a man whose whole character is plainly so nobly fashioned that such impulses either do not stir in him, or if they do, he reacts so instantly with his whole being that they die immediately. For the former, lustful behaviour *is* a live option in a way that it is not for the latter. Most people would feel, I think, that whilst the second is morally the higher type—the sort of being one ought oneself to be— the first, paradoxically, is morally the more commendable. Indeed, they might even feel that the second man does not really, at least so far as lust is concerned, exemplify a distinctively moral life and activity at all.

---

[28]Compare the following statement of W. G. de Burgh (some of which Farmer quotes and subsequently deletes): "Moral obligation and the consciousness of faith alike imply that a man has the power to choose between good and evil, to will either in the line of duty or against it. In the moment of willing he cannot question the possession of this capacity; doubt arises, if at all, on subsequent reflection, and is doomed to vanish on the next occasion that he sets himself to act. In Miss Dorothy Sayers trenchant words: 'Christians (surprising as it may appear) are not the only persons who fail to act upon their creed; for what determinist philosopher, when his breakfast bacon is uneatable, will not blame the freewill of the cook, like any Christian? To be sure the philosopher's protest, like his bacon, is pre-determined also; that is the silly part of it. Our minds are the material we have to work upon when constructing philosophies, and it seems but an illogical creed, whose proof depends upon our discarding all the available evidence.' Yet—here is the difficulty—side by side with this freedom of choice, man is aware of another type of freedom, displayed in the spontaneous and yet inevitable determination of his will by the thought of duty and of the good. Here there is no possible alternative; he could not, being the man he is, have done otherwise, have betrayed a trust or sacrificed his children to his own interest. It is...in action directed towards good rather than in action from a sense of duty that this compelling force of the ideal is most manifest" (*From Morality to Religion*, pp.227-8).—Ed.

Now it is not difficult so to formulate the relation of these two types of freedom to one another, that there would not appear necessarily to be any real contrariety between them. Considered merely as defined concepts, that is, without regard to actual situations in which they attain concrete exemplification, there would appear to be no reason why the freedom of choice for which good and evil in certain directions are live options, and the freedom of realised and established good character for which good and evil in other directions are not live options should not coexist in the same person together, the former representing an important creative point in the development of experience and character—a kind of *natura naturans*—the latter, except in so far as it may be the result of inborn disposition and temperament, embodying the funded results of such creativity in the past—*natura naturata*. In the illustration just given, to the man to whom sensuality is no temptation there are temptations of another sort, temptations on the level of his realised nobility; such are the growing points of *his* being, where failure would be as morally reprehensible (possibly more so) as the sensually tempted man's failure on his level. Thus even Christ is pictured as subject to temptations, real temptations; but they are on the level of his superlative character and the high messianic vocation for which it fitted him.

This way of thinking of the matter is in a measure in accord with the facts: it is a commonplace that men's characters are in some degree created by, are the *depositum* of, their own previous choices. Nevertheless, I cannot help feeling that this involves a considerable oversimplification of the facts of man's actual situation.[29] It is such an over simplification because, in point of

---

[29]The statements I have just made about the relation of the two freedoms can obviously, without difficulty, be taken up into the religious, and in particular the Christian, apprehension of the divine purpose in relation to man. From this point of view, it is part of the distinctive essence of man as created by God that freedom in the second sense of that realised perfection of being in which hard decision and strenuous wrestling with evil have no place can only be had through the exercise of freedom in the first sense, that is to say, through such hard decision and wrestling with evil. If we ask the question why freedom of choice enters thus into the divine scheme as the condition of man's progressive realisation of his divinely appointed end—why did not God so fashion men as to possess at once the liberty of perfected being, to which evil, having so to speak no psychological pull upon it, is never a live option?—it may be that, in the last resort, no answer can be given except to say that that is how God has willed things to be and so they are. But in point of fact the Christian revelation

fact, no act of the will, no matter with what vivid sense of freedom and responsibility it may be accompanied, ever takes place "in a sheer vacuum of unrelatedness". It is always, in some measure, the expression of the whole self; in some measure the result of an interplay of processes which lie outside explicit awareness and are not subject to volitional control. It is this fact that imparts some of its plausibility to a deterministic account, particularly from the side of the psychology of human behaviour. Though I do not think it is

---

has something more to say than that. Let me put it in this way. Many people faced with such a question in a cool hour of reflection would fall back upon a direct judgement of value to the effect that a freedom of perfected personal being achieved through the freedom of personal choice is of greater value than one immediately bestowed. But, such a judgement of value, I suspect, would belong too much in the realm of abstract morality, amidst the actualities of man's historical existence. In the actual concrete struggle of the moral life, its frequent weariness and defeat, the manifest dreadful consequences in suffering and corruption that men's wrong exercises of their freedom bring about, the secular mind has no protection against the thought that the price is after all too high, and that the judgement of value just referred to is therefore not really so inescapable and determinative of the issue as it seemed. If, however, the judgement is taken out of this abstract isolation into the context of the Christian revelation and faith, it receives powerful and continually renewed attestation in a way that involves much more of the whole man: what was already known in some way comes to be known in a different and better way, to use Collingwood's phrase again. In this we meet another aspect of the power of the Christian revelation and faith to penetrate reconcilingly to fundamental predicaments of man. The attestation is rooted in the central Christian faith in the Incarnation and is along two lines at least. First, it is attested by the fact that this is the divine method of succouring men in their misuse of freedom and all the consequences that brings. The wavering and vacillating hold of a man's mind on freedom as a value, amply witnessed in the history of mankind, is evidenced even in the sphere of religion, including Christianity itself, in the craving to be made perfect at a clap, to use Bunyan's phrase, by some overriding exercise of divine power; but the fact that according to the Christian faith God chose the infinitely slower and more costly method of entry as a human person into all the conditions of men's finite existence as moral existence as moral person's, exposing himself to all the risks and consequences of their freedom of choice is a final rebuke to such craving and a signal affirmation of the indefeasible value of human freedom. Second, it is attested by the fact that in Christ the Christian believes himself to be confronted with the fully realised perfection of a human personal life, and behold even from it, as I said a minute ago, the necessity to make costing choice between real options of good and evil to meet temptation and to wrestle with it even in the presence of God with such strenuousness that sweat fell from him as blood, is not absent. Moreover, such necessity is clearly discerned to be not an inexplicable dark point in what is otherwise the glory of his perfection, like a spot in the sun, but an essential element in it. Thus, once again the value judgement concerning freedom is attested and reinforced. Perhaps the following words from the epistle to the Hebrews express, in part, this insight: "In bringing many sons to glory, it was fitting that God, for whom and through whom everything exists, should make the author of salvation perfect through suffering." "Because he himself suffered when he was tempted, he is able to [succour] those who are being tempted" (Heb. 2:10, 18).

Furthermore, in concrete experience the distinction we have made between the determination of conduct by what we feel at the moment of serious moral decision to be a free choice between the higher and the lower course and the determination of conduct by the necessitation of what we already are, or have become over our whole being, is by no means so obvious and clear cut as the discussion so far may have made it appear to be.

anything more than plausibility, I am far from wanting to minimise the results of modern psychological enquiry into the unconscious determinants of choice and decision or the problems they raise for a doctrine of human freedom, which, on other grounds, we are bound to assert. However, it is not my purpose to discuss these problems. I do not wish to go beyond the plain evidence of everyday experience, evidence of which most people are probably dimly aware at some time or other, and people with intense and deep moral natures and some capacity for self-observation are often very keenly aware indeed. Faced by some really testing situation in which impulse and inclination urge strongly in one direction and moral judgement points in another, they are conscious that their situation is not such that they can make, as it were, a jack-in-the-box leap onto the side of the right from some vantage point outside their whole interior self; rather they must summon and mobilise powers from deeper levels of their being, and how to do that they do not know—indeed they are not at all sure, in their view of past experience, that such powers are there to summon. This awareness of their real situation finds expression in a feeling of irritation when well-meaning folk address moral homilies to them exhorting them to do their duty. They sense that such homilies are somehow wide of their problem; what they need is to be different people from what they now are. Similarly if they are able to make, even after a struggle, a right choice, they are not unready to admit, looking back on it afterwards, that there went into the making of that choice factors and influences of which they were not conscious at the time, and which in any case it is not possible to trace back to their source. Nevertheless, the choice seemed to be a real choice, veritably their own, one for which their awareness of themselves as moral agents requires them to take responsibility just as it would have required them to do had the choice in fact been of the opposite kind. This antithesis finds striking expression in the Sermon on the Mount, wherein alongside the lofty ethical injunctions which would seem to have little point if they did not presuppose a capacity in man to respond if he will, there occur words which seem equally to imply a considerable qualification of such a presupposition. "No good tree bears bad fruit, nor does a bad tree bear good fruit. Each tree is recognised by its own fruit. People do not pick figs from thorn bushes, or grapes from briers. The good man brings good things out of the good stored up in his heart, and the evil man brings evil things out of the evil stored up in his heart. For out of the overflow of his heart his mouth speaks." [30]

This has brought us to the point where living religion, particularly in its Christian form, penetrates and informs moral experience. When this happens, the antithesis discloses itself in an even more obvious and acute form. On the one hand, a man's sense of moral answerability for his decisions and deeds is rendered more solemn and inescapable by the fact that the moral imperative is now apprehended as carrying the claim of God with whom in the end all accounts must be settled. On the other hand, because the moral imperative is now apprehended as the demand of God it is apprehended as claiming the whole man and so reaching to the innermost thoughts and intents of the heart, that is to say, precisely to those regions and springs of activity in the self over which, whilst they play a part in every decision and choice, the fully conscious will appears to have no direct control. What God requires is now seen to be "truth in the inward parts" and a lustful desire, like a lustful act, is similarly felt to be evil. In such a living encounter with God, a man cries out for that which no man by an act of the will can ever give himself, a clean heart and a right spirit, a cry that God should make the tree itself good. Further, as we have seen, the religious person is deeply imbued with the sense of his utter dependence and the dependence of all things and all good upon God: such a sense is the core of worship and worship lies near the heart of the living encounter with God. Yet, on the other hand, as we have also seen, the radical personalism of the Christian apprehension of God, as well as its whole understanding of the divine way of succouring man through a historic personal revelation and not by an exercise of overriding might, insists that the saved man must stand on his own feet in a free, responsible, personal I-Thou relation with God. But there is no need to labour the point. The acuteness of this

---

[30]Lk. 6:43-45.

tension in the moral-religious life has made itself apparent throughout the history of Christian thought in the debates concerning Augustinianism and Pelagianism, Calvinism and Arminianism, total depravity and moral responsibility, a debate which is still going on today. It is, I think, not unimportant to realise that these problems and debates are not the creation of subtle, speculative theologians, though a good deal of subtle speculation may have entered into their treatment of them; nor again are they simply the product of religious belief, so that a man could rid himself of them simply by surrendering such belief; they are already, as I have indicated, deeply rooted in the moral experience of ordinary men as they are confronted by the high imperatives of conscience in their sense of responsibility and by the ineluctable facts of their own nature and of the forces which operate both within and upon it.

Once again, I do not myself think that a theoretical resolution of the contrariety will ever be found, though, no doubt, we must go on seeking it. Just how real choice, involving the sort of moral responsibility which is essential to man's status as a person, can coexist with that immense complexity of unconscious factors—internal, external, psychological, physiological and sociological—which manifestly condition choice, and indeed apart from which a man has no concrete historical existence at all, it is impossible rationally to formulate. More particularly, what is the nature of that divine saving relationship to a man, which can only save him as a moral personality *with* his consent, and yet apparently cannot gain his effective consent without working with those forces which lie outside his consciousness and control, and concerning which, therefore, he has no consent to give, the tree and its fruit being in fact inseparable from one another—these are mysteries which do not yield their secret to the analytic intellect, partly because it is analytic and by its very nature splits up the unity and continuity of reality into segments and oppositions.[31] I want, however, to suggest that through the Christian revelation and the relation with God it calls into being, it

---

[31]See H. H. Farmer, *The World and God*, pp.32-4.—Ed.

is possible to have an *inward* sense of the actual unity of these opposites which goes deeper than, and persists in spite of, the problems which rise up and baffle the mind directly it begins to reflect on these matters. The difficulty, of course, is how to state such a discernment in words, for words involve concepts, and concepts, as we saw earlier, necessarily involve opposites and often seem merely to exhibit the opposition as soon as they are used. If we do try to state it, the best way to approach it is to call attention in the first instance to the apprehension of him, in New Testament experience and thought, as the indwelling Spirit at work within the hidden deeps of the personality.[32] I have always thought that this virtual identification of the divine Christ in all the vivid, concrete individuality of historic personal life, and the divine Spirit within—which otherwise, as the history of religion shows, is so easily thought of as merely an occult, overriding, impersonal power—without, however, any loss of the sense of their distinctive sphere and function in salvation, constitutes one of the most profound and fundamental of all the synthesising insights of the Christian revelation and faith. But we must insist again that it is not a synthesis reached by the rational or speculative explication of ideas, but one which springs out of the divine saving revelation itself. It is sustained by, as it also helps to sustain, the real and increasing integration of the personality which that revelation makes possible. The fact that, in the New Testament, Christ and the Spirit are distinguished from one another and sometimes apparently used interchangeably, is not the result of looseness or confusion of thought, but a piece of profound synthetic intuition: it is one aspect of the uniqueness of Christianity as a reconciling faith. To apply this to our particular problem, the fact that the Christian revelation requires that the Christian should direct his obedience, trust, loyalty and devotion which he owes to God and to God alone upon the concrete, historic figure of Christ apprehended as God incarnate, insures that the relationship to God is all the time kept centrally within the sphere of the personal. It insures

---

[32]See H. H. Farmer, *Revelation and Religion*, pp.66ff.; "Christian Truths in Daily Experience: Of the Holy Spirit", in *The Presbyterian Messenger* (November, 1933), pp.180-2.—Ed.

that it is an I-Thou relationship in which the "I" is aware, in the most explicit way, of itself as "I" and of God as "Thou", a relationship in which the human person stands upright upon his own feet conscious that he has a responsible part to play in it. He is fully conscious of the responsibility, which no one can discharge but himself, of keeping his whole being thus centred upon God in Christ. This sense of free, personal self-direction and responsibility of being called (in the words of the New Testament) to have "the mind of Christ", is reinforced by the fact that Christ, as apprehended through his concrete, historic self-manifestation, imposes no code of precisely defined moral duties and instructions. Instead, the Christian is confronted by the concrete, historic Christ—apprehensible, in some measure, through his recorded teaching, but most of all through the total impact of his person. It is perhaps not superfluous to say that in order to be in this kind of fully personal relation to God in Christ, it is not in the least necessary to achieve anything approaching perfection, to be in fact already the good tree. It is a matter of setting the whole being in a certain direction, and of a continuous re-affirmation in spite of every failure of the resolve so to do. Such a resolve expresses the deepest commitment of which the self, in its consciousness of being a self, in some degree in charge of its own destiny, is capable. Nor does the self in this relationship lose that sense of dependence upon God without which it would not be a religious relationship. For he is fully aware that such a response of self-commitment is only made possible by God's own initiative of self-disclosure in Christ.

On the other hand, the Christian revelation and faith declare that the same divine saving purpose of love, which through Christ meets man in the area of his fully conscious responsible self-awareness, and calls for self-conscious decision and choice, is also through the Spirit at work in relation to those depths of his being which lie outside that area. And this is not just a gratuitous additional dogma imposed upon his belief, but one that enters into the closest connection with the I-Thou relation to God in Christ to which he is called and in which he stands. For this I-Thou relation which he is under obligation to maintain inevitably makes him increasingly aware of how deep-seated in his nature and beyond the reach of his conscious volition the roots of evil are, of how corrupt the tree is, and of how precarious, therefore, even the relation to Christ must be, if it depends simply on his own resolve to maintain it. In short, the facts of experience make plain that if God himself is not recreatively at work in the deeps of the personality, making the corrupt tree good, the very saving purpose of his own historic revelation in Christ will not be achieved; therefore faith in Christ involves faith in the Spirit also. Thus the self is enabled to make a comprehensive act of self-commitment to God. It can commit itself to him alike in his hidden working within and in his outward disclosure of himself through Christ, for in both he is one and the same saving purpose directed to the one end of giving to the whole man his true life as a personal being. And God can be trusted to complete the work he has set himself to do in a way that is fully consistent with that end. In his inward working there will be no mere taking by assault those personal defences which, by the whole manner and content of his revelation in Christ, he has shown that he intends to respect. On the other hand, in personal relation to Christ a man is not left to the thin, feeble straining efforts of an unsupported will destined always to be at the mercy of alien forces springing from a corrupt, immature and impoverished nature.

To conclude then, it is in this total act of personal faith in, of commitment of the whole being to, God revealed as Father, Son and Spirit, one God, that the contrariety of which we have been speaking is no longer felt to be a contrariety. But, it must be repeated that the mystery of the whole process, of the interaction of the conscious will with the unconscious deeps in a way that leaves the person intact as a free and responsible person, remains impenetrable to theoretical reason; it is, I suppose, part of the mystery of God and of the way in which the human person is rooted and grounded in him.

PART FOUR
THE SELF
and

THE WORLD

6

THE SIGNIFICANCE AND
THE NON-SIGNIFICANCE OF THE SELF

We come now to the third of our three main classes of duality—"The Self and the World". Under this heading I propose to consider four forms of a certain basic conflict or contrariety which underlie and pervade all human experience. This may be called the conflict or contrariety between the significance and the non-significance of the self.

The Problem with Theoretical Treatments of Evil

Perhaps we may best approach what is intended by this title by saying at once that we are not proposing to discuss what is often called the problem of evil, at any rate in the direct way that is usually followed in expositions of a theistic worldview.[1] This indeed should be evident from the whole purpose and direction of our thought hitherto in these lectures. In accordance with this purpose, we shall consider the contrarieties I have in mind primarily in their interplay with living religious experience and more particularly in their relation to the Christian revelation and faith as uniquely integrative and reconciling. I am not implying that the sort of discussion of the problem of evil with which we are familiar in, what one might almost call, the standard texts of philosophical theism are of little value. Clearly such discussion must have a place in any attempt systematically to expound and interpret the world

---

[1]As, for example, in the classic eighth chapter of the second volume of F. R. Tennant's *Philosophical Theology* (Cambridge: Cambridge University Press, 1931).

in terms of the good purpose of God, and it may even play some part in enlightening the perplexities and easing the burdens of religious faith for those who are capable of following the arguments used.[2] Nevertheless, I venture to think that the line we are going to take, whilst not unrelated to the theodicies of theistic thinkers, really goes deeper, penetrating more to the fundamentals of the human situation—I hope it does not sound presumptuous to say that; it is really only one way of calling attention to the necessary limitations of the usual abstract, theoretical approach to these problems, and, therefore, of the need for it to be supplemented by some study of religion itself, if the full case for a specifically Christian theism is to be presented. Surely I am not alone in having the vague feeling of disappointment and disquietude, which, I confess, I nearly always feel when I read a treatment of the problem of evil presented as part of the theoretical formulation of a theistic viewpoint. It is not merely, or even mainly, that there seems so little that is fresh in such treatments, one having a pretty good idea in advance of the broad lines that will be followed[3] (though that may have something to do with it), it is rather that the considerations adduced are so abstract and theoretical—necessarily so no doubt, but that does not affect the point. To anyone actually *in profundis* wrestling with evil in its concrete manifestation, its actually felt power and threat to crush, destroy and corrupt, for whom, for one reason or another, the whole of existence seems at the moment to be on the edge of a pit of utter meaninglessness and futility, such considerations might well seem so thin, glib and superficial, so utterly without either the reach or the power to lay hold of the soul, as to be almost insulting—comparable perhaps to the twittering of birds over an earthquake. On the other hand, to one who has been in the

---

[2] For Farmer's own discussion of the subject, approached from a fundamentally teleological and eschatological angle, see *Towards Belief in God*, ch.13; and also *The World and God*, chs. 6, 13 and 14. See also J. Hick, *Evil and the God of Love*, pp.260-1.—Ed.

[3] One might say *must* be followed, for it appears that these days it is not possible to say anything new in a theoretical way on the problem. One gets the impression that the main paths have long since been marked out, not to say beaten flat, hard and smooth; to be sure a man's gait and pace and conversation *en route* will bear the stamp of his individuality, and that may mean a good deal; still it is in the main the same path that has been trodden so many times before that he is following.

depths and has been lifted out of them into faith in God, the considerations adduced seem equally thin, glib and superficial. He will know well enough, that it was not a theoretical theodicy which saved him or could have saved him, and, being now presented with it, he gains but little in conviction from it; it reaches neither to the despair in which he once was, nor to the source and origin of the faith he now has. The theistic philosopher may reply to this by saying that the philosophy of theism is one thing and the victories of religious faith another, and that to rebuke the first for not doing the work of the second is mere confusion of mind. There is some justice in that; nevertheless one has the uncomfortable feeling that it may be too easy a way of escape. For if the human situation appears to be of such a kind that, on the one hand, it is but superficially touched by such a discussion of the problem of evil and, on the other hand, is radically transformed by some other sort of transaction of man with this world, then that would seem, in the interest of theism, to call for a much more profound analysis than is usually offered of that situation and of the way in which it is so transformed.

Substantially the same point can be approached from another angle. It has sometimes been said that, from the standpoint of formulating a theoretical philosophy or worldview, the theist, to an extent, creates the problem of evil for himself by setting himself too obstinately to interpret the world in terms of an omnipotent divine purpose of good. From the strictly theoretical standpoint, it is argued that an earthquake or a cancer poses no greater problem than the fall of a tree; it is one piece of the jigsaw puzzle to be fitted into whatever scheme of thought our minds may devise, and the fact that we do not happen to like its jagged edges and ugly colours is of no consequence—at most it is another piece of the puzzle which must take its chance along with the rest. If we cannot fit it, or indeed any other fact, into the theistic hypothesis there is nothing to prevent us from dropping the hypothesis and seeking another, or perhaps from giving up the quest for a worldview as a waste of time. The point, I think, must be granted from the perspective of abstract theory, and it must be granted *too* that the theistic apologetic often discusses the problem of evil in a way that appears to concede it also. But it is precisely here that we find such discussion unsatisfactory. We have the feeling of being invited to take up a detached theoretical attitude just at the point where to do so is to ignore the full reach and depth of the problem with which we are dealing, just at the point where the question of the nature of ultimate reality becomes concentrated and focused in the most fateful way on the problem of our own existence and significance as self-conscious persons in the world. It is this existential situation of "self-in-world" that calls for exploration, and so long as it is not explored, it is hard to see how any discussion of the problem of evil could fail to give in some measure the impression of a certain glibness and superficiality.

It is to some of these deeper and more fundamental tensions of the "self-in-world" situation, tensions which no man can escape any more than he can escape being a "self-in-world", that I wish to draw attention. All of them arise out of the fact that personal self-consciousness, by virtue of the fact that it is personal self-consciousness, is *implicitly* aware of its own unique status and significance in the world and yet, at the same time, it is implicitly aware, by virtue of the fact that it is in the world, that it has no such unique status and significance. When I say that the self is *implicitly* aware of this contrariety of significance and non-significance I mean: first, that the awareness of it does not enter into *all* states of consciousness, but may at any moment make itself felt in one or other of its various forms; second, that when it does so make itself felt, it may not do so in an explicitly realised form, but rather as a subconscious determinant of the mental state imparting to it, in varying degrees, a distinctive, if fluctuating, feeling-tone of insecurity, dispeace and anxiety; third, when it is more explicitly realised and faced, it need not be formulated in the neatly antithetical formula of "significance and non-significance of the self" which I have used. I would add, that awareness of the contrariety is apt to come much nearer to the surface of the mind, and to be much more strongly determinant of its mood at those points where what we are accustomed to call the problem of evil takes concrete form for the individual in one or other of the serious burdens and afflictions of human life. At the heart of such experiences there is always some awareness of the threat which they constitute either directly or indirectly to the significance of the self in the world, and if any kind of genuinely reconciled adjustment to them is made, as distinct from merely grimly enduring them because there is no option to do otherwise, one element in such an adjustment is usually a recovery in one way or another of the sense of the significance of the self.

We turn now to our four forms of this basic contrariety between the significance and non-significance of the self. We shall first describe each in turn after which we will go on to the discussion of the relation of religion to them.

The Tension Inherent in the Relationship of Knowledge Between the Self and the World

This tension has to do with that relationship of the self to its world which we may call, generally speaking, "knowledge". Or to put it in a slightly different way, it has to do with knowledge considered as a function of rational and reflective self-consciousness. An animal, of course, may be said to know its world, but the animal does not have knowledge of it in the sense in which I here use the term. For what I have in mind is not simply a subject-object relation, but a subject-object relation in which the subject is always indirectly aware of itself as knowing subject, and may at any moment become directly aware of it. Now in this relation of knowledge, considered thus as a function of reflective self-consciousness, there is implicitly this opposition of the significance and non-significance of the self. To take each side of the opposition in turn:

(1) We begin with an examination of the implicit sense of the significance of the self. This may be exhibited through two aspects of the relationship of "self-knowing-its-world". In the first place, the world is only "there" and can only be there as an object of apprehension or knowledge by being "there" for the single, particular self which apprehends it and knows it. It exists only as *my* world; only as an object of *my* knowledge is it "there" for *me*. Annihilate me as knowing subject, and you annihilate *my* world. The point is that, so far as I as a knowing subject am concerned, there is no other world. In

short, self and world from this angle are inseparably correlative terms; there *is* no objectivity without *subjectivity*, in Kierkegaard's sense of the term; in the sense, that is to say, of there being a particular self or subject who is active in knowing. It may be said, "but surely the world I apprehend is there in its own right, an object of knowledge for any self and all selves and not merely for me, and still existing even if not known by any self at all." That is, of course, how we do think of the world. However, to raise the point at this stage is in fact to pass over to the other side of the paradox, namely, the relative non-significance of the self in the relationship of knowledge, and does not affect what I am now saying. For even when I apprehend the world as thus independent of me and as the permanent object of knowledge for all selves, the world as so characterised is still my world and there wholly and solely through its relation to me. Whatever be the character of the world I know, I am, as the self knowing it, to use Karl Heim's phrase, the absolute perspective-centre to whom alone the whole vast panorama is disclosed. If I vanish, everything vanishes. Heim made the point many years ago in his usual vivid way:

For us all, including the scientist who explores the objective world of nature by induction, experiment and measurement, the primary datum which is given us is not even the content of our sense experience and the measurements which we base on them. The vault of glittering stars above us, which we can only dimly grasp through the notion of thousands of light-years, the electric impulses which throb in the atom, the miracle of life which unfolds itself before our astonished eyes through millions of years from the first plant life up to man, all that we think of as constituting primary and permanent reality is nevertheless not what is primarily given at all. The nearest and most intimate reality when we apprehend the world is, so to speak, the observation point where we stand and from which alone the immense panorama of the world, becomes accessible to us. That observation point is just ourselves. For each one of us it is our "I" which stands on this side of the whole objective universe and upon which the impressions stream in almost overwhelming profusion.[4]

The second thing which discloses the unique significance of the self in the relationship of knowledge, is the fact that, though I am self-conscious, I can never in the nature of the case make my self as knowing subject an object of knowledge in the way I make my world, including even my mental processes in interpretation, the object of knowledge. To suppose that I could, would be to be involved in an infinite regress, for the self as knowing is the absolute presupposition of all knowledge and therefore slips out of sight directly the attempt is made. The knowing self cannot, therefore, be apprehended simply as an object within a bit of the world that it knows, nor can its relation to the world that it knows be comprehended and stated in the same sort of judgements and propositions which it uses to express its knowledge of that world. Thus the self transcends the world and its objects, stands apart from it, over against it, above it, beneath it, at its centre—we can only use spatial terms derived from the world and so instantly falsify the relationship. The self is the invisible, inaccessible observer, never to be observed; to that invisible and inaccessible point the "whole choir of heaven and furniture of earth" are disclosed.[5]

(2) On the other hand, there is, in my coming to know my world, that which equally seems to imply and assert the non-significance of my particular selfhood and its self-consciousness, insists, as it were, on my withdrawal from the scene. Thus, in the first place, there is the fact that the inherent and irresistible movement of the mind, in its endeavour to apprehend and manage its world, away from the particular to the universal and general. I cannot, in

---

[4]Source not traced. Possibly Farmer's own translation of a passage from *Glaube und Denken*. Cf. K. Heim, *God Transcendent: Foundation for a Christian Metaphysic*, tr. by E. P. Dickie (London: Nisbet, 1935) pp.86-7. See also pp.57, 91, 152, 145, ch.5.—Ed.

[5]The point is not unfamiliar to students of philosophy: the act of knowing can never be comprehended and stated in the same sort of judgement and proposition as that which comprehends and states relationships between objects and events in the world that is known. This is the Achilles heel of all purely naturalistic theories of reality; they cannot account on that basis from the relationship of knowledge itself.

fact, think effectively on any other terms. I have to universalise, conceptualise, categorise the "here" and the "now" of my particular observation point (for example, all those vivid sensory and valuational experiences which are mine and mine alone and through which my world becomes my world) until the "here" and the "now" fades out of the picture.

Thus I find myself inevitably confronted and tied up with a world whose reality can only be expressed in general truths in relation to which my particularity, my "here-and-now-ness" as an experiencing self, must be thought of as progressively more irrelevant and non-significant. Co-operating in this process there is the intuitive apprehension of the existence of other selves, other knowers, each of whom are also perspective-centres and observation points. Hence, there is also the sense of a public world existing independently of all selves, and in relation to which, therefore, my particular self has no special significance. And finally, there is the fact which experience soon makes plain to us, that the world we thus come to know, although being in one sense our world and depending upon us for its "thereness" as our known world, nevertheless appears to hold us ultimately and absolutely in its power. We realise that we are after all part of it, even though in another sense, as knowing subjects, we are not part of it and cannot comprehend ourselves in terms of it. Although, to all appearances, the world has brought us into being and at any moment may destroy us, it remains true that the being it has apparently bestowed transcends it, and that in taking away that being it destroys itself—everything vanishes into a pit of absolute nothingness, the thought of which, if we can entertain it at all, shakes our being to its foundations.

It might be thought that all these statements are merely the product of the lucubrations of metaphysicians, and that there is nothing corresponding to them in the consciousness of the ordinary man, and nothing therefore that has anything to do with living religion and its integrating work. But I want to suggest that that is mistaken, even though it is true that the specialised aptitude and training, and the specialised vocabulary perhaps, of the philosopher is required to isolate and express, and still more to explore the implications of, these aspects of human experience. Most of the ultimate philosophical problems are, after all, rooted at some point in contrarieties which are latent in the everyday experience of ordinary people and which either operate there, below the surface, as unconscious and fluctuating determinants of consciousness, or, more rarely, emerge into explicit awareness. Many of us have experienced the way in which even a child will suddenly, with a look of perplexity on its face, blurt out a question which holds implicitly within it some of the most difficult problems with which profound philosophic minds have struggled. In respect of the particular opposition we are considering, I should not wonder—I will not say more than that—if many quite ordinary folk, have on occasion, had their minds at least brushed by that strange and disturbing experience of "isolement" (isolation as a self), as it has been called.[6] And with some, no doubt, the experience, even if on rare occasions, has not been a mere brushing of the mind, but an overwhelmingly explicit awareness. It is significant that the more explicit sense of "isolement" often seems to come in childhood just about the period when the child for the first time vividly realises its own selfhood. This would indicate that the experience is bound up with self-consciousness, and more particularly with that consciousness of the self as the *sole centre* of its own world which I have been trying rather lamely to describe. The best expression of it that I know is to be found in John St Loe Strachey's biography, *The Adventure of Living*. It deeply impressed my mind when I read it many years ago because it put into much clearer language than I can command a similar, though perhaps less vivid, experience of my own which took place when I was about the same age. He describes "a psychological incident" from his early childhood.

Then suddenly there came over me a feeling so strange and so different from anything I had ever felt before as to be almost terrifying. It was

---

[6]Farmer seems to have got the term from John St Loe Strachey who discusses it at some length in the sixth chapter of his *The Adventure of Living: A Subjective Autobiography* (London: Hodder & Stoughton, 1922). Strachey himself attributes it to the composer H. Berlioz (p.77).—Ed.

overwhelming in the true meaning of the word. Incredible as it seems in the case of so small a child, I had the clearest and most poignant feeling of being left completely, utterly alone, not merely in the world, but in something far, far bigger—in the universe, in a vastness infinite and unutterable. As with Wordsworth, everything seemed to vanish and fall away from me, even my own body. I was literally "beside myself." I stood a naked soul in the sight of what I must *now* call the All, the Only, the Whole, the Everlasting. It was no annihilation, no temporary absorption in the Universal Consciousness, no ingression into the Divine Shadow, that the child experienced. Rather it was the amplest exaltation and magnification of Personality [the self] which it is possible to conceive...The effect on me was intensely awe-inspiring—so awe-inspiring, indeed, as to be disturbing in a high degree.[7]

Strachey concludes: "though I was this isolated, I had no sense of smallness or of utter insignificance in face of the Universe. I did not feel myself a miserable, fortuitous atom, a grain of cosmic dust. I felt...that I was fully equal to my fate. As a human being I was not only immortal, but *capax imperii*—a creature worthy of a heritage so tremendous. From that day to this, talk about the unimportance, the futility of man, and his destiny has left me quite cold."[8] Here obviously is the sense of the significance of the self, of which I have spoken. But what of the other side of the contrariety, the sense of the insignificance of the self? That appears to have been in abeyance in Strachey's experience, as it was in my own earliest experience of a similar kind. But that may have been due in part to the fact that at that very early age the fact of death, with its apparent annihilation of selfhood, had not come home either to him or to me. In my own case, however, if I may venture to be so autobiographical, the two thoughts did a year or so later confront one

---

[7]J. S. Strachey, *The Adventure of Living*, pp.78-9.
[8]Ibid., p.80.

another in my mind in an acute and painful sense of their opposition. An old uncle who had been staying with us for some months suddenly died. I came into the room, in which he used to spend most of his time, and on the seat of the chair which he always occupied was no longer himself but his old skullcap. That simple object instantly became the precipitating agent of the experience of "isolement" which I had had on an earlier occasion. I felt again, though of course I could not have put it into words, the awful fact of being the sole midpoint of my world. Moreover, I suddenly realised with horrible clearness that selves vanish leaving perhaps only a forlorn skullcap, and that I might vanish in the same way at any time at the behest of forces over which I had no control, and that when I vanished everything and everybody would vanish: father, mother, home, the trees, the sky, the sun—the whole of the world would vanish and instead there would be a void and pit of absolute nothingness. Of course, I knew in a sense that the world would still be there, just as it was still there after the disappearance of my uncle, but to have reminded me of that would have left the essential centre of the experience quite untouched. This queer, awful feeling soon passed; indeed, if it had not, it would have been intolerable. But I have often thought that at that moment I experienced in a peculiarly intense way something of that "angst" of which some of the existentialist philosophers have spoken. To grasp it, one has to give full weight to both elements, namely, the sense of the utter significance of one's own self-conscious selfhood as the solitary centre of one's world, and the sense of one's insignificance as having no security of existence even as that centre. The sense of one's significance is augmented by the fact that one is conscious of one's insignificance, and the sense of insignificance is made the more burdensome because of the sense of one's significance.

John Oman, incidentally, has one or two interesting passages on this theme. He frequently appealed to childhood experience as providing data for the understanding of man's situation of "self-consciousness-in-the-world" and its relation to the theory of knowledge as, for example, in *The Natural and the Supernatural*. But I quote only one simpler selection from his earlier work

Vision and Authority which expresses what I have been saying, particularly about isolement. Speaking of that way in which a child at times becomes finally aware, in its own way, of ultimate questions, he writes:

> Roused by a word or by an incident, self-consciousness awakes. No slow process has accustomed him to the change. With awful suddenness, he realises that he too must go out alone upon the great stream of time, his own pilot through the storm and the dark. Already he hears the booming of the vast and dangerous ocean on eternity. He looks upon the white face of death, walks in the funeral *cortège*, watches the filling up of man's last narrow and solitary home. Careless people drop hints of how the worms feast below and the angels fail to rejoice above. Ghastly images haunt him as he lies in his chamber at night. After much speculation on the soul, he remains amazed at its invisibility, and goes round the world with his own as if it were a bird insecurely fastened in a cage. Forgetful and unsympathetic people may be able to think of child-likeness as freedom from speculation and satisfaction with authoritative instruction, but it is only because they have themselves lost the sense of mystery.[9]

The Tension Between the Inner Felt and the Outward Known

The second illustration I take of the contrariety between the significance and the non-significance of the self may be thought of as the conflict between—to use a phrase of Julian Huxley's—the inner felt and the outward known. The point is in a way a very familiar one, partly because it refers to what is a more or less obtrusive element in the experience of all men, though perhaps not many could state it in the generalised form which we propose to give it; rather they feel the contrariety only as it presents itself in the particular experiences of their life. At the same time, for a reason which I shall give in a moment, I

---

[9]J. Oman, *Vision and Authority or the Throne of St. Peter*, second edition (London: Hodder and Stoughton, 1928), p.45.

think it is true to say that a great many more are today conscious of the contrariety in its more comprehensive and generalised form than was once the case, and this awareness certainly enters into, and accentuates the more immediate and distressful sense of the contrariety which comes through particular experiences.

It is obvious that the human person's sense of his significance as a self is centred in and inseparably bound up with his interior private feeling-life, with all those values, ideals, imperatives of conscience, longings, ambitions, aspirations and personal affections which he alone directly experiences. These, and these alone, give meaning to his life and being as a self. Yet this living, palpitating interior life of feeling and meaning finds itself in the midst of an outward environment, a world, which appears to be indifferent to it and indeed perpetually to frustrate and contradict it; and that not simply in the form of obstacles against which a man of spirit might zestfully measure his powers, but in a way that seems in the end, no matter what his purposes may be, to stamp his personal being with a final meaninglessness and non-significance. It is hardly necessary to draw the picture in detail. The world of nature with its almost unthinkable immensities dwarfing the tiny human embodied person almost into nothingness, the mechanical fixity of its processes which, though they sustain and bless man's life, can, and so often do, break into it with undiscriminating destruction, the impression of sheerly irrational and impersonal mindlessness being accentuated, rather than lightened, by the apparently capricious contrast. The world of history in all its tumult and chaos, its apparent unending "going on and getting nowhere"; the wicked prospering, the virtuous suffering, or both indiscriminately lumped together in a common fate; the great causes into which men, under the prompting of their inward being, have poured their very lifeblood coming to naught. Moreover, the contrariety of which we are speaking penetrates even into man's inward being itself. Within the boundaries of his own being he finds a like contradiction and conflict. The innermost sanctuary of his ideals and aspirations seems to be set like a beleaguered fortress in the midst of violently insurgent passions, hereditary weaknesses, obscure compulsions, which, like the hosts of Midian in the hymn, "prowl and prowl around". But I must not allow myself to grow rhetorical. Let us go back rather to a quiet and lucid statement in more abstract terms—Kant's famous utterance in the *Critique of Practical Reason*, the full force of which is unfortunately often completely lost because it is quoted only in part:

> Two things fill the mind with ever new increasing admiration and awe, the oftener and the more steadily we reflect upon them: *the starry heavens above and the moral law within.* I have not to search for them and conjecture them as though they were veiled in darkness or were in the transcendent region beyond my horizon; I see them before me and connect them directly with the consciousness of my existence. The former begins from the place I occupy in the external world of sense, and enlarges my connection therein to an unbounded extent with worlds upon worlds and systems of systems, and moreover into limitless times of their periodic motion, its beginning and continuance. The second begins from my invisible self, my personality...The former view of a countless multitude of worlds annihilates, as it were, my importance as an animal creature, which after it has been provided for a short time with the vital power, one knows not how, must again give back the matter of which it was formed to the planet it inhabits (a mere speck in the universe). The second, on the contrary, infinitely elevates my worth as an intelligence by my personality, in which the moral law reveals to me a life independent of animality and even of the whole sensible world.[10]

There you have it in cool phraseology: the outward world annihilates my significance, the inner world exalts it. It is the conflict between the inner felt and the outward known.

---

[10]I. Kant, *Critique of Practical Reason And Other Works on the Theory of Ethics*, tr. by T. K. Abbot (London: Longmans, Green & Co., 1889), p.260.

I said a minute ago that the contrariety of which we are speaking has for the modern mind assumed a more comprehensive and generalised form, so that it has become a more or less vaguely felt and disquieting background to his whole personal existence. Three reasons for this may be mentioned. (1) The first is the domination of the modern mind by the outlook and results of what is vaguely called "science". That view of the world as a nexus of impersonal rigidly determined relations, which prima facie seems to be presupposed and implied by science, has become part of the mental furniture of the ordinary man, or, to change the metaphor, has become, as it were, a pair of spectacles through which he sees all things without being aware that he is wearing them. From the work and conclusions of physical, biological, sociological, psychological, and economic science, often presented in half-baked, popular form, he continually receives the impression that he is but the product and meeting place of natural forces. Even the values and the directing of will and desire towards them which otherwise would seem to constitute the very essence of his being as a person are understood to be but the result of such forces. This, of course, was precisely Kant's problem—how to relate the world of Newtonian physics to the moral consciousness. My point, however, is that it has now become everybody's problem, even if it is not precisely formulated. (2) The second is the popularisation of astronomical knowledge, as, for example, purveyed recently over the radio by Mr Fred Hoyle. Here again is Kant's problem—his sense of personal annihilation and non-significance in the presence of the starry heavens above has now become more than ever before a permanent element in the consciousness of the plain man. (3) The third is indicated by the way there has entered into current jargon the adjective "global". It indicates perhaps that men are conscious in a new way that the forces which determine history—and therefore, because of the close-knit texture of modern life, determine their own individual destiny—are immeasurably vast, complex and apparently beyond control. On the one hand, national policies and political decisions now penetrate much more than they have ever done before into the personal life of the individual, and, on the other hand, politics has increasingly become geopolitics or, as the phrase is, "global". No doubt men's lives have always been determined by historical processes and events wider in their origin and scope than they have realised. However, the point is that today they do acutely realise the situation. Consider, for example, the almost instantaneous dissemination of news. Almost every news bulletin over the radio helps to build up the impression of the non-significance of the very ordinary person who listens to it.

Nevertheless no man, as I have said, can really rid himself of the sense of his own significance, for it is bound up with the fact of his self-consciousness and bound up with the inward world of feeling and valuation which alone gives meaning to his existence. The result is that there is produced in the modern person a deep-seated cleavage and conflict which, in some measure, colours his whole self-awareness and which enters as a factor into the more particular distresses and afflictions of his life. This cleavage and conflict has, I suspect, something (perhaps a good deal) to do with the widespread restlessness and discord of human life today from the large-scale relations of groups down to the more intimate personal relations of daily life. Lacking that resolution of the conflict which only a religious faith can provide, and in particular lacking that deep and final resolution of the conflict which, as I believe, only the Christian revelation and faith can provide, men seek to alleviate it in dangerous and perverted ways. I hazard the generalisation that people are today suffering from feelings of inferiority and the results of such feelings in a much more acute and profound way than the prevalent cliché use of the term might suggest—a way that goes to the roots of their beings as self-conscious persons. Everybody seems, in one way or another, to be fighting against a sense of personal insignificance and diminishment, defending or asserting their own importance. But it is a hopeless and endless fight, for, as I have said, so much in the world's relationship to us shouts it at us. So far as religious faith is concerned, the modern man seems to be caught in a vicious circle. It is this sense of his insignificance *vis-à-vis* the world that makes it difficult for him to have religious faith, and it is the absence of religious faith that accentuates a pathological self-assertiveness and readiness to take offence.

The Tension Which Arises as a Result of Reflection upon
the Accident of Birth

This third instance of the contrariety might between the significance and the non-significance of the self be indicated in by calling attention, on the one hand, to the well-nigh universal custom of men at all levels of culture to celebrate their birthday, and on the other hand, to the almost equally universal habit to take note, in one way or another, of the "sheer accident of birth". Although, of course, into the former many elements enter, I suspect that one central element is that the anniversary temporarily makes more explicit and intense that sense of the self's unique significance as the irreplaceable centre of his own world. To have come into existence is to have entered into that unique and mysterious status, and the giving of gifts to you and to you alone on that particular day recognises, expresses and emphasises this truth. I remember the slight but distinct shock which I received as a youth, the feeling of—I do not quite know how to express it—diminished personal significance and status, when I discovered that someone whom I knew had been born on the self same day, almost in the self same hour as myself. I do not think that this was merely a manifestation of egotism and self-importance, of the desire to have all the limelight to myself, for indeed, his limelight, so to speak, did not interfere with mine in the least. Rather it touched a deeper nerve in my self-awareness. In particular it confronted me for the first time, with all the force that attaches to concrete fact rather than to abstract truth, with the other contrasting factor of which I have spoken, namely, the "sheer accident of birth". Chucked into existence on the same day, almost the same hour, why was I not he, and he I; or if that is a foolish question, bringing with it a kind of mental vertigo from which one can only turn away as quickly as possible (for if I were he, I should not be I to be he), why was not I, this self same I, born of his parents, into his home, with his heredity and environment and all the rest, instead of my own. Thus at the very point where my own significance as a self was being asserted, a sudden question mark was put against it: apparently I am not significant enough for there to be any discernible reason why I did come into existence as myself at that point in time and space.

This last thought has, of course, often found expression. Many years ago now I wrote some words which perhaps I may be permitted to repeat.

Surely any sensible and reflective mind must ask itself this ultimate and inescapable question: why am I just I and not somebody else? Why am I an Englishman and not a naked Hottentot ranging in the forests of Africa? Why was I born into a comfortable and gracious home, and not, as so many, into a miserably poor and bitter one? Why am I clever, taking all the rewards of cleverness, while somebody else is stupid; or stupid while someone else is clever? Why am I privileged to go to public school and university, when a lad in Bermondsey must play in the gutter, sleep in a basement, and at fourteen years of age work in a factory? There was a child born of a drunken mother in prison; why was not I born of a drunken mother in prison? These are not absurd questions to ask. They spring from the very heart of reason itself, that faculty within us which must ask for a reason and purpose in things. It seems an absolute affront to reason that the most important things in life should apparently be apportioned with no more principle than the parcels from the bran tub bazaar. And the more a serious view of life is taken, the greater the affront becomes.[11]

The words still express well enough my point, but I have since come to feel that the impact of this contrariety is not merely on reflective minds who ask themselves questions and habitually seek a reason and purpose in things, though they inevitably feel it in a more explicit and therefore more acute way; it also thrusts itself into the consciousness of quite ordinary minds producing a real, if passing, sense of bafflement and disquiet, because it arises out of the fact of self-consciousness itself as it confronts the inescapable facts of its situation in the world. In the words of Georges Bataille, as given by Paul Foulquié, "If I think of my coming into the world—bound up with my birth,

---

[11]H. H. Farmer, *The Healing Cross* (London: Nisbet, 1938), pp.88-9.

and beyond that, with the union of a man and a woman, and with the moment of that union—a unique chance decides the possibility of this self that I am; indeed, the wild improbability of the mere being, without which, *for me*, nothing would exist. The slightest change in the series of which I am the term, and instead of the self avid to be myself, there would only have been some other, and as for myself, there would have been only a nothingness as complete as if I were dead." [12]　Foulquié adds, "the sense of the infinite, grievous improbability of the sequence of chance events that occasion my birth, and with it, the consciousness of the irreplaceable being that I am, since without me nothing would exist for me, and that to exist is to be for me; this is the double and contradictory sentiment to which reflection on its own existence gives rise to the mind." [13]　However, that said, Pascal's discussion of the point seems to me to come somewhat nearer to the facts in that there appears to underlie all that he says a feeling that there is something positively monstrous and unnatural in any man who has not felt, and does not feel, the pressure of this contradiction between the significance of his own being and the apparent meaninglessness of the factors which have determined his appearance in what he calls "one corner of the vast expanse of the universe", in just this spot rather than another, at just this point of time rather than another of the whole eternity which went before or shall come after, and which will in the end determine its disappearance from the scene.　He plainly suggests that those who affect to be unconcerned about it are merely posing in a way that he finds intensely irritating.　It is not merely irrational—it is unnatural, a word which he uses several times. [14]

That the awareness of this contrariety is not remote from the consciousness of ordinary people is perhaps evidenced by the grip that the belief in the

---

[12]G. Bataille, *L'expérience intérieure*, p.109.　Quoted by P. Foulquié, in *L'Existentialisme* (Paris: Presses Universitaires de France, 1948), p.45; Eng. tr. by K. Raine (London: 1948). [See also P. Roubiczek, *Existentialism: For and Against* (Cambridge: Cambridge University Press, 1966), pp.118-9—Ed.]

[13]P. Foulquié, in *L'Existentialisme*, p.45.

[14]See B. Pascal, *Pensées*, tr. by W. F. Trotter (London: Dent, 1931), pp.16-21.　Cf. also H. F. Stewart (ed.), *Pascal's Apology for Religion: Extracted from the Pensées* (Cambridge: Cambridge University Press, 1942), pp.11ff.—Ed.

transmigration of souls has had on the minds of men, particularly in that form which explicitly relates the place and circumstances of birth to the moral quality of the life lived in a previous existence. This is obviously, in part, an attempt to assert the significance of the self and, at the same time, to overcome its apparent non-significance in view of the factors which determine its appearance at "just this spot rather than another". The theory has attracted a number of thinkers who have consciously sought a rational solution of the problem of man's existence and status in the world, from Pythagoras and Plato to Lessing, Goethe and MacTaggart, not to speak of the sages of the East. But the way in which it has laid hold of the mind of the masses in India, for example, shows that it is not merely an answer to a thinker's problem, but has to do with a real element in the felt situation of every man, in whom, therefore, it finds at once a point of attachment. In India, of course, the problem is accentuated and brought into the foreground of consciousness by the rigid caste system.

We may perhaps surmise that the main reason why belief in metempsychosis has never laid hold of the western mind to the same degree has not been that the contrariety was not felt, but rather that the dominant tradition has been Christian and this, as we shall see, has taught another answer to the problem. That the decline in the influence of the Christian tradition has not resulted in the spread of belief in transmigration is no doubt due in part to the fact that the forces of secularisation which have brought about the former inhibit the latter also. A positivistic age which has so largely lost the sense of the spiritual background of life is clearly not going to find a doctrine of the soul and its morally determined destiny congenial, even if the other difficulties which are inherent in the theory could be overcome. Nevertheless, some sense of the contrariety of which we have been speaking remains, and we may perhaps conjecture that it bears some relation to the unreflective and often embittered egalitarianism which so often characterises an otherwise legitimate protest against social injustice. Such egalitarianism is, once again, an assertion of the significance of the self against the apparent non-significance of the factors which determine the so-called accident of birth.

The Tension Inherent Within Moments of Serious Moral Decision

Every man at some point in his life has to make really critical decisions and choices which he knows will determine for good or for ill the whole course of the future both for himself and for others. At such a point the awareness of the significance of the self can take possession of the mind in an unusually intense form. He knows that according to his decision events will unfold in one way rather than another, with possibly unforeseen fateful results. But, on the other hand, in proportion as this sense of responsibility possesses the mind, it is apt to bring with it a burdened and lonely sense of inadequacy to sustain such a responsible role. Shut up within the inaccessible loneliness of choice, for no one can make the decision for him, he is conscious that in himself alone he cannot, and does not, possess the knowledge and wisdom which would entitle him to make such a critical decision, not to speak of making it with any confidence or peace of mind: the historical and world process of which he is a part, and which for a moment concentrates and narrows itself in his decisive choice, is altogether too vast, complex and incalculable. Here obviously, and once again, is an occasion for a lively sense of the contrariety between the significance and non-significance of the self, bringing with it a distressful feeling of anxiety. The situation so plainly declares the critical importance of the decision of the self and yet at the same time, it is clear that the factors which actually determine the unfolding of events utterly transcend the limits of the self and its knowledge.

I would wish to emphasise that this awareness is bound up with, is the inevitable accompaniment of, man's self-consciousness. In one way it is a perfectly obvious truth, almost a truism, that a man's choices and actions are only a small factor in the infinite network of happenings which constitute the world process, just as the activities of other finite entities, animals, plants, and things are. We can, indeed, state this truth in a quite cool abstract way in the detached seclusion of the study; or perhaps contemplate it at the theatre as part of the fascinating drama of life, setting alongside one another as determinants of destiny Caesar crossing the Rubicon and even the length of Cleopatra's nose, or perhaps commenting in no more serious mood than that in which

Pope wrote in *The Rape of the Lock*, "what mighty conflicts rise from trivial things". But to the man actually confronted with the necessity to make a critical decision, nothing could seem farther removed from the truth than to equate what he is doing, even though it is in fact but one factor amongst countless others, with the merely instinctive activity of an animal or the physiological structure of a woman's face. Just because he is a rational self-conscious person, he is not merely an item in the process of events, but also, *he knows that he is*, and that makes all the difference, for it puts an inescapable responsibility of decision upon him so that the cry "what ought I to do" can be one of real anguish. Yet because he is a rational self-consciousness, he also knows that, in another sense, the equation just referred to is perfectly correct, and that he is but one tiny factor along with countless others. We must not indeed exaggerate the extent to which ordinary men feel these things; some people seem to be surprisingly lacking in a serious sense of responsibility, even in what are manifestly important choices and decisions, and in others, I suspect, the sense of this contrariety is continuously alleviated by a kind of dim and undeveloped religious faith in providence, a faith that if a man does his best, and no one can do more, all the other factors will co-operate for good on the whole. Nevertheless, situations may arise at any time, for anybody, in which the burden and anxiety of decision cannot but be acutely felt and not so easily disposed of. But even apart from such special situations of crisis, we can perhaps see some evidence that this conflict is not remote from the everyday consciousness of people in the way in which so many are ready to surrender themselves absolutely to an external director of conduct, whether in the form of a dictator or of an authoritarian church. One element in this readiness is undoubtedly a flight from the burden of decision in the midst of a world as complex and unpredictable as ours manifestly is.

It is, of course, serious moral natures who feel most acutely the burden of responsibility in a world where so little is in their knowledge and control. Such natures are frequently extremely puzzled and perplexed by the moral problems with which the concrete situations of life confront them. Nor are they likely to get much help from the various ethical systems which have at different times been formulated by ethical writers. Hartmann suggests that such puzzlement and perplexity is due to the fact that the moral sense, like every other mental function, needs to be developed and educated, that the more it is developed and educated the less the perplexity becomes, and that nothing more can be expected of the moralist than to help in this development and education. There is, of course, truth in this. Nevertheless, I think it greatly over-simplifies the situation. The more morally sensitive a man becomes, the more likely is he to feel acutely the burden of his own significance as a responsible self in the midst of an infinite number of factors which he cannot know, or knowing cannot control, and in relation to the working out of which, therefore, he has but the smallest significance. It is coarse moral natures which find decision easy and lightly bear the thought of mistake, whereas it is a developed sensitivity to moral values that makes a man aware of how complex a situation is and how fraught with incalculable consequences anything he decides to do may be, both for himself and for others.

Religion and Self-consciousness

We now ask how this broad and basic contrariety between the significance and non-significance of the self, which we have set forth in the last lecture through four instances of it, is related to living religion and especially to the Christian revelation and faith. That the relation is close will be evident from what has been said from a number of different angles throughout these lectures.

The ultimate objective source of religion we have maintained and must continue to maintain is the self-revealing activity of God. Nevertheless, a subjective condition which the divine revelation both creates and speaks to is the self's awareness of its significance as a self and its need to maintain that significance in the midst of a world that at so many points seems to deny it. This awareness and need is related to the apprehension of God as the final succour and security of man's being and life. The divine succour may, under the pressure of need, be thought of primarily and predominantly in terms of the immediate, natural necessities of life, but one may surmise that there enters into even the most primitive eudaemonistic approach to God an underlying sense of the significance of the self and of the need to affirm it in the face of the threats of the world. For such a sense is bound up with the fact of self-consciousness, and certainly without self-consciousness there can be no religion. But the awareness and need are also connected with the apprehension of God as absolute demand, for, as we have seen, it is only through the impact of such a demand that man is released from the flux of a purely instinctual life and begins to stand upright on his own feet as a self-conscious person, with all the needs of a self-conscious person, in the midst of the world.

These, of course, are not new thoughts. Apart, however, from our own particular approach, one could quote a number of statements from modern authorities in religion, which in one form or another express the view, based on their studies, that living religion and the establishing and succouring of man as a self-conscious person in the midst of his world are closely bound together. Albrecht Ritschl's well-known statement may be taken as typical:

> In every religion there is a solution of the contradiction in which man finds himself as both a part of the world of nature and as a spiritual self-conscious personality claiming to rule nature. For in the former role he is part of nature, dependent on her, subject and confined by other things; but as spirit he is moved by his impulse to maintain his independence against them. In this situation religion springs up as faith in divine spiritual powers, by whose help the power which man is conscious of possessing in himself to be a self, is in some way supplanted and elevated into a unity of its own kind which is a match for the pressure of the natural world.[15]

---

[15]This seems to be Farmer's own translation. See A. Ritschl, *The Christian Doctrine of Justification and Reconciliation*, tr. by H. R. Mackintosh & A. B. Macauley (Edinburgh: T. & T. Clark, 1900), p.199. See also H. R. Mackintosh, *Types of Modern Theology*, pp.147f.; and J. Richmond, *Ritschl: A Reappraisal* (London: Collins, 1978), pp.83f.—Ed.

Or, again, one might give a catena of quotations from a number of deeply experiencing thinkers who have come at the same essential truth simply by probing the underlying deeps of their own consciousness as religious men— Augustine, Pascal, Hegel, Schleiermacher, Kierkegaard. The thoughts of all these men are led along different paths to this same strange paradoxical situation of man in the world, standing over against it in the independence of its own interior self-awareness, so little merely part of it that he can know it, and know that he knows it, and intends to know it, and by knowing it to rule it; and yet, on the other hand, he is so utterly part of it that, as Pascal says, a vapour, a drop of water can utterly obliterate him. Augustine's 26th and 27th chapters of Book II of *De Civitate Dei* wherein, having anticipated Descartes' *cogito ergo sum* (though in a wholly religious context) he then goes on to speak of "existence and the knowledge of it and the love of both." Pascal's famous paragraphs where he speaks of the greatness and littleness of man as a self-conscious thinking being. Hegel's baffling discussion in the *Phenomenology of Mind* of what he calls "the unhappy consciousness" of the self, tracing it back even into the simplest act of sense-perception. Schleiermacher's insistence, in his *Christliche Glaube*, that religion is essentially bound up with self-feeling and that we can only grasp its essence in the feeling of absolute dependence if we take note of the dual position in which man finds himself as he confronts his world: namely, of freedom and mastery over it, on the one hand, expressing the existence of the subject for himself, and of the dependence upon it, on the other hand, expressing the self's coexistence with the "other" of the world. Finally, there is the centrality in Kierkegaard's thought of the notion of "subjectivity" to which reference has already been made. All these thinkers appear to be hovering around the central truth. But the fact that they are men of profound mind does not mean that they are out of touch with the experience of ordinary men, even though they express themselves in terms which the latter would find completely incomprehensible. On the contrary, they are doing what they certainly believe themselves to be doing, namely, uncovering and giving expression to a fundamental element in the actual situation of any self-conscious person in the world.

We turn now to a striking illustration of the reality of the close connection between religion and the need of the self-conscious person to maintain his status in the world; it is the more striking because it might seem, at first sight, to run completely counter to it. It is found in mysticism, particularly in the highly developed speculative mysticism of India. Bowman is thus surely right to contend that the key to Indian mysticism is its emphasis on the soul, the self, the *Atman*. The conception of Brahma or world-unity is, of course, of the highest significance as a philosophic idea, but Brahman knowledge only becomes mysticism through a prior pre-occupation with the self. This dominant starting point (whatever the outcome) must not be forgotten. Mysticism has come to be widely known as a gospel of self-renunciation, a cult of indifferentism or quietude, the merging of the self in the cosmos. This is, in a sense, its final outcome when *Atman*-lore merges in Brahman-lore. However, when the mystic loses his individual self to Brahman, the whole experience must be interpreted in the light of the idea that it is only in this way that he can attain to that fullness of selfhood, which has been from the beginning the object of his endeavours.[16] In short, the mystic quest *is* the yearning for selfhood notwithstanding the fact that it is presented as a yearning to be rid of selfhood. By a not unfamiliar psychological process, the very denial of the significance of the self is really a disguised form of asserting it, and this is shown by the fact that it issues in the stupendous pronouncement that the soul is All, and all is the Soul, one self without a second. Thus the world, with all its dualities, and in particular its threat to the self, has completely disappeared.

Returning now to the four instances of the contrariety of the significance and non-significance of the self, I want briefly to consider the relation of religion, and in particular of Christianity as a reconciling faith, to each.

---

[16]See A. A. Bowman, *Studies in the Philosophy of Religion*, vol.1, pp.377-80, 391-98.—Ed.

Reconciliation and the Relationship of Knowledge Between the Self and the World

Again, we begin with that form of the contrariety which is implicit in the relationship of knowledge and which sometimes manifests itself in the experience of "isolement". That the ordinary man does not become *explicitly* conscious of this contrariety is no doubt due in part to his absorption in the sheerly practical task of getting to know and manage his world, as well as to the fact that he lacks the power of self-observation and self-analysis and, even more, the abstract concepts which such self-observation and analysis require. But I venture to think that there is in fact a deeper reason, namely, that the contrariety is continually being resolved by something in the nature of religious awareness, which may be only dimly conscious of itself—the belief, that is to say, in the dependence of all things, the world and the self together, upon an all-creating and all-sustaining divine will which posits and affirms both together; and along with this a belief in the continued existence of the self and its world beyond their apparent annihilation in death. Such a faith, dim and obscure though it may be, prevents, even in those who would not ordinarily count themselves religious believers, the sense of isolation (the sense of the self as being the unutterably lonely centre of its world and as being, nevertheless, under constant threat of being annihilated, taking the world along with it into nothingness) from taking possession of the mind. Of course, where there is an explicit and continuous rejection by the *conscious* mind of such a faith, this is bound, to some extent, to work inhibitingly upon these deeper and more immediate responses of the self. When that happens the sense of the contrariety between the significance and the non-significance of the self can enter much more powerfully as a determinant into a one's consciousness, bringing with it a sense, not the less unhappy for being vague and intermittent, of being down to the roots of one's selfhood profoundly isolated and insecure. Such an "unhappy consciousness" (to use Hegel's phrase) I suspect has something to do with the psychological troubles from which so many suffer in these days.

I believe that we here touch upon one at least of the internal conditions and sources of the belief in a divine creator and the belief in life beyond death which men have held from the earliest ages of which we have any record. To all appearance the two beliefs emerged simultaneously with the emergence of human self-conscious personality. If we speak simply in terms of such internal conditions and sources, and leave out of consideration the divine initiative of self-disclosure (which, of course, in any complete understanding of the situation, we must not do), then we can say that the belief in the divine creator and sustainer of all, and the belief in continued existence after death, which we find at the most primitive levels of culture, are the indispensable defences of human personal consciousness as it comes to know the world.

Perhaps I may digress for a moment to make a comment on each of these two points. (1) In relation to belief in God as the creator and sustainer of the world. If what I have just been saying is correct, it is possible perhaps to see that Berkeley's argument for the existence of God (that it is necessary to posit the divine mind as the permanent source and basis of the persistence of the world even when men cease to perceive it) is, like other traditional proofs of God's existence, really an attempt to transpose into a rational medium a need and an insight which have other and much more profound roots in the soul. We may surmise that it was because of this deeper need and insight, rooted in the fact of his self-consciousness *vis-à-vis* the world, that Berkeley felt the argument to be more convincing than, in strict logic, it actually was.

(2) With regard to belief in the continued existence of the self after death, no doubt a number of elements have always entered into this, as we have seen in other connections. But one root of it, I suggest, is man's peculiar situation as the self-conscious "perspective-centre" of his world. Thus we can accept the statement, which has so often been made, that men believe in life after death because of an incapacity to contemplate their own annihilation. But, and this is the point, the implication, expressed or unexpressed, which often goes with it, that such incapacity arises simply from a feeble and irrational egotism, we do not accept. On the contrary, we believe that to draw such an inference is to reveal, once again, the superficiality which characterises so

much thought about the world and its relation to man and, in particular, the superficiality which ignores the unique fact of the self-consciousness of man as he stands in the midst of, and apprehends, his world. It ignores "subjectivity". Before such an inference can have any weight, there must be a much more careful and deep-going analysis of precisely this incapacity of a self to contemplate its own annihilation. We might say that what is called for is a metaphysic of self-consciousness.

Finally, I must say a brief word on the relation of the Christian revelation and faith to all this. I want to suggest that the particular contrariety between the significance and non-significance of the self that we have been exploring *is* overcome in the Christian revelation and faith in a profound and distinctive way. In the first place, the dim and undeveloped religious beliefs of which I have spoken, and which I am sure are deep within people's minds far more than they realise or would acknowledge, are made fully explicit; and thus, be it noted, not merely in abstract theological statement, but also, and much more importantly, in regularly repeated acts of worship, in which the deepest feelings, attitudes and responses of the whole self down to its subconscious depths are engaged. Thus God is continuously and livingly apprehended as the transcendent creator and sustainer, whose power and wisdom have established, indwell, work through, and hold together both self and world in an inseparable, mutual dependence-independence relation with one another. That is to say, the world is not simply "there" for me, my world, a function of my self-consciousness, though it may appear to be so if I think only of the lonely observation point which I occupy, or rather am, in the activity of knowing. Nor, on the other hand, is my self-consciousness merely "there" because of the world, a mere product or function of it, though it may appear to be so, if I think only of its brief temporality and utter helplessness in the face of the world. Rather, both are "there" because of, and for, and in God, who transcends both. Each, therefore, having significance for God, has significance independently of the other, and yet they both also have significance in relation to one another; for the world is affirmed by the Christian faith to be the sphere in which God is at work and encounters the self, and the self's true life is affirmed to be its co-operation with, or rather service of, God in his work in the world.

In the second place, the Christian faith makes quite explicit and central (so that it forms the permanent and clearly apprehended background and context of self-consciousness) that dim and instinctive belief in the persistence of the self beyond its apparent annihilation in death, which in the ordinary man's mind goes some way to allaying the contrariety we are discussing. The Christian revelation, however, meets the situation in an ever more thorough and distinctive way. It establishes the self in a personal I-Thou relationship with the ultimate reality which is the source of its existence and of the existence of the world, a relation which it characterises as one of love on the part of God and an answering trust and self-commitment on the part of the self. In such a relation the sense of *isolement*, the sense of being the lonely centre of one's world and, at the same time, always under threat of extinction, is overcome at the deepest possible level with a finality not otherwise possible. We must emphasise the phrase "not otherwise possible". The isolation of the self in its selfhood *vis-à-vis* the world connotes a quite fundamental and essential loneliness which no companionship with other human selves or "thous", who are plainly in exactly the same situation, can really touch. What is required is precisely what the Christian revelation makes possible, the living apprehension of being in relation to a "Thou" of a different order, one who is the ultimate source of the self's own existence and significance as a self and of all selves and all being whatsoever, in short, all that is meant by the term "God".

It might perhaps be said that, after all, these two affirmations (the affirmation of the significance of both the world and the self, in themselves and in relation to one another under the one creative purpose and will of God who transcends both, and the affirmation of the continued existence of the self and world beyond death) are not, even as explicitly formulated religious convictions, distinctive of the Christian revelation and faith. On the contrary, they tend to characterise all religious faith that has moved towards an ethical monotheism. This no doubt is true; and certainly one would not suggest that, in order to maintain and exhibit the distinctiveness and uniqueness of Christianity as a reconciling faith, we must deny that there are any elements in it which are paralleled elsewhere. Indeed, our finding of the normative concept of religion in Christianity, which has been at the basis of our thought throughout both series of lectures, implies the contrary. At the same time, however, the Christian revelation *has* its own deep-going and distinctive way of presenting these two truths, of putting them right at the heart of the religious consciousness and so of overcoming, once and for all, the contrariety we are considering. It does this by its central and distinctive faith in the incarnation as the manifestation of divine love.

The incarnation, or as we have preferred to put it, the "inhistorisation" of God clearly means that God himself *entered the world in the form of human selfhood itself.*[17] One aspect of the "inhistorisation" is that it sets forth a final resolution of the self and the world antithesis without denying the reality of either. For, on the one hand, it affirms that not only does God draw near to the self in its isolation and establish it in an I-Thou relation of fellowship with himself, but also that the medium of his drawing near is a human self. There could be no more unequivocal and emphatic assertion right at the heart and centre of living religious faith of the significance of selfhood against everything in the world which would seem to deny it. On the other hand, the doctrine of the incarnation does not affirm the significance of the self at the expense of the significance of the world, as acosmic mysticism tends to do. On the contrary, it asserts the latter just as much as it asserts the former, and also their contrariety with one another, for both are within the one all-encompassing, redeeming and creative purpose of God. This double implication of the dogma finds expression in the New Testament in the thought of Christ the incarnate Son being the one true perfect human self and also the creative principle at work in the world, the Logos, by whom the world was made. It is important to realise (and to make this clear is part of the

---

[17]See J. Baillie, *The Sense of the Presence of God* (London: Oxford University Press, 1962), p.86.—Ed.

purpose of these remarks) that such statements as these are not the formulations of abstract theologising, though they may have that appearance; rather, they spring right out of the Christian experience of reconciliation at a very deep level, the level, that is to say, of the self-in-world opposition—this explains, in part, the glow with which they are written. Perhaps we come nearest to the heart of this experience in the words attributed to Christ at the end of Matthew's Gospel: "All authority in heaven and on earth has been given to me...And surely I am with you always, to the very end of the age." [18] The incarnation, as the central and supreme manifestation of divine love towards the self, approaches its accomplishment, so far as the self is concerned, in the establishment of the self in fellowship with God through Christ, a fellowship which nothing in the world, not even death, can destroy. In this relationship, any hint of "isolement", any sense of being the lonely centre of one's world and at the same time under threat of extinction so that everything, self and world together, dissolves into a void of nothingness, is finally overcome at the deepest possible level and in a way that brings the whole self to a final completion and fulfilment.

Reconciliation and the Tension Between
the Inner Felt and Outward Known

We turn now to that form of the contrariety between the significance and the non-significance of the self which we have called the contrariety between "the inner felt and the outward known", the profound contrariety between the inward ideals and aspirations of the self and the ineluctable outward facts. How is this fundamental brokenness in human experience to be healed?

The two opposed elements in the duality indicate two broad lines along which the religious mind has sought a solution of the problem. In the first place it has sometimes sought the solution by, in effect, reinterpreting the outward facts of experience. It has refused to accept the apparent outward facts as conclusive; there is more to reality than meets the eye; so far from it

---

[18]Matt. 28:18,20.

being true that "all is vanity",[19] the vanity of life is not all. Thus Job, confronted by the apparent failure of the facts of experience to harmonise with his inward sense of right and wrong, cries "I know that my Redeemer lives..."[20] Something of this faith enters into all living religion, and is, we may again surmise, not altogether absent from the minds of ordinary men and women enabling them, as we say, to "keep going", however dim and unformulated it may be and however little they may be ready to acknowledge it in explicit thought. But its weakness is that it is always a flying in the face of facts and, therefore, is precluded from appealing to experience for confirmation. Hence, it is very apt to have within it a continuous strain of effort, an effort which, in the presence of the worst contradictions and the most exacting tests, may break down or else become a piece of pathological make-believe—which is far from being a deep and genuine reconciliation and peace.

In the second place, the religious mind has sought a solution of the problem by a readjustment of the self. The chief source of the contradiction between the self and the world is declared to be the inward state of the soul, its corruption and confusion as a result of the false values which rule there. External reality in its relation to the self clearly does have within it elements which remain dark and inscrutable and concerning which the direct counter-affirmation of faith must still be made. But these elements appear more dark and inscrutable than they really are, and the affirmation of faith made correspondingly more difficult to sustain, because they are judged by false standards springing from the impurity of the self. The shadow which lies across the world comes from within and what is required, therefore, is primarily an inward purification. Mysticism has laid almost exclusive emphasis on this approach to the problem. However, it also represents a strand of thought which, in one form or another, appears in nearly all religion, running alongside and interacting with the more simple and outwardly

---

[19] Ecc.1:2
[20] Job 19:25.

directed faith-declaration that the external reality with which man has to deal is, in its contradiction of his inner being, not what it appears to be.

The Christian revelation and faith, however, moves along *both* the lines I have just indicated. In doing so, it makes its own distinctive contribution to each, and at the same time unites them inseparably with one another. The result is unification, a reconciliation which, while of course not disposing of all mysteries, is of a peculiarly deep and inclusive kind. And once again it does this because of its central affirmation of the incarnation.

In the first place, the self-disclosure of God in the historic person of Christ brings together the inward and the outward aspects of human experience in such a way that faith is no longer merely a strained flying in the face of facts, but is succoured and established in their very presence and midst. How is this so? Well, to begin with, the revelation continually calls forth in the believer the conviction that, in Christ, he encounters the full and perfect realisation and embodiment of all those highest values which have disclosed themselves, however dimly and intermittently hitherto, in his inward being.[21] He is constrained to say, "this is perfect spirit, this is the living completion and fulfilment of every dim vision of, and movement towards the ideal that my soul has ever had." Thus the inward values cease to be merely inward, a dim and intermittent vision of the interior self; rather, they now confront the self, so to say, from "out there", both in their fullest perfection and also concretely objectified amidst the actualities of the world-process of nature and history itself. This is obviously a first and important step in the overcoming of the contrariety. The values of the inward being are no longer what we bring, in their dim and clouded intermittency, to the external reality, but meet the self in full realisation in the midst of external reality, as veritably there as any other fact. Here the concrete, historical reality of Christ, the fact of Christ, is of crucial importance. But that is not all. There is another element in the Christian reconciliation which goes deeper. It is that the values which are thus seen to be concretely objectified and fulfilled in Christ are manifested in and

----

[21]Cf. H. H. Farmer, *The World and God*, pp.196ff.—Ed.

through the very kind of external fact which seems most to run counter to them. They are not manifested merely alongside those facts, or in spite of them, but *in and through* them; that is to say, they make them the vehicle and means of their manifestation. Thus again, the contrariety is overcome. Here the fact of the passion of Christ, which the Gospel narratives and the New Testament generally make dominant and central in the revelation, is of crucial importance. But again, that is not all. There is still a further step. That in Christ the values of the inward being are concretely manifested in their perfection in external reality and use the contrary facts as their vehicle and means of self-manifestation is not a final overcoming of the contrariety, for there may still await them a final defeat and eclipse. In particular there remains the fact of death—that last question mark which nature and history set against all the values of personal life. This also is met in the Christian revelation. It is met by the fact of the resurrection, attested by eyewitnesses as historically objective—just as historically objective as the passion and crucifixion. In the resurrection, the reconciliation of "the inner felt and the outwardly known" is completed.[22]

But now, in the second place, it is obvious that all this assumes the capacity to discern in Christ the perfect realisation and fulfilment of the inward values and ideals which alone give meaning and dignity to man's life, and that is manifestly a very large assumption to make. The values to which men aspire even in their more idealistic moments, still less those which actually rule their lives, are not, as a rule, those which do in fact find their concretion and realisation in Christ. Hence, as an indispensable element in its reconciliation of the inward and the outward, the Christian revelation and faith also requires a purification and reordering of the self, a transformation of its

---

[22] This final point was originally written as follows: "Revelation did not culminate in the crucifixion; if it had done it would have no distinctive reconciling power in this matter of the inwardly felt and the outwardly known. The culmination of it is the resurrection of one who in his perfect personal life was apparently utterly defeated and crushed by the outward order—the resurrection is presented and affirmed as concrete and empirically attested fact in history as much as the crucifixion itself. The resurrection as credibly attested historical fact is the final answer of the Christian revelation to the conflict between the inner felt and the outward known."—Ed.

values, which may have to be so radical that the metaphor of "new birth" is not felt to be inappropriate. But the important thing, from our point of view here, is that according to the Christian understanding, the cleansing and reordering of the self and its values is not separate from the divine revelation in Christ. Such cleansing and reordering is not something which a man can and must first accomplish for himself by a process of self-purification before that revelation can speak to him. On the contrary, the revelation is understood and experienced to be itself the chief and quite indispensable means of purification; it is itself the light which penetrates the darkness and confusion of man's interior being, and calls into activity, with the co-operation of the divine spirit which is at work in the deeps of the soul, the very power of discernment to which it appeals. We will not pursue this farther. It is enough to note that the whole process of reconciliation in respect of the contrariety between internal and external reality is a quite unitary process. At one and the same time (and in inseparable unity with one another) it brings together the two needs which make themselves apparent in one form or another throughout the whole history of religion—the need for faith to be succoured in face of the outward facts, and the need of the self to be cleansed and purified in its inward being. It brings them together so that the satisfaction of the one is part of, and indispensable to, the satisfaction of the other.

Reconciliation and the Tension Which Arises as a Result of Reflection upon the Accident of Birth

We come now to the third contrariety between the significance and non-significance of the self—that which we summed up in the phrase the "accident of birth". The relation of the Christian revelation to this, and the way in which it is overcome in Christian faith and experience is to a large extent implicit in what was said in the earlier chapter on time and eternity, and I do not think it is necessary to set forth again what was there said.

It might be thought that the doctrine of divine providence provides sufficient answer to the problem of the accident of birth in relation to the sense which the self has of its own significance, in that it asserts that one receives one's personal existence and the particular point in the continuum of nature and history into which one is born *by the appointment of God*, despite the fact that both appear to be the result of irrational and meaningless chance; and no doubt this is broadly the answer of the Christian faith. But obviously, merely to assert a doctrine of providence need have little to do with that profound reconciliation of the man himself, touching the deepest feeling insights and responses of the self, which the Christian faith claims to make possible in a distinctive way and which it is our concern here to grasp. We are interested here, as throughout both these series of lectures, with living religion and its unifying power, and only in doctrines in so far as they meet us in and arise out of, or make possible, such living religion. I pointed out at the end of our discussion of time and eternity that a belief in the divine providence may have a number of different sources and meanings and correspondingly different bearings on men's lives; and it was in part the burden of that chapter that the Christian man's faith in providence has a quite distinctive content and strength because it is a faith rooted in the incarnation.

The point I want now briefly to make may be approached through the idea of divine election which came before us in the above-mentioned chapter on time and eternity. It has to do with one aspect of the biblical belief in divine election which was not mentioned in that chapter, namely, that it is always understood as election, not to privilege, but to service. We need not expound this, for not only, when once it has been pointed out, is it apparent everywhere in both the Old and New Testaments, but it has also been done in great fullness by H. H. Rowley in his *The Biblical Doctrine of Election*.[23] What we need especially to notice is the distinctively Christian interpretation which is given to this doctrine through the suffering and death of Christ as this is set before us in the New Testament. In accordance with the fundamental truth of the "inhistorisation" of God in Christ, the redeemer himself is apprehended as appearing at a quite particular point and place in history, not by any accident of birth, but by the determinate counsel and foreknowledge of God. He is sent

---

[23]H. H. Rowley, *The Biblical Doctrine of Election* (London: Lutterworth, 1950).

to inaugurate the Kingdom and to be the saviour of mankind, and thus he appears in history as the supreme example of election to service; he is the elect servant of God. But, and this is the point, as elect to be the saviour of mankind, he is by that very fact elected to suffering, for by his suffering and by it alone he fulfils the divine saving purpose towards mankind in him. We may here quote Rowley: speaking of the figure of the suffering servant in Isaiah, through which this profound and revolutionary thought is first adumbrated, later to be given its fullest and clearest expression in concrete actuality in Christ, he says,

> The uniqueness of the Servant is that whereas others suffered in consequence of their mission, his suffering is the organ of his mission. The service for which he was chosen was a world-wide service...The complaint against the Biblical doctrine of election that it is unjust is here more than anywhere shown to be beside the mark. For what is commonly meant by the complaint is that it is unjust that the elect should be favoured...But here it would appear that if there is injustice it is directed against the elect and not in his favour. His is a heritage of suffering, and to others—even to those who inflict the suffering on him—it brings a heritage of blessing. For justice is not the only Divine principle, or even the highest principle. That man should treat his fellow-men with injustice is sin, and an offence to God. This means that the maltreating of the Servant by men is sin, and therefore an offence against God. But that the Servant should willingly accept that suffering in obedience to his vocation is something far higher than justice. It is the fruit of his standing in the counsel of God, and the mark of his oneness with God.[24]

Now this transcending of the category of justice in the relation of oneness with God in the service of his will is, I believe, a unique element in the

---

[24]Ibid., pp.117-8.

Christian revelation and experience of reconciliation and is closely related to the problem we are discussing. It is to be noted that it is not a transcending of it merely in idea, as though it were forced upon us as a theoretical postulate in order to ease the otherwise insoluble problem of the injustices of life; rather it is compellingly exhibited in the process of history itself; and, in particular, it is exhibited as the very centre and consummation of that "saving history". As we saw in the discussion of time and eternity, a man is one with God when he takes his place alongside Christ within this saving history and knows himself to be also elect and called of God to serve him in it, and to have the fellowship with God which that service brings. Nothing else matters but this. Even suffering can, like the suffering of Christ, be taken up into and become the organ and means of service to God in his saving purpose. Thus for the reconciled man also, the category of justice is transcended, and this profoundly affects his thought concerning the accident of his birth. For this, in the context of the divine election and the call to service becomes, along with the category of justice, of no further interest. It loses its significance in the larger significance of the divine purpose. This constitutes the Christian reply, at the level of the living experience of reconciliation as distinct from argument in the realm of ideas, to the doctrine of *karma*. The latter, from the standpoint of the Christian revelation, is overly concerned both with the accident of birth and with the category of justice. We might put it like this: we cannot read the meaning of our birth situation, least of all in terms of justice. But God bestows meaning upon it by taking it up, through his revelation in Christ, and supremely through his suffering, into saving history. And this meaning can be bestowed on any situation. Thus all are brought onto a level with one another. Or we might put it thus: it is an essential part of the reconciliation of the Christian man that he is enabled to say (which we may properly make to echo the words of Christ) "for this cause was I born when I was born and for this cause I came into the world at the place where I came into the world, that I should bear witness to the truth."

Reconciliation and the Tension Highlighted in
Moments of Serious Moral Decision

The fourth instance of the contrariety between the significance and non-significance of the self was concerned with those moments of serious moral decision which come to all men at some time. At such moments the self is conscious of the critical significance of its decision in the unfolding of events, and yet also of the infinite complexity of the forces which constitute the world process into which his decision is immediately taken up, and by which its consequences are in considerable measure determined. At such a time a serious moral nature is oppressed with the sense of being forced, as it were, into a role which it has not the knowledge and insight to sustain. To this also the Christian revelation and faith has something distinctive to say, and once again, it is centred in the affirmation of the incarnation. I make three brief points:

(1) Faith in the incarnation establishes Christ as, in some sense, the final authority in the moral sphere. This at once imparts and sustains the sense that amidst all the complex perplexities and relativities of moral action there *is* an absolute, a finality for the self. This itself helps to quicken and cleanse the moral insight, for there are few things, in the long run, more calculated to paralyse and blind, to undermine and destroy the capacity for moral judgement than to have an underlying scepticism as to whether there is anywhere, in a form accessible to the human spirit, a moral absolute, a firm moral ground under the feet, a really reliable and supporting moral medium and environment. This is precisely the situation of countless people today. They are bogged down in moral relativity.[25]

---

[25]No doubt it is partly the desire to escape this situation that impels men to choose out from amongst the relativities of history some element on which they can bestow an artificial absoluteness such as a fascist dictator or a Marxist orthodoxy—artificial because so long as man chooses his own absolute from among the relativities, he knows deep down that it is not a real absolute and that it is liable to be exposed as such at any moment by other facts in the historical process with which it is fundamentally on a level. This perhaps explains the bitter and cruel fanaticism with which they adhere to it. Fanaticism springs from fear, and fear, in this instance, springs from the underlying sense that an element in history, elevated to the rank of an absolute over history, is at bottom a fraud. This is avoided in the Christian revelation by the explicit presentation of Christ as the divine incarnation or inhistorisation,

It is evident, however, that whilst much is gained for the moral life by the acknowledgement of Christ as the absolute for it, the problem of moral perplexity remains. The absolute standard acknowledged in Christ has still to be translated into the practical decisions and choices of daily living amidst all the infinite multiplicity of factors of historical reality, and in the absence of precisely formulated instructions, such as Christ significantly never gave, and of which there is little hint in the New Testament, the situation would still seem to remain the same. It is here that the other two points become relevant.

(2) The Christian faith in the Incarnation implicitly carries with it the conviction that Christ is not merely a historical figure external to the self and receding farther and farther into a remote and increasingly alien past; rather he is apprehended as embodying the true universal of human nature, and therefore is deeply related to the inward being of the self at all times, including particularly those times when the self is most conscious of its responsibility as a self in moral choice and decision. Christ, according to the Christian revelation and faith, is true man, he is the realisation of that norm which is already inherent in human personality or selfhood as such. He is the embodiment of the original *imago dei*, which, in whatever degree and in whatever sense it may be held to be defaced by sin, remains essentially constitutive of it. Hence, it is not merely an utterance of pious devotion and aspiration, but a factual statement about human selfhood, a basic element in a Christian anthropology, that there is latent within the self a hidden Christ-principle continually pressing towards realisation and expression in a life after the type of the "Son of man". Or (in the thought of the New Testament) Christ is, for every human self, in a final sense, "the Way, the Truth and the Life". This obviously connects with the Christian doctrine of the Holy Spirit, and in particular with what was said in an earlier chapter concerning the

---

that is, the self-disclosure into history, as well as in and through history, of the absolute reality which transcends history and rules it. Man, as an item in the process, does not bestow absoluteness on Christ, another item in the process; rather, in Christ, the absolute which is above the process and at the same time at work in it, bestows itself on him. There is a greater significance in relation to the human situation than might at first sight appear in the following simple statement of Christ as recorded in the fourth gospel: "You did not choose me, but I chose you..." (Jn. 15:16).

interplay of the Spirit working in the unconscious deeps of the self with the directing of the mind, on the conscious level, to the historic figure of Christ. It is part of the faith in the Incarnation to declare that such interplay *is* possible, and that where it takes place there is a quickening of moral insight, which constitutes, amidst all the confusion and perplexity of life, real and available guidance.

Nevertheless, the burden of the situation is still not wholly lifted. For, firstly, the guidance, as we have said, certainly does not take the form of detailed instruction miraculously imparted as each new situation arises, which instruction I have only to obey in order to be saved from every possibility of mistake. I am still under necessity, as a self, to make my own decision by my own judgement, and though that decision and judgement are necessarily different from what they otherwise would be were I not committed to faith in Christ, they are the decision and judgement of one who is still, to some degree, immature and sinful and liable seriously to err. Secondly, this is reinforced and illustrated for me by the fact that the ethical judgements of men who seem equally committed to the Christian way of life often appear to differ radically from one another, and from my own judgement, in what seem to be fundamentally the same critical situations and problems.[26] Though this may be explained as being due to the fact that, after all, a man's situations and problems, as lived, never are the same as anybody else's, but always peculiarly his own, this cannot be taken to be the whole explanation without strengthening the very sense of being lost in moral anarchy, confusion and relativity from which relief is desired. Thirdly, the Christian believer, in making his ethical decisions even according to the standard given in Christ, may well still be oppressed with the sense that his knowledge of the operative factors in nature and history which he has and on which must be based, in some measure, a responsible decision is utterly disproportionate to what may be the far-reaching consequences of that decision. This brings us to the third point.

---

[26]Farmer will no doubt be thinking of his costly pacifism.—Ed.

(3) The Christian faith in the incarnation implicitly involves the conviction that Christ is not only uniquely related to the inward being of the self, but also is uniquely related to the whole natural and historical process. The world process, in all its vastness and complexity, is in its ultimate constitution, and therefore at the point where it narrows, as it were, into my personal situation and decision and then widens out again into the broader stream of events, Christ-patterned or Christ-grained. The Christian, in making Christ the standard of decision, is therefore fortified and sustained by the thought, implicit in his faith in Christ as the self-disclosure of God himself, that in so doing he is, in spite of all the appearances, moving with the grain, along the pattern, in harmony with, the unalterable divine structure of the whole creation.[27] The metaphor of graining or patterning, however, is not fully appropriate, for it does not sufficiently express the personal, active nature of the divine will, which has not only bestowed on the world its structure, but is actively operative within it and holds all the infinite complexity of its process, including the choices and decisions of men, in its grasp. According to the Christian revelation and faith, the character and direction of that divine will have been once and for all disclosed in Christ. Hence, the reconciled man, as he seeks to make his decisions in the light of that disclosure, is made conscious of being (despite all the immaturity and ignorance and sinfulness of his being and all the possibility of mistake that these involve) in real rapport and fellowship with a wisdom, power and love to which he can commit himself and his acts and all the consequences of his acts, in his own life, in the lives of others and in the most far-reaching developments of history. Although this, of course, brings us back to the fundamental religious faith in providence in its specifically Christian form, I hope it has brought us back to it in a way that enables us to see, once again, how deep and distinctive the reconciling power of the Christian revelation is in respect of the duality of the self and the world.

---

[27]This conviction comes to expression in John 1 and Colossians 1.

PART FIVE
THE SELF
and
OTHER SELVES

CHAPTER SEVEN

THE SELF AND OTHER SELVES

We come now to fourth and final main class of duality and contrariety, namely that concerned with the relation of the self to other selves. Although the phrase "self and other selves" naturally brings to mind the sort of perplexities with which our relations with one another continually confront us and which it would, to some extent, fall to a Christian morality or ethics to consider, these are not our concern. In accordance with our plan throughout, our interest is in the more general and fundamental contrarieties which underlie particular problems. What follows is a brief consideration of two such contrarieties. These are contrarieties which are implicit in ordinary human experience in this sphere of the self in relation to other selves, but only become of importance to the self when it is interpreted by and asserts an ideal which Christianity lays down for selves in relationship, namely, the ideal of love.

It is characteristic of the Christian revelation that it centres the whole problem of man's unification/reconciliation in all its various aspects in the personal relationship of God with man and man with his neighbour. And this means that it centres it in the problem of sin, sin being understood to be a radical discord or estrangement in those relationships—sin has its source in man and affects the whole of his being.[1] So long as this discord and estrangement is not overcome, so long as man is not reconciled at this central point, there is no possibility of his being fully and finally reconciled elsewhere. That is why in the Christian revelation, the central emphasis is placed on the forgiveness of sin, both God's forgiveness of men and also

---

[1]Cf. H. H. Farmer, *The World and God*, ch.11.—Ed.

men's forgiveness of each other.[2] Now, it follows from this that in addressing our minds to the relation of the self to other selves, we come particularly to the source and centre of man's whole ununified and unreconciled state and are dealing with relationships which are in a very direct and radical way darkened and perverted. One result of this is that men are apt to be either not conscious at all of the contrarieties of which we are going to speak, or, in so far as they are conscious of them, they do not feel that they have any particular significance or urgency. The Christian revelation, therefore, has often first to evoke an explicit awareness of these contrarieties or tensions and of their significance and urgency before it can reconcile them, or, in so far as there is some awareness of them, it has to clarify and intensify that awareness and to insist that it be taken seriously.

The reason why the Christian revelation raises these problems in an explicit form and insists on their importance, is that it places the self in all its dealings with other selves under an absolute obligation to love. The word "love", however, is much too vague and even sentimental to be of use to us without further explication of its meaning. Let us then seek to explicate its meaning along a line which will help to make clear how necessary it is to pass into the sphere of the Christian revelation if the contrarieties we are to discuss are to be felt as real problems. To this end we may distinguish between three different ways in which it is, broadly speaking, possible for us to apprehend another self and to be related to him.

Three Forms of Inter-personal Relationship

(1) It is possible for me to apprehend the other self simply as another self, or, as Cullberg puts it, as a "*Fremd-Ich*." That is to say, I may apprehend him, in effect, as one of a certain class of objects among and along with all the other various classes of objects which constitute my world. Like the other objects of my world, he has his own distinctive kind of being and activity which I must take into account when dealing with him. In distinction from, say, table-

---

[2]Cf. H. H. Farmer, *God and Men*, ch.3; *The Word of Reconciliation*, ch.3.—Ed.

objects or tree-objects or animal-objects, he is a human-object, a specifically *human* mind-body organism, the activities of which spring from certain vital and psychical processes which I must, so far as possible, get to know and adjust myself to in dealing effectively with him.

It is obvious that this way of apprehending the other self does enter largely into men's dealings with one another, and, up to a point, is unavoidable. It is the attitude of the scientific observers of human behaviour in such sciences as psychology or sociology, which must, for their own purposes, regard selves as highly complex meeting points and vehicles of various forces which impinge upon them and produce results in accordance with the distinctive psycho-physical constitution of that particular sort of entity. It is the attitude which, consciously or unconsciously, underlies a great many relationships which appear to be necessary to the normal functioning of human society: in the moulding of children through educational processes of various kinds, in providing economic incentives and rewards for work, in the threat or imposition of punishment as a deterrent to wrongdoing, in military training and discipline, in advertisement and salesmanship, in all these there is obviously, and quite unavoidably, much that is little more than the bringing to bear of forces and influences upon the plasticities, the instinctual responses, of given human nature; it is simply, in part, a kind of conditioning of the human dog to beg. These things find their most extreme and unqualified expression in the policies and principles of totalitarian police states, wherein human selves are regarded as fundamentally no more than so much raw stuff to be processed by methods presumed to be appropriate to the human material involved, or, if resistant, to be disposed of as so much dross or waste.

(2) It is possible for me to apprehend the other man as having certain claims upon me which I recognise that I am under obligation not to ignore in my dealings with him. This is obviously a vastly different attitude from the one just indicated and brings us at once into the sphere of ethical reality. We may indicate the change by saying that at this point the other self ceases to be merely an object-self, or a self-object, a *Fremd-Ich*, and is apprehended as a person-self. According to this usage, the word "person" and the word

"claim" or "right" are correlative terms. An object-self becomes a person-self to me precisely at the point I recognise that he has rights which bind me, for no other reason than that he is "there" within my sphere of activity. If I do not recognise this, then he is not a person to me, but rather once again merely a self-object or entity in the sense just described. It is obvious, however, that this sort of attitude to the other self (immensely important as it is in human affairs and great as the advance is on the previous attitude) has serious limitations. Thus, I may recognise that although the other self has claims upon me, at the same time I may (either deliberately or if not deliberately then in effect) regard my responsibility to him as limited to those claims. I neither recognise any necessity, nor have any desire, to give him more than his due. The most meticulous meeting of his moral claims may go along with an indifference, and even a positive unfriendliness and enmity towards him; outside the area of those claims I may "wash my hands of him", with no desire, or will to have any other sort of relation with him. Indeed, I may even regard myself as entitled to make use of him simply for my own purposes and without regard to his purposes, provided only that his claims, or what I regard as such, are not infringed.

(3) The final way in which it is possible to be related to the other self has already been indicated in what has just been said. It is the relation in which I am not satisfied simply and solely to meet his minimal ethical claims upon me, but recognise an obligation, and have a real concern, to go a good deal farther than that. I am conscious that the meeting of his claims upon me must be the expression of a relationship which is much deeper, much more comprehensive of his whole being as well as of mine and much more difficult to achieve and to preserve. It indicates a relationship which is essentially involved in the highest good of each of us as selves in relationship, namely, the relationship of being, in the fullest attainable degree, in genuine fellowship with one another. In this third type of relationship, my desire and my will are the desire and will to fellowship with the other self. We may distinguish this attitude by the use of the word "thou", in that the other self is not apprehended merely as a human-object, nor yet merely as a person-self, but as

a thou-self. The appropriateness of this is not so evident in English as it would be in German, wherein the word *"du"* in distinction from the second person plural *"Sie"* carries the accent of fellowship and amity and is normally reserved for family and friends.[3]

The Will to Fellowship

Now it is this "thou" attitude, this desire for and will to fellowship, that the Christian revelation sets up as normative for all the relations of the self with other selves. It, or rather the obligation to have it, is the essence of the Christian ideal, or law, of love. It must be admitted that the word "fellowship" is a very much overused and somewhat cliché one, but the meaning of the phrase "the will to fellowship" will, I hope, be sufficiently clear for our purpose. The phrase, whilst it lacks some of the warmth of the word "love", has the following advantages: (a) It emphasises the element of volition in the relationship and so avoids any suggestion that Christian love is merely, or mainly, a matter of feeling, of emotional gush, so that the idea of an obligation to love becomes nonsensical. (b) It emphasises that the relationship sought must be on the highest ethical level—it must be based on a real community of values, and above all on a common recognition of the claims of all other selves. Finally, (c) it emphasises the will and desire for reciprocity, for mutuality, for a real union and communion of spirit with spirit—the end in view is *fellowship* and not merely a one way movement from the self to the other self without regard to what sort of response, or lack of response, there may be in the opposite direction. One, two, or possibly all three of these elements are apt to be lacking from the meaning of the term "love" as commonly used.

It is perhaps not superfluous to add that all this does not mean that it is always illegitimate from the Christian point of view to be related to the other

---

[3] We may recall the usage of the word "thou" and "thee" in The Society of Friends, a society which in an impressive degree has achieved the kind of relationship we have in mind in the relation of its members with one another, and has also steadfastly and costingly sought it in their wider dealings with men and women.

self as a human-object or as a person-self, in the sense in which I have used these phrases. I have already said that such relations have their inevitable place and importance in the complexities of human life. What the Christian revelation condemns is an attitude to the other self which is content to apprehend him merely as a human-object, or merely as "a person" to whom certain duties are owing. If the awareness of him as "thou", if the will to fellowship is not also present informing the relationship, no matter how great the obstacles to its expression and fulfilment may be, the relation is not one of Christian love.[4]

The Tension Between Egoism and Altruism

We turn now to the two contrarieties which it is our purpose to discuss.

The first contrariety is that between egoism and altruism. To make clear what we have in mind by this I must emphasise that the term I use is "egoism" and not "egotism". By egotism we mean egocentricity, or, put simply, plain selfishness—the attitude of mind which, in one way or another, and to the extent to which it is present, enthrones the self and ignores or overrides the claims and needs of other selves. Egoism, however, in the sense that I am using the term, is a quite different concept from egotism. It is something essentially bound up with selfhood *per se*, with being an "I", and very particularly with being a moral subject.

Concerning this latter point, some elucidation is required. It is obvious that consciousness of the self *is* of the very essence of the personal life. There are, of course, certain fixed routines of behaviour, habits, skills which have to be acquired as the basis of effective living, and these can function without our being aware of ourselves as active in them; yet even so, they can only be thought of as specifically human personal functions in distinction from the habits and skills acquired by sub-personal animals because they are neither a

---

[4]The treatment of the other as an other self easily passes over into a gross and degrading impersonalism, and though this may be kept in check, in some measure, by the recognition of him as a person who has certain ethical claims upon me, even this, without the will to fellowship, can decline into a hard and unsympathetic legalism which is almost as chilling as not recognising those claims at all.

deposit of, nor continuously incorporated into, a total activity which has been and *is* characterised by self-awareness. At the other end of the scale there are those absorbed states of mind wherein we seem completely to lose ourselves in the objective reality with which we are dealing; but even into these self-awareness assuredly enters as an underlying ground-tone or accompanying background without which they would not be what they in fact are. But leaving on one side such states of mind, it is obvious that it is in specifically moral activity (activity where there is valuation and deliberate choice of the ends to be pursued) that human existence is most sharply characterised by what we think of as "personal". Furthermore, it is obvious that such activity is inseparably bound up with a quite explicit element of awareness of being a self, of being, to use Oman's formula, "a being who is self-determined according to its own self-direction, in the world of its own self-consciousness."[5] Because of this self-awareness, even choice and action which are directed to the most altruistic ends, are *not* possible without an underlying sense that, in the seeking and achieving of those ends, the good of the self is also inseparably bound up. The sought-after good is felt to be, in some sense, *my* good, good for me; by seeking it I am, or shall become, a better and more worthy self than by not seeking it. Along with this there goes a sense of direct, unshared and unshareable responsibility for being, or becoming, this sort of self rather than, of being, in an inescapable way, in charge of my own destiny as a self. I am not, of course, suggesting that the ordinary man apprehends these things in a way that would enable him to formulate them in the kind of statement I have just made. Nevertheless, I cannot doubt that something corresponding to them is implicit in the experience of us all.[6]

---

[5]J. Oman, *Grace and Personality*, p.48.

[6]It is perhaps necessary to add that I am not here raising the question in theoretical ethics as to whether, and if so in what sense, self-realisation can rightly be considered to be the end or standard of moral decision. I am merely drawing attention to a factor which inevitably enters in whenever the self is functioning morally, whatever may be the ends or standards by which it is determining its behaviour. Nevertheless, it is because of this factor that the ideal of self-

There is then no escaping this implicit self-reference or self-concern, this egoism, which characterises self-consciousness, and characterises it not least at its highest moments of moral self-direction, responsibility and decision. And that being so, the question is unavoidable, in what relation does it stand to the ideal of the self's relation to other selves? Of course, this is an ideal which is generally required by humanity in one form or another, and given explicit expression in the Christian ideal of love, which consists in the going out of the self to the other self in a pure and immediate will to fellowship with him. Is there not a real contrariety between this ideal and the self's relation to other selves? It might be said that this is not the case—that there is no reason *in principle* (that is, apart from the complicating factor of the egocentricity of sin) why the self should not give itself wholly to the other self in a pure will to fellowship, and, at the same time, be conscious that in so doing it is fulfilling its own highest life and destiny as a self. Ideally speaking that may be so, but we have to look at the human situation, and particularly at the moral situation in its present concrete actuality, for it is only in its relation to that that we are interested in Christianity as a reconciling revelation and faith. When we do look at that situation, we find that we are actually confronted with a very real problem. There are two reasons for this: (a) Man, as a finite self, is not given moral perfection ready-made, but has to achieve it. It is of the essence of man's moral situation that he has to grow towards his full stature as a self, to some extent, by his own moral choices and decisions. In relation to this fact of man's situation, the contrariety can be stated thus: one is under obligation to seek to give oneself wholly to the other self in that love which is a pure and perfect will to fellowship. Yet the seeking to do that necessarily involves one in that concern for oneself which is the form of all moral activity; as a moral being one has increasingly to win selflessness through exercising a form of self-concern. It would seem that the self has to look in two directions at once—to develop a sort of squint—an eye on oneself as responsible for

---

realisation (whatever be its deficiencies as a standard, deficiencies which have often been pointed out) always rings a bell in the mind: it is always, as Herrmann somewhere says, "a quickening thought to the human heart."

oneself, and an eye away from oneself to others at the same time. (b) The situation is further complicated by the fact of sin and the fact that man is *egotistic* in the sense defined. The right concern for the self (egoism) and the wrong concern for the self (egotism) continually merge and mix with one another in the confusion of man's interior life. The difficulty is made all the greater by the fact that the wrong self-concern continually excuses and justifies itself by appealing to the right. We speak of "proper self-respect", a name which sheer pride is always ready to adopt.

I think that ordinary people are often vaguely conscious of this problem of egoism and altruism. They recognise, in themselves and in human nature generally, the presence of impulses of self-love and benevolence, to use Butler's terms, and feel constrained to give them both, as Butler did, moral standing. But for the most part they are content to accommodate them both according to the play of circumstance and the inclination of the moment. Indeed, even when there is something of a conflict between the impulses, little of genuine moral assessment and decision enters in; the two kinds of impulse are left to fight it out. If men do think about it, they find themselves unable to do more than make the highly general and (from a practical point of view) useless judgement that an unspecified amount of self-interest and self-concern is right and necessary, and that, on the other hand, any excess over an unspecified amount of benevolence is foolish and not to be expected of any man. In short, they shelve the whole problem.

The Christian revelation and faith, however, makes it impossible to do this. It forces the problem into the open. On the one hand, it accentuates a man's sense of his responsibility before God for what he does with his own being and life, he being the only one with control over it. On the other hand, it imparts to the ideal of love, of self-forgetfulness, of the complete giving of the self to the other in the will to fellowship, all the absoluteness of the divine will. The reality of this is borne witness to by the New Testament: on the one hand, the rightness of self-concern, the need for a keen sense of responsibility for the conduct of one's own life, of answerability before the judgement throne of God, appears again and again in one form or another; on the other hand, the idea of the self making its own moral perfection its supreme end, of seeking to achieve its own salvation, in short, anything in the nature of self-concern in its dealings with other selves seems clearly contrary to its whole outlook. Thus the question, "What must I do to inherit eternal life?" is not repudiated as an improper question to ask. And the question, "What good will it be for a man if he gains the whole world, yet forfeits his soul?"[7] obviously only makes sense if a man is concerned with *not* losing his own soul. Yet, along with these passages, there are also such sayings as, "seek first his kingdom and his righteousness, and these things shall be given to you as well",[8] as well as the general call for a total self-giving to God and to the neighbour which the New Testament writers derive, not only from the example of Christ's life, but also from the incarnation itself. In the familiar passage from Philippians, the Christian man is called to have the same mind as was in Christ Jesus, "Who being in very nature God, did not consider equality with God something to be grasped, but made himself nothing, taking the very nature of a servant, being made in human likeness. And being found in appearance as a man, he humbled himself and became obedient unto death— even death on a cross."[9] This is the perfect expression of divine *agape* (the divine love and will to fellowship) which the Christian is called to manifest in his dealings with selves. "Be perfect," said Christ, "as your heavenly Father is perfect."[10]

The way in which this tension is overcome in the Christian revelation and faith must be indicated only briefly.[11] In the first place, it is overcome by the lifting of the self, as a moral subject out of the lonely sense of responsibility for the pursuit of its own true life and worth, and into the context of a divine will which is wholly directed to the *same end*. This is the first step. For a

---

[7]Matt. 16:26.
[8]Matt. 6:33.
[9]Phil. 2:6-8.
[10]Matt. 5:48.
[11] The reason he limits himself to such a "brief" comment is, of course, because of the time constraint imposed on him as an evening Gifford lecturer at Glasgow University. This chapter, along with some of the others, is taken directly from his lecture notes.—Ed.

purely humanist and secular morality, however high its professed ideals, there is (as Irving Babbitt, the great American humanist, came to see) no way out of the egoistic predicament, no means of preventing the egoism inherent in selfhood from continually passing over into, and feeding the egotism of self-centredness. This is the source of the following frequently observed paradox: the more earnestly a man seeks to base his life on a secular ethic, the more he is apt to give the impression of an egotism which even his manifest pursuit of the highest ends and devotion to the most altruistic causes cannot remove.

In the second place, God is apprehended as the wholly trustworthy purpose of love in which the highest good of the self is already secure, and to which, therefore, it can be wholly committed. To put it in other terms, the demand and succour of God are inseparably fused with one another so that in the doing of the will of God and in the fellowship with him that that brings, the highest good of the self is already in principle realised. Hence, as soon as one becomes aware of the self and of its good in the deliberate responsible setting of the self towards an ideal, it becomes possible to be instantly lost in an act which affirms the divine will, rather than the good of the self, and which commits the whole self and its good to God, to a divine love which is known to be much more effectively and more wisely concerned for the good of the self, than ever the self can be for its own. This at once purifies and releases the will to fellowship with the other self and brings it nearer to the divine perfect will to fellowship, the divine *agape*, which it is bidden in the New Testament to imitate, and which is historically manifested in Christ's keeping company with publicans and sinners. It is only on the basis of such an apprehension of God as love and self-commitment, and of one's self-commitment to God, that it can be morally right for the self to avert its attention away from the achievement of its own true end and to surrender concern for its own worth.

All this is well summed by Oman from a somewhat different angle in one of what he called "the antinomies of grace". I bring some of his separated phrases into juxtaposition, but not altering the meaning intended. "Morality", he says, "must rest on the reverence for our moral selves, and our moral worth is necessarily our own achievement; yet our moral end is not our moral progress nor our moral worth, but simply God's will of love. Though God's grace is wholly concerned with our salvation, that is with the worth of our moral selves and its achievement through ourselves, its whole working is to direct attention from ourselves and our achievement simply to the doing of his will. To enter the kingdom is to be concerned with God's rule not with our selves, and for the very reason that our salvation is so exclusively God's end, his will alone needs to be our end." [12]

The Tension Between Solitude and Society

We now come to the second of the two tensions or contrarieties, the contrariety between the essential solitariness or inaccessibility of the self and the need of the self for communion with other selves. We take each point in turn.

(1) It is evident that the self *is* characterised by a certain inaccessible solitude *vis-à-vis* other selves. Each self has a secret, interior life into which, in the nature of the case, no other self can penetrate. It is true, of course, that I can, through imagination and sympathy, seek to enter another self's thought and feelings, to project myself into his situation on the basis of similar situations in my own experience, to put myself in his shoes; but the extent to which I can do this is obviously extremely limited. [13] The infinitely subtle and complex interplay of the other person's thoughts, images, motives, feelings, memories, desires and aspirations; his holding of all these together in the unity of his own, his very own, particular selfhood and self-consciousness; the emergence in his inward being of this or that insight, or this or that responsible willed decision (insights and decisions which are entirely and exclusively his

---

[12]See S. Bevans, *John Oman and his Doctrine of God* (Cambridge: Cambridge University Press, 1992), pp.72ff.—Ed.
[13]Cf. Farmer's discussion of "productive empathy", Georg Wobbermin's method of studying the religious experience of others: "...the method, that is to say, of penetrating to the living essence of religion, as it lies behind and within its manifestations, by feeling our way into it on the basis of our own inner religious faith and experience." (*Revelation and Religion*, p.45.)—Ed.

seeing and deciding, impregnated with his own utterly incommunicable self-feeling and self-awareness) lie utterly beyond me, hidden behind a wall or partition as impenetrable as would be a two foot thick concrete wall to my body. Even my most vividly imaginative thoughts and sympathies are distinctively *my* thoughts and feelings and are themselves involved in the inaccessible loneliness of my own interior being; they are not and never can be, in any sense whatever, the actual thoughts and feelings of the other self as lived through by him; they are elements in my personal biography and not his.[14]

This privacy and solitude of the self, this imperviousness to other selves, is obviously essential to its very existence as a self. Without it, our psychical being would be merged in a collective or generic consciousness, flowing into and out of it like a stream of water flowing into, and out of, and through, a collection of porous pots. A self without walls or frontiers would not be, and could not be, a self at all. It is in accordance with this that a capacity for solitude and a high degree of individuation and independence in the self do seem to go together, as has not infrequently been pointed out. Nicolai Berdyaev writes of the sense of solitude as springing from man's endeavour to develop his personality regardless of the life of the species. "Only when man is alone", he says, "...does he become aware of his personality, of his originality, of his singularity and uniqueness, of his distinctiveness from everyone and everything else." Similarly, Karl Mannheim says, "a privacy and inwardness are perhaps the strongest means of individualisation and one of the greatest assets in the growth of independent personality. It is in this realm of seclusion and partial isolation that our experiences gain in depth and that we become spiritually different from our fellowman." It is of great

---

[14]It is this that invests, it seems to me, the work of the novelist or biographer, in so far as they set out to give a detailed and realistic account of the mental processes of their subject, with a certain bogus quality, a certain air of make-believe, of which I find myself always faintly conscious as I read, and from which I sometimes turn with a sense of relief to an author who is content to tell a plain story with no more psychological analysis than that necessary to explain the course of events and which any intelligent person uses in dealing with his fellows in the ordinary business of life.

significance in this connection that human beings are only able to communicate with one another through words or other signs and symbols.[15] Words are like signals through the wall of partition; they reveal the existence of the partition in the very act of seeking to overcome it, like taps on the wall by prisoners in contiguous cells. I cannot break through the wall that divides me from another self and pour my thoughts directly into his mind; I can only signal my meaning and that meaning can only become his after he has interpreted the signals and taken it into the otherwise inaccessible privacy of his own inward being. Thus, paradoxically, speech and the essential solitude and individuation of selfhood are closely bound together. Of course, people do greatly influence one another by processes of suggestion and imitation of which they are not explicitly aware, and telepathic communication is an accredited, if relatively rare, phenomenon. However, it is true to say, I think, that it is this "open" side of man's being which is most inimical to the development of individuality and independence; high suggestibility and a low and unstable mental life tend to go together.

(2) If the necessity to communicate through signs illustrates the essential seclusion of the self, the need to communicate at all illustrates the other and opposed truth, namely, that the self, in the profoundest possible way, needs other selves, needs to commune with them, to have a shared life with them, just as much as it needs to have an essential and inviolable solitude over against them. This is so obvious that it hardly needs to be developed. It is enough to say that the need goes deeper than the mere fact that the human being, like some other sentient creatures, is equipped with powerful social and gregarious impulses and feelings and, therefore, has an abhorrence of being without contact with others of its kind, though, of course, such impulses and needs are related to it; rather it touches the very core, the very existence of selfhood as such. Selfhood, as we know it and have it, presupposes and implies some sort of consciousness and communication with other selves. In Berdyaev's words, "the self is social in the depths of its metaphysical being."

---

[15]See his discussion of symbol in *The World and God*, ch.4.—Ed.

Or in Martin Buber's pregnant little sentences: "*Ohne Du keine Ich; Ich werde am Du.*" The self's hunger for a shared life with other selves is in fact one expression of the impulse to affirm and preserve its own distinctive being as a self; or to put it negatively, it expresses a recoil from that which is an implicit threat to its own existence as a self. If, *per impossible*, a self could be completely lifted out of this world, out of this order of selves in relationship, it would at that moment cease to exist as a self. We get at least a hint of the truth of this in the observable mental disintegration and collapse which follows upon an extreme degree of isolation from other selves. That is why solitary confinement is the most monstrous and wicked of all punishments and, in principle, far worse than the death sentence. Whereas death kills the body, solitary confinement, if not in intention then in effect, is an attempt to annihilate selfhood.

There is then this fundamental and inescapable tension or contrariety in the relation of the self to other selves: on the one hand, it is essential to being a self to have a profound inward and inaccessible solitude; on the other hand, it is equally essential to it that it should be linked to other selves in a life of mutual communion and understanding. It would be foolish, however, to suggest that the ordinary man is explicitly conscious of the contrariety as constituting a central problem in his relations with others for which he must find a solution. He appears to be content for the most part merely to establish such rapport with other selves as the ordinary means of communication permit, and as is necessary for the practical business of daily life; as for anything beyond that he is on the whole satisfied with the superficial camaraderie and bonhomie of social occasions in which the problem is not so much solved as submerged. Wherever it seems impossible to establish real understanding and rapport, he is content to leave it so, and feels no call to do anything about it. Nevertheless, the problem of the isolation and solitude of the self is certainly there beneath the surface, whether men realise it as such or not, and is, by no means, a negligible factor in the many and persistent misunderstandings and conflicts in human life. It would be a fantastic oversimplification to suggest that this difficulty of communication between selves is the only factor (or even the prime factor) in the strains and estrangements of human relationships. However, that it is a factor (albeit one that is always greatly aggravated by human sinfulness) nobody who has ever sought to be a reconciler and peacemaker could doubt. It is significant that if the ordinary man ever does become aware of this as a pressing problem which he cannot lightly brush on one side, it is at the point where he feels something of genuine love, a genuine will to fellowship towards another self. The desire to enter into closer and deeper rapport with the other self which characterises even natural love, in spite of its many perversions, is continually frctted by the essential inaccessibility and solitude of the inward being of the other self; and this can rise to a pitch of real agony when the one thus loved is apprehended to be at a crisis point of decision or need.

This brings us to the Christian revelation and faith. The Christian revelation and faith brings the problem right out into the open and makes it both central and urgent. It does this by the ideal of love which it lays down for the self in relation. How can my will to fellowship be any other than continually frustrated by the inaccessible solitude of the other's inward being, and this even apart from the aggravation which may be caused by the fact that an answering will to fellowship may be wholly lacking in him, or, if present, may be, like my own, impure and perverted by the sinful egocentricity and false values of human nature? Faced by such a question, and in default of any answer to it, one might well conclude that the Christian ideal of a universal and persistent will to fellowship runs hopelessly counter to the insurmountable obstacles and limitations of the human nature and the human situation, and that it would be better to be content with those more modest working accommodations with which ordinary men, in their combined need for, and isolation from one another, have to be (and for the most part are) content. The answer which the Christian faith gives to the problem, it is hardly necessary to say, is once again bound up with the whole apprehension of God.

In the first place the Christian revelation says that if we think of the world of human selves in relationship as consisting *only* of human selves in relationship we utterly misconceive it; we in fact leave out the most important element. According to the Christian revelation, selves in relationship are always selves in relation with God, in and through their relationship to one another; and selves in relation with God are always selves in relation with one another through their relation with God. The self does not stand in two relations, one to God and one to his neighbour, but in one relation with, as it were, two poles; he is related to his neighbour in God and to God in his neighbour; it is a single and personal continuum or order.[16]

In the second place the Christian revelation declares that God, with whom selves in relationship are thus inseparably bound up, is himself perfect love, the perfect will to fellowship with persons. Hence, the Christian's will to fellowship is never merely *human* functioning, but rather is caught up in the activity of God in the world of persons, and in his infinite wisdom and knowledge and power. The Christian's will to fellowship, which the divine self-revelation in Christ calls into action, *is* the divine will to fellowship in action in the world of selves in relationship. In the third place, and this is the point that especially concerns our problem, it declares that God, being *God*, has access to and knows the inward being of selves in a way that human selves, in the nature of the case, can never do in their relationships with one another. Inaccessible to one another, they are nevertheless not inaccessible to God; in an ultimate solitude and seclusion in relation to one another, they are in no such solitude and seclusion in relation to God; the thoughts and desires which selves can only fumblingly and partially signal to one another by means of symbols need no such expression in relation to God. This all-comprehensive and all-comprehending interior access and knowledge of the self belongs to God, and to God alone; it belongs to him because he is *God*.

Manifestly the reality of this divine knowledge of selves cannot be empirically demonstrated; the assurance of it is part of that living religious apprehension which, as we have indicated so often, rests on God's disclosure

---

[16]This is why, in the New Testament, men are called upon to be perfect even as God is perfect. Divine forgiveness and human forgiveness are united inseparably together, and the refusal of even a cup of cold water to a needy man is declared to be the refusal of something to God in a way that affects the whole destiny of the self.

of himself as God. By the same argument, it is a mystery which baffles the mind, being one aspect of the transcendent otherness, the sheer Godness of God. The truth finds expression both in the Bible[17] and in other religions. It is connected with the apprehension of God as an inward presence and power which, as we saw earlier, is an element in all living religion, and in Christianity finds expression in the doctrine of the Holy Spirit. The thought of the openness of selves to God in contrast with the closedness to one another is perhaps most often associated in men's minds with his judgement upon sin— "Our thoughts lie open to thy sight, And naked to Thy glance; Our secret sins are in the light, Of Thy pure countenance". But it is distinctive of the Christian revelation to assert a deeper truth (which, however, does not exclude the thought of the divine judgement), namely, that God's full knowledge of the self is the knowledge of a perfectly pure and holy love. It is this truth which is especially connected with the point under discussion. The tension between the self's will to fellowship and the inaccessible solitude of the other self is continually resolved by the faith that its own will to fellowship is taken up into, is at one with, the divine will to fellowship, to which such a limitation of interior solitude does not apply. In a sense, the self *has* access to the interior being of the other self, not directly, however, but only through God and in God; it is conscious of having, as it were, a hidden divine ally there, and so the temptation to falter in its own will to fellowship, in so far as the temptation arises out of the awareness of the essential limitations of finite selfhood, is removed. It is important to state that the duality or opposition as such is not removed—it cannot be, for it is essential to the existence of finite selves, as we have seen, that they should both need, and be impervious to, one another; and in any case it is not the way of the Christian revelation to expunge dualities (which is the way of mysticism).

That these abstract statements, despite their abstractness, are nevertheless closely related to the actualities of the Christian experience of reconciliation, is evidenced by the central place which the New Testament gives to the prayer

---

[17]See, for example, Pss. 139; 51:6; Heb. 4:12-13.

of intercession, and the place which such prayer has always had in the highest Christian living. The will to fellowship, in so far as it arises in and out of the specifically Christian revelation and faith, must express itself, must go out towards the other self, in prayer for him, and for its own fulfilment in relation to him through the fulfilment of God's purpose in relation to both. From this point of view, the prayer of intercession is the deliberate and focused uniting of the self's own will to fellowship with the divine love. It is the self finding access to the interior being of the other self in the only way in which it is either possible or safe for it to have such access, namely, through God. In other words, in such prayer my love is joined to the divine love which is already at work in the innermost being of the other self, it is filtered and purified through it; and since it is precisely part of the divine purpose that selves should find fellowship with one another in God, my prayer plays a part in the fulfilment of that divine purpose. Failure to pray would evidence a failure in love, a failure in the will to fellowship, as defined by the divine revelation in Christ. "As for me, far be it from me that I should sin against the Lord by failing to pray for you."[18] In these words the whole biblical and Christian understanding of the world of selves in relationship is succinctly and concretely expressed. With this we conclude our studies.

Concluding Comments

The first is to express the hope that the course of our thought has, in some measure at least, made plain what I believe to be the quite distinctive reach and depth and adequacy of the Christian revelation and faith when viewed from the angle of the profound need of the human spirit for reconciliation. At the same time, I hope it has helped to make plain the close-knit unity of all that it has to say in the various problems we have been considering, a unity which has its centre in the central Christian faith in the incarnation. In this also its power to unify is made manifest.

---

[18]1 Sam. 12:23.

Secondly, by virtue of the all-comprehensive unification or reconciliation which it makes possible and which we have explored, the Christian faith confronts us as a true and consummated monotheism. For, religiously speaking, and indeed philosophically speaking also, we only believe in one God in the measure in which we believe in the oneness of the world and our experience of it, in the measure in which we can discover all experience, for all its chaos and complexity, all its dualities and contrarieties, to be one—not within the unity of pantheism, but within the one steadfast purpose and manifold wisdom and all-controlling providence of sovereign love. We may sum this up in another way. We began these studies, it may be remembered, with an examination of the Christian worship of God under the Triune name— Father, Son and Holy Spirit—and again and again our thought has continually circled around that formula and brought us back to one or other element in it.[19] This means that the doctrine of the Trinity is not a puzzling theological speculation, but a tremendous affirmation of monotheism in the only form that religiously matters, namely as an expression of a reconciled life which does not run away from the dualities and contrarieties of life.[20] The doctrine of the Trinity will never be understood if it is not understood as fundamentally an expression of integration, unification, reconciliation in its specifically Christian form. My hope is that these Gifford lectures may have helped toward such an understanding.

---

[19]See H. H. Farmer, *Revelation and Religion*, chs.3 and 4.—Ed.
[20]See further Farmer's important article, "Monotheism and the Doctrine of the Trinity", in *Religion in Life* 29 (1959-60), pp.32-41.—Ed.

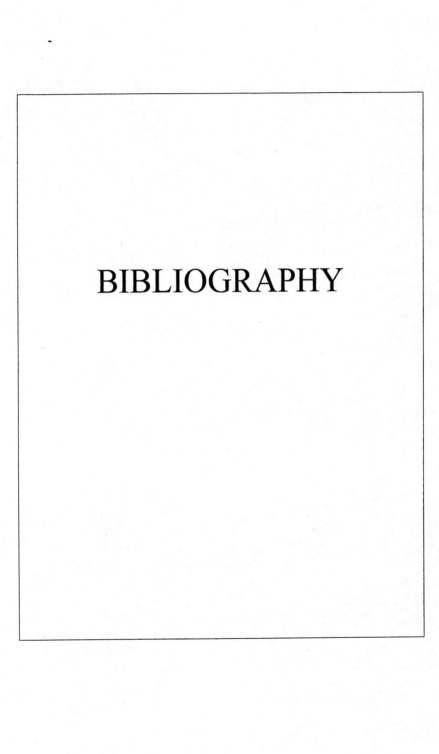

BIBLIOGRAPHY

THE WRITINGS of H. H. FARMER

1. Books & Pamphlets

Things not Seen: Studies in the Christian Interpretation of Life, second edition (London: Nisbet, 1929)—first edition (London: Nisbet, 1927).

Experience of God: A Brief Enquiry into the Grounds of Christian Conviction (London: SCM, 1929).

The Dimension of the Eternal (Hartford: 1932).

The World and God: A Study of Prayer, Providence and Miracle in Christian Experience, second edition (London: Nisbet, 1936)—first edition, (London: Nisbet, 1935); Fontana Library edition (London: Collins, Fontana, 1963).

The Healing Cross: Further Studies in the Christian Interpretation of Life (London: Nisbet, 1938).

The Servant of the Word (London: Nisbet, 1941).

Towards Belief in God (London: SCM, 1942).

The Westminster Confession of Faith After 300 Years (London: The Presbyterian Church of England, 1944).

God and Men (London: Nisbet, 1948).

The Bible and Preaching, (Birmingham: Berean Press, 1952).

Revelation and Religion: Studies in the Theological Interpretation of Religious Types (London: Nisbet, 1954).

Reconciliation and Religion: Some Aspects of the Uniqueness of Christianity as a Reconciling Faith, ed. by C. H. Partridge (Lampeter: Edwin Mellen Press, 1998)

The Christian Person and Morality (London: Fellowship of Reconciliation, 1957).

Are Miracles Possible? (London: SPCK, 1960).

The Word of Reconciliation (London: Nisbet, 1966).

Preaching and Worship (London: Carey Kingsgate Press, n.d.).

Forgiveness, Divine and Human (Research Commission of the Pacifist Council of the Christian Church, n.d.).

2. Articles, Sermons & Lectures

'Christ and the Sickness of Humanity', in J. Marchant (ed.), *British Preachers 1925* (London: Putnam's, 1925), pp.233-44.

'The Worship of Jesus Christ', in *The Modern Churchman* 16 (1926-1927), pp.552-63.

'The Danger of Getting What We Want', in *The Presbyterian Messenger* (1927), p.19.

'The Severity of Jesus', in *Reconciliation: Working Towards a Christian World* (1928).

'The Ministry of Reconciliation in the World Today', in *Reconciliation: Working Towards a Christian World* (1928).

'Christ's Right *to* Our Worship', in J. V. Bartlet (ed.), *The Lord of Life: A Fresh Approach to the Incarnation* (London: SCM, 1929), pp.268-304.

'The Permanent Element in Apocalyptic', in *The Congregational Quarterly* 8 (1930), pp.265-78.

'What is Sin?', in *The Spectator* 144 (8 March, 1930), pp.357-8.

'Science and God', in *The Spectator* 146 (7 February, 1931), pp.173-5.

'Two Sorts of Religion', in *The Intercollegian* (December, 1931), pp.83-84.

'The Lonely Christ', in *The Christian World Pulpit* 122 (1932), pp.85-7.

'Christian Truths in Daily Experience: Living Beliefs', in *The Presbyterian Messenger* (Jan. 1933), pp.236-7.

'Christian Truths in Daily Experience: Of Divine Providence', in *The Presbyterian Messenger* (Aug. 1933), pp.98-100.

'Christian Truths in Daily Experience: Of God in Jesus Christ (1)', in *The Presbyterian Messenger* (Sep. 1933), pp.122-4.

'Christian Truths in Daily Experience: Of God in Jesus Christ (2)', in *The Presbyterian Messenger* (Oct. 1933), pp.150-2.

'Christian Truths in Daily Experience: Of the Holy Spirit', in *The Presbyterian Messenger* (Nov. 1933), pp.180-2.
'Experience of God as Personal', in *Religion in Life* 2 (1933), pp.237-46.
'The Dictatorship of Love', in *The Christian World Pulpit* 125 (1934), pp.301-3.
'America, After Four Years. Things I Have Loved' (Hartford Seminary Library: Item No.11955, 1935).
'Pearls for Pearls', in *The Christian World* 78 (1935).
'The Christian and War', in *Religion in Life* 4 (1935), pp.250-8.
'Christianity and the World To-Day', in *Missionary Review of the World* 58 (1935), pp.113-7.
'Two Kinds of Religion', in *The Christian World* 79 (1936).
'Leaving Too Little to God's Care', in *The Christian World* 79 (1936).
'Judging in the Light of the Cross', in *The Christian World* 79 (1936).
'The Last Judgement', in *The Christian World* 79 (1936).
'Duty and Reward in the Christian Life', in *The Christian World* 79 (1936).
'To Serve the Present Age', in *The Christian World* 79 (1936).
'Victory Over the Common Place', in *The Christian World* 79 (1936).
'Justice and Gospel', in *The Christian World* 79 (1936).
'Manger and Cross', in *The Christian World* 79 (1936).
'Doubts or Certainties', in *The Christian World* 80 (1937).
'Unrighteous Mammon and True Riches', in *The Christian World* 80 (1937).
'The Passion Not Passive', in *The Christian World* 80 (1937).
'Christ at the Door', in *The Christian World* 80 (1937).
'Receiving Without Giving', in *The Christian World* 80 (1937).
'The Hope of Gain and Fear of Loss', in *The Christian World* 80 (1937).
'The Dilemma of Goodness', in *The Christian World* 80 (1937).
'Vows', in *The Christian World* 80 (1937).
'Keep My Commandments', in *The Christian World* 80 (1937).
'Like a Lost Sheep', in *The Christian World* 80 (1937).
'Faith, Probability and Immortality' (Drew lecture), in *The Congregational Quarterly* 15 (1937), pp.13-26.
'The Oxford Conference: The Church and the People', in *The Presbyterian Messenger* (1937), pp.323-4.
'The Hidden God', in *The Christian World* 81 (1938).
'Crucified Unto the World', in *The Christian World* 81 (1938).
'His face towards Jerusalem', in *The Christian World* 81 (1938).
'The Cost of Discipleship', in *The Christian World* 81 (1938).
'Called of God', in *The Christian World* 81 (1938).
'Follow Me Yourself', in *The Christian World* 81 (1938).
'Comforted of God', in *The Christian World* 81 (1938).
'The Beauty of Holiness', in *The Christian World* 81 (1938).
'Belief and Love', in *The Christian World* 81 (1938).
'The Revelation in Christ and the Christian's Vocation', in *Christian Faith and the Common Life* (London: Allen & Unwin, 1938), pp.143-72.
'Doctrine in the Church of England', in *Journal of Theological Studies* 39 (1938), pp.113-25.
'The Authority of the Faith', in W. Paton (ed.), *The Authority of the Faith*, Tambaram Series, vol.1 (Oxford: Oxford University Press, 1939), pp.163-80.
'The Faith By Which the Church Lives', in *International Review of Missions* 28 (1939), pp.174-84.
'The One Foundation', in *The Christian World Pulpit* 135 (1939), pp.205-7.
'Death of Dr John Oman: An Appreciation', in *The Christian World* 82 (25 May, 1939), pp.9, 19.
'Mirage', in *The Christian World* 82 (1939).
'Rejoice', in *The Christian World* 82 (1939).
'The Word is Very Nigh Thee', in *The Christian World* 82 (1939).
'The Salt of the Earth', in *The Christian World* 82 (1939).

'The Sorrow of the World', in *The Christian World* 82 (1939).
'Confidence in God', in *The Christian World* 82 (1939).
'God Near and Far', in *The Christian World* 83 (1940).
'Might in the Cross', in *The Christian World* 83 (1940).
'Sin the Parasite', in *The Christian World* 83 (1940).
'Footmen and Horses', in *The Christian World* 83 (1940).
'But if Not', in *The Christian World* 83 (1940).
'Who For Us Men', in *The Christian World* 83 (1940).
'The Christian Message *to* Men and Nations', in *The Christian World Pulpit* 136 (1940).
'The "Good" and the "Right"', in A. Sampson (ed.), *This War and Christian Ethics*
     (Oxford: Blackwell, 1940), pp.59-79.
'Memoir of the Author', in John Oman, *Honest Religion* (Cambridge: Cambridge University
     Press, 1941), pp.xxvi - xxxii.
'The Mind We Bring', in *The Christian World* 84 (1941).
'Unworldliness', in *The Christian World* 84 (1941).
'Victory Over Arithmetic', in *The Christian World* 84 (1941).
'Anger', in *The Christian World* 84 (1941).
'Power', in *The Christian World* 84 (1941).
'That They May Be One', in *The Christian World* 84 (1941).
'In His Light', in *The Christian World* 84 (1941).
'Conjunctions', in *The Christian World* 84 (1941).
'His Own Received Him Not', in *The Christian World* 84 (1941).
'What Shall It Profit?', in *The Christian World* 84 (1942).
'Forward', in O. Wyon, *Radiant Freedom* (London: Lutterworth, 1942), pp.5-7.
'The Notion of Desert Bad and Good', in *Hibbert Journal* 16 (1943), pp.347-54.
'Thanksgiving and Adoration', in J. S. Boys Smith et al. *Prayer and Worship* (London:
     Hodder & Stoughton, 1945), pp.17-28.
'The Most Important Question', in *Current Religious Thought* 6, (1946), pp.10-13.
'Fundamental Causes of Failure', in J. Marchant (ed.) *Has the Church Failed?* (London:
     Odhams, 1947), pp.46-64.
'Some Reflections on Professor Wieman's New Book', in *The Journal Religion* 27 (1947),
     pp.114-9.
'Preaching and Worship', in *The Review and Expositor* 43 (1946), pp.243-60.
'The Preacher and Persons', in *The Review and Expositor* 43 (1946), pp.403-18.
'The Preacher and Culture', in *The Review and Expositor* 44 (1947), pp.34-49.
'The Christian and War', in *The Church, the Gospel and War* (New York: Harper & Row,
     1948).
'Doubt and Faith', in G. P. Butler (ed.) *Best Sermons 1947-1948* (New York, Harper, 1949),
     pp.144-9.
'Personality in God and Man' (1), in R. C. Walton (ed.), *Man and His Nature: Broadcast
     Talks in Religion and Philosophy* (London: SCM, 1949), pp.64-71.
'Personality in God and Man' (2), in R. C. Walton (ed.), *Man and His Nature: Broadcast
     Talks in Religion and Philosophy* (London: SCM, 1949), pp.72-79.
'John Wood Oman', in L. G. Wickham Legg (ed.), *The Dictionary of National Biography
     1931-1940* (London: Oxford University Press, 1949), pp.657-9.
'The Bible: Its Significance and Authority', in G. A. Buttrick et al (eds.), *The Interpreter's
     Bible*, vol.1 (New York: Abingdon, 1952), pp.3-31.
'John Wood Oman', in F. L. Cross (ed.), *The Oxford Dictionary of the Christian Church*
     (London: Oxford University Press, 1957), p.983.
'The Bible and Preaching: The Church's Word to the World', in *Encounter* 19 (Indianapolis,
     1958), pp.151-67.
'Monotheism and the Doctrine of the Trinity', in *Religion in Life* 29 (1959-60), pp.32-41.
'Vocation', *Hartford Quarterly* (1961).
'Sense of Vocation in the Christian Ministry', in *Princeton Seminary Bulletin* 55 (1962),
     pp.12-8.
'Where is Your God?', in *Faith and Work* (1962).
'John Wood Oman', in *The Expository Times* 74 (1963), pp.132-5.

'The Courage of Christ', in *The Expository Times* 75 (1964), pp.176-8.
'Against Principalities, Against Powers', in *Our Work Overseas: A Monthly News Sheet Issued by the Foreign Missions Committee of the Presbyterian Church of England* (n.d), pp.271-3.
Jeremiah 12.5 (New Barnet: St Augustine's Presbyterian Church, n.d).
1 John 3.18-20 (New Barnet: St Augustine's Presbyterian Church, n.d).
John 4.35 (New Barnet: St Augustine's Presbyterian Church, n.d).
Deuteronomy 34.4 (New Barnet: St Augustine's Presbyterian Church, n.d).
Matthew 5.9 (New Barnet: St Augustine's Presbyterian Church, n.d).
2 Timothy 1.12, 14 (New Barnet: St Augustine's Presbyterian Church, n.d).
Colossians 3.17 (New Barnet: St Augustine's Presbyterian Church, n.d).
Luke 24.31; John 20.14; 21.4 (New Barnet: St Augustine's Presbyterian Church, n.d).
Galatians 6.14 (New Barnet: St Augustine's Presbyterian Church, n.d).
Hebrews 12.1 (New Barnet: St Augustine's Presbyterian Church, n.d).
Psalm 29.2 (New Barnet: St Augustine's Presbyterian Church, n.d).
Luke 23.28, 21 (New Barnet: St Augustine's Presbyterian Church, n.d).
Ephesians 4.18, 21 (New Barnet: St Augustine's Presbyterian Church, n.d).
Matthew 13.45-6 (New Barnet: St Augustine's Presbyterian Church, n.d).
Revelation 3.20 (New Barnet: St Augustine's Presbyterian Church, n.d).

3. Reviews

J.-J. von Allmen, *Worship: Its Theology and Practice*, in *The Ecumenical Review* (1966), pp.397-9.
G. W. Broomfield, *Revelation and Reunion: A Response to Tambaram*, in *The International Review of Missions* 32 (1943), pp.96-100.
W. A. Brown, *Church and State in Contemporary America*, in *The International Review* 27 (1938), pp.258-60.
H. P. van Dusen (ed.), *Church and State in the Modern World*, in *The International Review* 27 (1938), pp.258-60.
N. F. S. Ferré, *Faith and Reason*, in *Theology Today* 4 (1947), pp.134-7.
R. S. Franks, *The Work of Christ*, and H. P. van Dusen, *The Vindication of Liberal Theology*, in *The Ecumenical Review* 16 (1964), pp.230-3.
A. C. Garnett, *Reality and Value*, in *Journal of Theological Studies* 39 (1938), pp.212-4.
T. Haecker, *Søren Kierkegaard*, in *Journal of Theological Studies* 39 (1938), pp.209-212.
G. Harkness, *Foundations of Christian Knowledge*, in *Theology* 60 (1957), pp.86.
W. E. Hocking, *Living Religions and a World Faith*, in *The International Review of Missions* 30 (1941), pp.259-64.
L. Hodgson, *For Faith and Freedom*, vol.1, in *Journal of Theological Studies* 8 (1957), pp.391-5.
D. T. Jenkins, *The Nature of Catholicity*, in *The International Review of Missions* 32 (1943), pp.96-100.
S. Kierkegaard, *Philosophical Fragments*, in *Journal of Theological Studies* 39 (1938), pp.209-212.
J. Oman, *Vision and Authority*, in *The British Weekly* (29/11/1928), p.194.
H. J. Paton, *The Modern Predicament*, in *Theology* 59 (1956), pp.204-7.
D. E. Trueblood, *Philosophy of Religion*, in *Theology* 62 (1959), pp.469-70.
J. E. Turner, *The Nature of Deity*, in *Journal of Theological Studies* 29 (1928), pp.422-5.
H. N. Wieman, *The Source of Human Good*, in *The Journal of Religion* 27 (1947), pp.114-9.

4. Unpublished Material
(a) Lectures
'The Doctrine of the Ideal Man', The Carew Lectures, Hartford Seminary (1929).
'Lectures on Marriage' (Hartford Seminary Library: Item No.11963, n.d).

(b) Letters
(i) Letters from H. H. Farmer to:

R. W. Barstow, 17/11/1930 (Hartford Seminary Library: Item No. 11875).
R. W. Barstow, 6/12/1930 (Hartford Seminary Library: Item No. 11879).
R, W. Barstow, 9/12/1930 (Hartford Seminary Library: Item No. 11881).
R. W. Barstow, 1/1/1931 (Hartford Seminary Library: Item No. 11888).
R. W. Barstow, 7/2/1931 (Hartford Seminary Library: Item No. 11895).
R. W. Barstow, 9/3/1931 (Hartford Seminary Library: Item No. 11902).
R. W. Barstow, 29/3/1931 (Hartford Seminary Library: Item No. 11907).
R. W. Barstow, 3/7/1931 (Hartford Seminary Library: Item No. 11914).
D. R. Porter, 29/7/1931 (Hartford Seminary Library: Item No. 11916).
R. W. Barstow, 26/7/1933 (Hartford Seminary Library: Item No. 11926).
R. W. Barstow, 5/8/1933 (Hartford Seminary Library: Item No. 11927).
R. W. Barstow, 14/3/1936 (Hartford Seminary Library: Item No. 11940).
R. W. Barstow, 2/5/1936 (Hartford Seminary Library: Item No. 11942).
R. W. Barstow, 22/9/1936 (Hartford Seminary Library: Item No. 11945).
W. A. Visser't Hooft, 5/9/1953 (World Council of Churches Library: Geneva).
R. W. Barstow, n.d (Hartford Seminary Library: Item No. 11947).

(ii) Letters to H. H. Farmer from:
E. E. S. Johnson, 11/11/1930 (Hartford Seminary Library: Item No. 11953).
D. Horton, 14/11/1930 (Hartford Seminary Library: Item No. 11870).
R. W. Barstow, 15/11/1930 (Hartford Seminary Library: Item No. 11871).
R. W. Barstow, 21/11/1930 (Hartford Seminary Library: Item No. 11877).
R. W. Barstow, 25/11/1930 (Hartford Seminary Library: Item No. 11878).
R. W. Barstow, 6/12/1930 (Hartford Seminary Library: Item No. 11880).
R. W. Barstow, 23/12/1930 (Hartford Seminary Library: Item No. 11885).
R. W. Barstow, 23/12/1930 (Hartford Seminary Library: Item No. 11886).
R. W. Barstow, 23/12/1931 (Hartford Seminary Library: Item No. 11887).
R. W. Barstow, 26/1/1931 (Hartford Seminary Library: Item No. 11893).
R. W. Barstow, 27/1/1931 (Hartford Seminary Library: Item No. 11894).
R. W. Barstow, 20/2/1931 (Hartford Seminary Library: Item No. 11897).
R. W. Barstow, 21/2/1931 (Hartford Seminary Library: Item No. 11898).
R. W. Barstow, 15/5/1931 (Hartford Seminary Library: Item No. 11906).
R. W. Barstow, 16/6/1931 (Hartford Seminary Library: Item No. 11908).
R. W. Barstow, 16/6/1931 (Hartford Seminary Library: Item No. 11909).
R. W. Barstow, 17/6/1931 (Hartford Seminary Library: Item No. 11913).
R. W. Barstow, 15/7/1931 (Hartford Seminary Library: Item No. 11915).
R. W. Barstow, 30/11/1931 (Hartford Seminary Library: Item No. 11921).
R. W. Barstow, 1/2/1932 (Hartford Seminary Library: Item No. 11922).
R. W. Barstow, 18/8/1932 (Hartford Seminary Library: Item No. 11923).
R. W. Barstow, 14/10/1932 (Hartford Seminary Library: Item No. 11924).
R. W. Barstow, 6/1/1933 (Hartford Seminary Library: Item No. 11925).
R. W. Barstow, 10/8/1933 (Hartford Seminary Library: Item No. 11928).
R. W. Barstow, 17/11/1933 (Hartford Seminary Library: Item No. 11929).
R. W. Barstow, 26/2/1934 (Hartford Seminary Library: Item No. 11931).
R. W. Barstow, 15/5/1934 (Hartford Seminary Library: Item No. 11934).
R. W. Barstow, 26/6/1934 (Hartford Seminary Library: Item No. 11935).
R. W. Barstow, 9/8/1934 (Hartford Seminary Library: Item No. 11936).
Anon. 4/12/1934 (Hartford Seminary Library: Item No. 11938).
R. W. Barstow, 3/4/1936 (Hartford Seminary Library: Item No. 11941).
R. W. Barstow, 2/6/1936 (Hartford Seminary Library: Item No. 11944).
R. W. Barstow, 2/12/1936 (Hartford Seminary Library: Item No. 11946).
W. A. Visser't Hooft, 28/8/1953 (Geneva: World Council of Churches Library).
R. E. Maxwell, 27/10/1954 (Geneva: World Council of Churches Library).

LITERATURE ABOUT H. H. FARMER

1. Books

Partridge, C. H. *H. H. Farmer's Theological Interpretation of Religion: Towards a Personalist Theology of Religions*, Toronto Studies in Theology, vol.76 (Lampeter: Edwin Mellen Press, 1998)

2. Articles

Bowden, J. 'Farmer, Herbert Henry', in *Who's Who in Theology* (London: SCM, 1990), p.47.

Donovan, P. 'Phenomenology as Apologetics', in *Scottish Journal of Theology* 27 (1974), pp.402-7.

Haymes, B. 'The Supernatural is Personal', in *Baptist Quarterly* 26 (1975), pp.2-13.

Healey, F. G. 'Introduction', in *Prospect for Theology. Essays in Honour of H. H. Farmer* (London: Nisbet, 1966), pp.7-33.

Hope, N. V. 'Herbert Henry Farmer: An English Presbyterian Who Influences American Thought', in *Church Management* (September, 1942), pp.19-20.

Langford, T. A. 'The Theological Methodology of John Oman and H. H. Farmer', in *Religious Studies* 1 (1966), pp.229-40.

MacKinnon, D. M. 'Herbert Henry Farmer (1892-1981)', in Lord Blake and C. S. Nicholls (eds.), *The Dictionary of National Biography 1981-1985* (London: Oxford University Press, 1990), pp.136-7.

Partridge, C. H. 'Herbert Henry Farmer (1892-1981)', in T. A. Hart (ed.), *The Dictionary of Historical Theology* (Carlisle: Paternoster Press, 1998).

Anon. 'Professor Herbert Henry Farmer D.D.', in *Who's Who: International Missionary Council, Madras, India, December 12-29, 1938*, p.25.

Anon. 'This Month's Author: H. H. Farmer' (including: Questions for Discussion on *Towards Belief in God* [Part 1]), in *The Religious Book Club Bulletin* 30 (London: SCM, September, 1942), pp.7-8.

Anon. 'Professor Herbert H. Farmer', in *Hartford Seminary Foundation Bulletin* (June, 1949), p.41.

Anon. 'Herbert Henry Farmer', in *The Christian Century* 98 (1981), p.257.

Anon. 'Herbert Henry Farmer' (Hartford Seminary Library: Item Nos. 11959/60/61, n.d).

Anon. 'The Validation of Faith', in *The Glasgow Herald* (8 February, 1951), p.3.

Anon. 'Experience Versus Theology', in *The Glasgow Herald* (10 February, 1951), p.6.

Anon. 'Revelation and Faith', in *The Glasgow Herald* (15 February, 1951), p.3.

Anon. 'Contrast of Eternity and Time', in *The Glasgow Herald* (17 February, 1951), p.6.

Anon. 'Christian Experience in Reconciliation', in *The Glasgow Herald* (22 February, 1951), p.3.

Anon. 'Christianity and Moral Consciousness', in *The Glasgow Herald* (24 February, 1951), p.4.

Anon. 'Christianity as a Reconciling Faith', in *The Glasgow Herald* (1 March, 1951), p.3.

Anon. 'Man's Sense of His Significance', in *The Glasgow Herald* (3 March, 1951), p.4.

Anon. 'Christianity and Reconciliation', in *The Glasgow Herald* (8 March, 1951), p.3.

Anon. 'Christianity's Moral Enterprise', in *The Glasgow Herald* (10 March, 1951), p.4.

3. Reviews

(a) Experience of God

Culpepper, W. J. in *Methodist Quarterly Review* 78 (1929), pp.660-1.

Hastings, A. W. in *The Expository Times* 40 (1928-29), pp.291-3.

Oakshott, M. in *The Journal of Theological Studies* 31 (1929), pp.302-3.

(b) The World and God

Bosley, H. in *The Christian Century* 53 (1936), p.939.

Brown, W. A. in *Religion in Life* 6 (1937), pp.317-8.

Hastings, A. W. in *The Expository Times* 47 (1936), pp.242-3.
Pittenger, W. N. in *The Living Church* 94 (1936), p.796.
Prichard, H. A. in *The Churchman* 150 (1936), p.325.
Tennant, F. R. in *Mind* 45 (1936), pp.241-6.
Tribble, H. W. in *The Review and Expositor* 33 (1936), pp.320-2.
Woodburne, A. S. in *The Crozer Quarterly* 13 (1936), p.302.

(c) Towards Belief in God
Balmforth, H. in *Theology* 46 (1943), pp.86-8.
Bennett, J. C. in *Christendom* 9 (1944), pp.121-3.
van Dusen, H. P. in *Westminster Bookman* (1943), pp.9-10.
Fosdick, H. E. et al in *Religious Book Club Bulletin* (1943).
Gardner-Smith, P. in *Cambridge Review* (1943).
Isherwood, T. W. in *Record* (22 January, 1943).
Knox, J. in *The Journal of Religion* 23 (1943), pp.95-6.
Lees, E. G. in *Hibbert Journal* 16 (1943).
Miller, R. C. in *The Churchman* 157 (1943), p.452.
Smith, C. R. in *The London Quarterly and Holborn Review* (1943).
Taylor, H. M. in *Religion in Life* 13 (1943-4), pp.156-7.
Tribble, H. W. in *The Review and Expositor* 40 (1943), pp.387-8.
Wilson, W. E. in *The Friend* (1943).

(d) The Servant of the Word
Douglas, H. P. in *Christendom* 8 (1943), p.291.
Nash, C. A. in *Bibliotheca Sacra* 96 (1943), p.330.
Train, L. E. in *The Journal of Bible and Religion* 11 (1943), pp.252-3.
Vidler, A. R. in *Theology* 44 (1942), pp.130-32.
Weatherspoon, J. B. in *The Review and Expositor* 40 (1943), pp.81-2.

(e) God and Men
Brightman, E. S. in *The Crozer Quarterly* 25 (1948), pp.158-60.
Caldwell, F. H. in *Interpretation* 2 (1948), pp.377-8.
Coffin, H. S. in *Religion in Life* 17 (1948), pp.476-7.
Grensted, L. W. in *The Journal of Theological Studies* 50 (1949), p.123.
Haroutunian, J. in *Theology Today* 6 (1949), pp.125-7.
Kantonen, R. in *Lutheran Quarterly* 1 (1949), pp.97-8.
Knapp-Fisher, E. in *Theology* 51 (1948), pp.315-7.
Muelder, W. G. in *Christendom* 13 (1948), pp.386-7.
Rhoades, D. H. in *The Journal of Bible and Religion* 16 (1948), pp.228-9.

(f) The Bible and Preaching
Barrett J. O. in *The Baptist Quarterly* 15 (1954), p.236.

(g) Revelation and Religion
Aldwinckle, R. F. in *The Canadian Journal of Theology* 1 (1955), pp.123-4.
Allen, E. L. in *The Northern Presbyter* (July, 1954).
Cocks, H. F. L. in *Congregational Quarterly* 33 (1955), pp.85.
Ferré, N. F. S. in *Interpretation* 9 (1955), pp.100-2.
Galloway, A. in *The Expository Times* (July, 1954).
Hastings, A. W. in *The Expository Times* 66 (1955), pp.130-1.
Hendry, G. S. in *Theology Today* 12 (1955), pp.113-5.
Jurji, E. J. *Westminster Bookman* (December, 1954).
Keene, J. C. in *Journal of Religious Thought* 12 (1955), pp.125-6.
Kegley, C. W. in *Lutheran Quarterly* 7 (1955), pp.174-5.
Lewis, E. in *Religion in Life* 24 (1955), pp.301-3.
Manson, T. W. in *The Manchester Guardian* (6 September 1954)
Root, H. E. in *Theology* 58 (1955), pp.15-20.

Rust, E. C. in *Review and Expositor* 53 (1956), pp.226-8.
Smith, J. W. D. in *Scottish Journal of Theology* 8 (1955), pp.87-9.
Wood, H. G. in *The Birmingham Post* (13 July 1954).
Anon. in *The Times* (30 July 1954).
Anon. in *The Church Times* (10 September 1954).
Anon. in *The British Weekly* (26 August 1954)

(h) The Word of Reconciliation
Dillistone, F. W. in *Church Quarterly Review* 168 (1967), p.536.
Edwards, D. L. in *Theology* 71 (1968), pp.227-8.
McConnell, T. A. in *Religion in Life* 34 (1967), pp.633-4.
Mueller, D. L. in *Review and Expositor* 65 (1968), p.352.
Wallace, D. in *Foundations* (Baptist) 11 (1968), pp.186-8.
Walvoord, J. F. in *Bibliotheca Sacra* 125 (1968), p.181.

4. Theses

Anderson, G. M. 'An Analysis of the Concept of the Personalism of God in the Theology of Herbert Henry Farmer' (unpublished doctoral thesis: South Western Baptist Theological Seminary, 1985).
Beasley-Murray, S. 'Development of the Concept of the Holy Since Rudolf Otto' (unpublished doctoral thesis: Southern Baptist Theological Seminary, 1980).
Boeke, B. B. 'The Knowledge of God in the Theology of H. H. Farmer' (unpublished doctoral thesis: Princeton Theological Seminary, 1987).
Donovan, P. J. 'A Philosophical Analysis of the Doctrine of Providence with Reference to the Theology of H. H. Farmer' (unpublished doctoral thesis: Oxford University, 1970-1).
Fisher, R. N. 'The World and God: H. H. Farmer's Theology of Personal Relationships' (unpublished doctoral thesis: Oxford University, 1993).
Haymes, B. 'The Theology of H. H. Farmer' (unpublished Master's thesis: Exeter University, 1972-3).
Hill, S. S. 'The Religious Thought of H. H. Farmer with Special Reference to the Doctrine of Providence' (unpublished doctoral thesis: Duke University, 1960).
Hinderliter, H. H. 'Biblical Interpretation and Historical Method: An Analysis of the Writings of C. H. Dodd, H. H. Farmer, and Alan Richardson' (unpublished doctoral thesis: Vanderbilt University, 1960).
Lapp, D. C. 'The Context and Contribution of the Theology of H. H. Farmer' (unpublished doctoral thesis: University of Ottawa, 1975).
Mallory, F. C. 'The Christian Philosophy of H. H. Farmer' (unpublished doctoral thesis: Southern Baptist Theological Seminary, 1963).
McBride, J. R. 'The Apologetic Method of Herbert Henry Farmer' (unpublished doctoral thesis: Southern Baptist Theological Seminary, 1960).
Niedenthal, M. J. 'Preaching the Presence of God: Based on a Critical Study of the Sermons of Paul Tillich, Karl Barth, and Herbert H. Farmer' (unpublished doctoral thesis: Union Theological Seminary, 1969).
Partridge, C. H. 'Revelation, Religion and Christian Uniqueness: An Appreciative Critique of H. H. Farmer's Theological Interpretation of Religion' (doctoral thesis: University of Aberdeen, 1995—see above for details of the revised and published version).
Wolf, H. C. 'The Inadequacy of Personalistic Language Regarding God: A Study Based on the Theologies of Barth, Tillich and Farmer' (unpublished doctoral thesis: Harvard University, 1968).

5. Unpublished Material Concerning H. H. Farmer

(a) Letters

From J. Shaw *to* W. D. Mackenzie, 12/7/1928 (Hartford Seminary Library: Item No. 11949).
From G. W. C. Hill *to* W. H. Day & W. E. Strong, 6/11/1930 (Hartford Seminary Library:

Item No. 11952.
From R. W. Barstow *to* E. Billings, 11/11/1930 (Hartford Seminary Library: Item No. 11861).
From R. W. Barstow *to* G. E. Haynes, 12/11/1930 (Hartford Seminary Library: Item No. 11863).
From R. W. Barstow *to* E. E. S. Johnson, 12/11/1930 (Hartford Seminary Library: Item No. 11864).
From R. W. Barstow *to* E. Billings, 12/11/1930 (Hartford Seminary Library: Item No. 11862).
From R. W. Barstow *to* H. E. Fosdick, 12/11/1930 (Hartford Seminary Library: Item No. 11865).
From R. W. Barstow *to* G. E. Haynes, 12/11/1930 (Hartford Seminary Library: Item No. 11866).
From R. W. Barstow *to* E. Billings, 31/11/1930 (Hartford Seminary Library: Item No. 11867).
From R. W. Barstow *to* D. Horton, 13/11/1930 (Hartford Seminary Library: Item No. 11868).
From E. E. S. Johnson *to* R. W. Barstow, 14/11/1930 (Hartford Seminary Library: Item No. 11869).
From R. W. Barstow *to* W. P. Merrill, 17/11/1930 (Hartford Seminary Library: Item No. 11872).
From R. W. Barstow *to* E. Billings, 17/11/1930 (Hartford Seminary Library: Item No. 11873).
From R. W. Barstow *to* G. E. Haynes, 17/11/1930 (Hartford Seminary Library: Item No. 11874).
From R. W. Barstow *to* D. Horton, 18/11/1930 (Hartford Seminary Library: Item No. 11876).
From R. W. Barstow *to* J. R. Mott, 10/12/1930 (Hartford Seminary Library: Item No. 11882).
From J. R. Mott *to* R. W. Barstow, 11/12/1930 (Hartford Seminary Library: Item No. 11883).
From D. Porter *to* R. W. Barstow, 15/12/1930 (Hartford Seminary Library: Item No. 11884).
From R. W. Barstow *to* D. Porter, 23/12/1930 (Hartford Seminary Library: Item No. 11886).
From R. W. Barstow *to* D. Porter, 12/1/1931 (Hartford Seminary Library: Item No. 11889).
From R. W. Barstow *to* D. Porter, 15/1/1931 (Hartford Seminary Library: Item No. 11890).
From D. Porter *to* R. W. Barstow, 20/1/1931 (Hartford Seminary Library: Item No. 11891).
From R. W. Barstow *to* W. J. Kitchen, 28/2/1931 (Hartford Seminary Library: Item No. 11899).
From F. A. Henson *to* R. W. Barstow, 5/3/1931 (Hartford Seminary Library: Item No. 11900).
From W. J. Kitchen *to* R. W. Barstow, 5/3/1931 (Hartford Seminary Library: Item No. 11901).
From P. Elliott *to* R. W. Barstow, 18/3/1931 (Hartford Seminary Library: Item No. 11903).
From C. D. Nelson *to* R. W. Barstow, 18/3/1931 (Hartford Seminary Library: Item No. 11904).
From R. W. Barstow *to* P. Elliott, 20/3/1931 (Hartford Seminary Library: Item No. 11905).
From R. W. Barstow's secretary *to* W. J. Kitchen, 17/6/1931 (Hartford Seminary Library: Item No. 11910).
From R. W. Barstow's secretary *to* H. R. Sweetman, 17/6/1932 (Hartford Seminary Library: Item No. 11911).
From R. W. Barstow *to* D. Porter, 17/6/1931 (Hartford Seminary Library: Item No. 11912).
From D. Porter *to* R. W. Barstow, 4/8/1931 (Hartford Seminary Library: Item No. 11917).
From R. W. Barstow's secretary *to* D. Porter, 6/8/1931 (Hartford Seminary Library: Item No. 11918).
From R. W. Barstow's secretary *to* D. Porter, 6/8/1931 (Hartford Seminary Library: Item No. 11919).
From U. Norelstrom *to* R. W. Barstow, 17/8/1931 (Hartford Seminary Library: Item No.

11920).
From R. W. Barstow *to* Mrs G. Farmer, 23/12/1933 (Hartford Seminary Library: Item No. 11930).
From C. F. Reisner *to* R. W. Barstow, 10/5/1934 (Hartford Seminary Library; Item No. 11932).
From R. W. Barstow *to* C. F. Reisner, 14/10/1932 (Hartford Seminary Library: Item No. 11933).
From L. B. Moss *to* R. W. Barstow, 4/12/1934 (Hartford Seminary Library: Item No. 11937).
From R. W. Barstow *to* L. B. Moss, 18/12/1934 (Hartford Seminary Library: Item No. 11939).
From W. A. L. Elmslie *to* R. W. Barstow, 2/5/1936 (Hartford Seminary Library: Item No. 11943).
From W. D. Mackenzie *to* Hartford Theological Seminary, n.d (Hartford Seminary Library: Item No. 11948).
From Johnson Shaw *to* W. D. MacKenzie, n.d (Hartford Seminary Library: Item No. 11949).
From L. Newbigin *to* C. H. Partridge, 25 August, 1993.
From G. M. Williamson *to* C. H. Partridge, 9 September, 1993.

(b) Miscellaneous material
Excerpts from the minutes of the meeting of the Executive Committee of the Board of Trustees of the Hartford Seminary Foundation (19/2/1931): H. H. Farmer's salary (Hartford Seminary Library: Item No. 11896).

5. *Other Relevant Material*
Edwards, D. L. review of F. G. Healey (ed.), *Prospect for Theology*, in *Theology* 71 (1968), pp.227-8.
Healey, F. G. 'The Writings of H. H. Farmer', in *Prospect for Theology. Essays in Honour of H. H. Farmer* (London: Nisbet, 1966), pp.237-8.
Richardson, A. review of F. G. Healey (ed.), *Prospect for Theology*, in *Expository Times* 79 (1968), pp.110-11.

INDEX

TEXTS AND STUDIES IN RELIGION

41. Aegidius of Rome, **On Ecclesiastical Power: De Ecclesiastica Potestate**, Arthur P. Monahan (trans.)
42. John R. Eastman, **Papal Abdication in Later Medieval Thought**
43. Paul Badham,(ed.), **Religion, State, and Society in Modern Britain**
44. Hans Denck, **Selected Writings of Hans Denck, 1500-1527**, E.J. Furcha (trans.)
45. Dietmar Lage, **Martin Luther's Christology and Ethics**
46. Jean Calvin, **Sermons on Jeremiah by Jean Calvin**, Blair Reynolds (trans.)
47. Jean Calvin, **Sermons on Micah by Jean Calvin**, Blair Reynolds (trans.)
48. Alexander Sándor Unghváry, **The Hungarian Protestant Reformation in the Sixteenth Century Under the Ottoman Impact: Essays and Profiles**
49. Daniel B. Clendenin and W. David Buschart (eds.), **Scholarship, Sacraments and Service: Historical Studies in Protestant Tradition, Essays in Honor of Bard Thompson**
50. Randle Manwaring, **A Study of Hymn-Writing and Hymn-Singing in the Christian Church**
51. John R. Schneider, **Philip Melanchthon's Rhetorical Construal of Biblical Authority: Oratio Sacra**
52. John R. Eastman (ed.), **Aegidius Romanus**, *De Renunciatione Pape*
53. J.A. Loubser, **A Critical Review of Racial Theology in South Africa: The Apartheid Bible**
54. Henri Heyer, **Guillaume Farel: An Introduction to His Theology**, Blair Reynolds (trans.)
55. James E. Biechler and H. Lawrence Bond (ed.), **Nicholas of Cusa on Interreligious Harmony: Text, Concordance and Translation of** *De Pace Fidei*
56. Michael Azkoul, **The Influence of Augustine of Hippo on the Orthodox Church**
57. James C. Dolan, **The** *Tractatus Super Psalmum Vicesimum* **of Richard Rolle of Hampole**
58. William P. Frost, **Following Joseph Campbell's Lead in the Search for Jesus' Father**
59. Frederick Hale, **Norwegian Religious Pluralism: A Trans-Atlantic Comparison**
60. Frank H. Wallis, **Popular Anti-Catholicism in Mid-Victorian Britain**
61. Blair Reynolds, **The Relationship of Calvin to Process Theology as Seen Through His Sermons**